GLIMPSES FROM
BEYOND

Questions from the Physical World
Answers from the Spirit World

Sondra Perlin Zecher
Charles E. Zecher

BALBOA.
PRESS

A DIVISION OF HAY HOUSE

Balboa Press books may be ordered through booksellers or by contacting:

Balboa Press
A Division of Hay House
1663 Liberty Drive
Bloomington, IN 47403
www.balboapress.com
1 (877) 407-4847

Print information available on the last page.

ISBN: 978-1-5043-8744-6 (sc)
ISBN: 978-1-5043-8746-0 (hc)
ISBN: 978-1-5043-8745-3 (e)

Library of Congress Control Number: 2017914100

Balboa Press rev. date: 09/22/2017

Contents

FOREWORD

GLIMPSES FROM BEYOND has been written an a result of many deep-trance channeling sessions that Sondra Perlin Zecher and Charles Zecher held during monthly meetings of the Coral Springs (FL) Metaphysical Group over a period of several years. As a medium, Sondra put herself into an altered state and allowed her spirit guide to speak directly through her. Members of the group were then able to ask questions directly to her spirit guide; questions about their personal lives, world events, ancient history, extraterrestrial influence, the future, etc. Her husband, Charles Zecher, the group leader, prepared approximately thirty questions in advance each month which he intermingled with the questions asked by the participants. Unlike the mostly on-the-spot questions asked by the others, his questions were prepared in advance in writing but not shared with his wife in advance of the channeling sessions. The channeling sessions were digitally recorded and then transcribed by Charles. The questions he asked and the answers given by the guide provided the basic material for this publication. After a great number of questions had been asked and the answers written down, he then sifted through them and classified them into different categories. Those groupings are the A to W sections in this book. In order to provide some understanding of the process of channeling, Sondra has included a few introductory explanations to provide a perspective to understanding the information.

Chapter 1

UNDERSTANDING SPIRIT COMMUNICATIONS

The material presented in this book is based on two underlying assumptions. The first is that our souls are immortal and continue to exist after we leave the physical world. Our existence continues in the astral world; that is, in the spirit realm where non-physical conscious entities dwell.

The second basic assumption is that there are open lines of communication available between the conscious entities of those in the physical world and the conscious entities of those in the astral world.

The information in this chapter is presented as a recounting of my personal thoughts, beliefs, observations and experiences regarding communication from those in the spirit world.

I want to make it clear at the outset that I understand that others may have had different experiences from mine or have beliefs or truths that are in opposition to mine. Please be assured that I am not trying to convince anybody of anything. All I want to do is to share my personal experiences with you. You can believe or not believe what I say.

You may or may not choose to incorporate anything I present into your own personal belief system. Nevertheless I avow that everything I am saying here is my own personal truth. I do not proclaim myself to be an expert in anything. All I can do is to talk about what I do.

When we die our personal individualities continue to exist in the spirit world. Only the physical part of us dies. The rest continues to exist. Spirits are conscious energy beings that are not encased in physical bodies.

1

Some of the spirits who inhabit the astral world were previously part of our physical world. Others never incarnated in the physical world.

Very few of the spirits who dwell in the astral realm have reached the state of perfection, or completion as my guide corrects me, and are able to move on to another dimension beyond the astral realm.

We must understand that these non-physical entities in the astral realm are not God (or whatever term you may want to use for the highest of all powers) and therefore they are not infallible. Just as in our physical world with some humans more knowledgeable, adept or skilled than others in what they do, so it is with the spirits.

If, for example, you are experiencing severe abdominal pains and you have tried everything you know to relieve the pain, the next logical step is to go to a more knowledgeable person; that is, a medical doctor. Some doctors are more knowledgeable than others but, for the most part, doctors can usually find the source of the pain, sometimes after conferring with other doctors or even researching available information. But doctors are not God. Sometimes the diagnosis is wrong. It is the same in the world of spirits.

Some spirits that channel information to mediums are from a lower energy level in the astral world, others from a higher energy astral level or any level between. The higher the level of the source of information, the greater the probability of the accuracy of the information that is transmitted.

If, for example, your Aunt Millie was someone whose advice you would not take seriously while she was in the physical, treat her advice the same way after she has crossed over to the astral world. In this world, if you had a question about the laws of physics, you could ask your cousin who took a physics course in high school. He just might be able to answer your question correctly. The likelihood of getting the correct answer might increase if, instead of asking your cousin, you asked your neighbor who majored in physics in college. The likelihood of the correct answer might even be greater yet if you asked a university professor of physics. Just as there are different levels of intelligence or abilities in our world, so it is in the spirit world. You might get some kind of answer to your question from Aunt Millie or you might even get an answer from the level of Albert Einstein.

Just because information is channeled from the astral world, this does not mean that you can take it as gospel truth. In fact the Bible says "Try the spirits.", meaning "Test the spirits." (I John 4:1 "Beloved, believe not every spirit, but try the spirits whether they are of God: because many false prophets are gone out into the world.") Spirits can be good or evil. They can be right or they can be wrong. Some try to deceive. Some try to help. The important thing is to be very cautious when dealing with the spirits and the information they provide.

Some spirits like to send messages to their loved ones and friends; information mostly about their experiences, relationships and feelings while on this plateau. Other spirits provide guidance in their communications. Their intent is to be helpful and guide the individual. We all have at least one guide who stays with us throughout our lives. Even though we may not "hear" them, they do have an effect on our intuition so that we will be more likely to make the right choices in the exercise of our free will.

The exercise of our free will takes precedence over spirit influence. Ideas that come from spirits often appear as thoughts that come from "out of the blue", or "inspired" thoughts or even what you might call "epiphanies". Sometimes a guide will appear for a specific occasion, such as to give help to a doctor during an operation, or even to give advice to a gambler.

In my book Scattered Glimpses: A Mosaic I wrote about an interesting case that occurred when one of my physician friends, Dr. Richard Neubauer, spoke to me about the quadruple bypass heart surgery that he needed. He was in considerable pain and was fearful that he might not pull through. He knew me well enough that he had faith in my predictions. My telling him that everything would be okay calmed his nerves. He had the operation and it was very successful. My guide had told me this.

Two or three days after the operation, a doctor whom I did not know came to me in spirit, telling me about what had taken place on the operating table. He told me that when he was alive in the physical world, he had done a great deal of work with heart surgery. From the other side he was guiding the doctor who was performing the surgery, helping him with what he called some kind of loop that he had invented when he was on this plateau. I never spoke to the doctor who performed the physical operation but was curious about how the doctor in spirit had exerted influence on him. Did he actually come to him in spirit as he came to me or did he influence the doctor=s thinking (or intuition, as my guide calls it) without the doctor even knowing so?

When I related this episode to my recuperating friend, I told him the name of the assisting doctor from the spirit world, Christian Bernard. Dr. Neubauer told me that Dr. Christian Bernard was probably one of the most famous heart surgeons ever. It was he who performed the first heart transplant many years ago.

I get the impression it takes spirits a lot of energy to make their presence known to those in the physical world, whether visually or auditorially. On several occasions, after communicating with them for a while, they began to fade or their voice became weaker. They have told me they don't have the strength (I suppose that means energy.) to remain with me any longer. I feel the spirits can sense when they are in the presence of someone like myself who can see or hear them.

In addition to the transmission of information from the spirit entities, the receiver (that is, the medium) must also be considered. Very often information from the spirits is not given in words but rather in symbols, or pictures, or moving scenes, or in languages other than English, or by other means less familiar to those in our dimension, such as telepathy. The mind of the medium must handle this information and translate it accurately into understandable verbal language.

The translation of information into verbal language involves the exercise of the medium's psychic ability. A great psychic must be able to shut his mind down, have no conscious thoughts and be devoid of all emotions when in the psychic mode. The same is not true of mediums. Mediums can be simultaneously fully aware of what is occurring in the astral world and the physical world at the same time. Not all mediums are psychics. Not all psychics are mediums. Here also is an area open to wide diversity. Some mediums are more adept in translating the messages with greater accuracy than other mediums because of their varying psychic abilities. A great medium may not be a great psychic. Likewise, of course, a great psychic may not be a great medium. Thus herein lies another possible reason that a medium might provide information that was different from that which was transmitted by the spirit; in other words, information that was wrong, distorted or incomplete. For truly reliable information, the channeler must be adept as both a medium and as a psychic. Of course, this is all predicated on the energy level of the spirit that is channeling the information.

With all due modesty, I feel that I can say that there are three major reasons for the exceptional level of accuracy of my relating communications from the world of spirits: 1. The high level of the guide that is the source of the information 2. My ability as a medium to clearly receive information from the spirits 3. My psychic ability to interpret the information from the spirits accurately.

Chapter 2

CHANNELING

For me, channeling information from unseen sources is a very natural process. It has always been part of my life on this earth. I receive both psychic and channeled information. By this I mean that thoughts, ideas, pictures, symbols, feelings, hunches etc. just come into my mind, often when I am thinking about a particular topic but also often when my conscious thoughts are unrelated to the information received. Perhaps this information does come from an outside source (that is, channeled) but I sense a difference between psychic and channeled information. I feel that psychic information comes from my higher self at the soul level or from a source that is not related to specific entities that channel information to me. This I feel but I do not know, nor can I explain the difference.

I do, however, sense four different ways of receiving information from outside sources that I channel. The first is that ideas just flow into my mind. These are not words, but rather concepts that I can easily convert into conscious speech. As I relax, the words flow very easily from my mouth. I sense a difference that I am unable to explain between receiving information through this modality and receiving information psychically.

The second way I receive information is that I actually hear someone speaking inside my head; words that I could repeat aloud if I so choose. I often have to pay careful attention because my mind must keep up with the pace of the voice of the speaker. If I am distracted or do not pay careful attention, the words are not repeated by the sender but are lost to me. This can, on occasion, be quite disconcerting. There could be gaps in what I hear or the information is so abundant that my memory cannot recall all that was said.

The third means of receiving information is when I am in an altered state and allow the channeler to speak through me. Although it appears that my consciousness is not in this dimension, it seems that both my awareness of this world and the voice of the speaker are inside my head. Although the channeler is speaking through me, I have the ability to censor, block or alter what comes out of my mouth. When I return to this reality, I am able to remember only certain parts of what I spoke aloud.

The fourth means of channeling, which I call deep-trance channeling, is when my consciousness appears to be fully dormant. I am speaking aloud but I am totally unaware of what I am saying and have no ability to control what I say. After channeling, I come slowly back to my everyday third dimension level of consciousness and have no memory or only foggy memories of what was said through me.

Chapter 3

MY SPIRIT GUIDE

I'd like to tell you a little about my spirit guide and my relationship with him. First, however, I will begin by mentioning a few things I have learned from him regarding spirit guides in general. You will find some of what I will say here, in abbreviated form, in the question and answer section which follows.

We all have a spirit guide who, before our incarnation, agreed to guide us throughout our lifetime. Some of us have two or three, perhaps even more. At times, other spirits guide us for specific situations or periods of time. Like humans in the physical, spirits have emotions and personalities. They vary in their ability to provide guidance; that is, some guides are better than others. Some are very good and helpful in the information they transmit to us and, at the opposite end of the spectrum, some guides can be not so helpful, often even providing information that is incorrect, not understandable, or incomplete.

All of our guides communicate with us. It is we who do not hear them. Unlike most people, but like many other people, I am able to hear the voice of my guide within my head just as if a person were speaking to me. It seems that the majority of humans receive guidance that appears to them as intuition or "thoughts out of the blue". Even then, many people do not recognize their intuition, but instead either misinterpret it or just ignore it. Usually intuition appears as your very first thought when you are focusing on a situation. This first thought is very fleeting and often escapes before it is captured. The secret is to recognize your first thought, hold onto it, and then act on it.

Spirits have varying degrees of energy. This is what is meant by "levels" in world of spirits. The higher the level, the greater degree of accuracy in their communications. I will try to tell you everything I know about my guide but I will not reveal his name. This is not by my choice, but by his. If many others were to call on him, he says that this would drain his energy.

My guide is a very old soul; that is, he has had many, many incarnations in the physical both on the earth and in other star systems. He states that the earth is not his home base. We may therefore assume that he is of extraterrestrial origin. He views life in the physical as very difficult and says that he has no desire to reincarnate. He does at times, at his discretion, manifest himself to me visually also but not always. He has told me that he can manifest himself to me in whichever of his incarnation experiences he chooses. He has said he does not come to me in the visual form of his last lifetime but rather when he was on Earth in Biblical times.

He appears as a prominent personage in the Old Testament of the Bible. It is his preference to show himself as an old man with a white beard, dressed in a robe, wearing sandals and holding a crook in one of his hands; often walking on sand such as a beach or on cobblestones. A few times he has shown himself to me as a younger, strong, muscular healthy man. I do not know if that was his younger self in his Biblical lifetime or if it was he in another incarnation. I know nothing else of his other lives in the physical. He told me his name as a Biblical personality. Actually, since I am not well versed in Biblical characters, his identity was of little significance to me. Practically all I know about his life as portrayed in the Bible was told to me by my husband, who had a strong religious upbringing. He did indeed play a significant role in the Bible.

Since spirits have distinct personality characteristics just as do humans, I will attempt to tell you what I know about his personality. He is a gentle soul, kind and caring. He has quite a sense of humor, which can often be misinterpreted as what we might call a big ego. Yet he is modest and unassuming. He takes pleasure in helping those on our plateau. I say "others" because he has told me that he is the guide for other people in addition to me. He is quite down to earth and at times can be even rather earthy, even having a sharp tongue.

When I am communicating with him I often question what he tells me and I dispute what I am told. When I am in the third form of channeling, as described in the previous section, I sometimes hold back and do not say aloud what he tells me, or I tone down what he says to make it sound more dignified or tactful. I sometimes cover up his earthiness. It seems that tact takes a backseat to truth in the information my guide provides. There's something almost like a childlike honesty in his communication.

He has told me that English is not his language and that on rare occasions it is difficult for him to understand what we are saying to him. To us his spoken English is quite good. His vocabulary is rather extensive and his speech is precise although his phraseology is sometimes slightly different from what we might use, almost bordering what one might think of as slightly old fashioned. For example, he would often say "'tis" instead of "it's" or in answering a question that would evoke a "yes" answer, he would say "indeed" to mean "yes". He often says "they are existing" rather than "they exist". Many people have told me that they particularly enjoy his down-to-earth type of speaking rather than the inspirational or lofty platitudes that are often channeled through other mediums.

When someone once asked him a question in English but with a thick foreign accent, my guide asked him to ask his question in Spanish, the questioner's native language. The man then asked the question in Spanish and the guide answered in English through me. I myself do not comprehend Spanish at all but his response was very clear to the questioner. When I asked him what language he was most comfortable speaking, my guide's response was "Tongues". He says that Tongues is a fantastic way of expressing oneself. It is something that is built into the system of everyone who has a brain.

It's interesting to note that some of what I know about him did not come from what he said to me or how I visually perceived him. Instead it came from what members of our group told me after I had concluded a deep-trance channeling session. Although I knew he liked me, it made me feel good to hear group members repeat all the nice things he said about me and some of my specific traits which he liked. When I would channel, he would refer to me as "she" or "her" but never by my name. Using my name could have pulled me back into this reality. The group enjoyed my disputing him and his earthiness. His sense of humor often evoked laughter from the group.

In addition to my guide, I sometimes allow others from the astral world to speak through me. Years ago, when I would deep-trance channel in front of a group, my listeners told me that I was speaking in a thick Irish brogue. I have often been told that there are very slight but perceptible facial changes when I channel certain entities. For more information about interesting experiences with other non-physical entities, I suggest you read my first book in this series <u>Scattered Glimpses: A Mosaic.</u>

Chapter 4

QUESTIONS AND ANSWERS

The remainder of this book consists of the questions and answers that were provided during the meetings of the Coral Springs Metaphysical Group over a period of several years as I was deep-trance channeling.

Please keep in mind that I was not aware of the words that I spoke while in a trance. I must say that when I listened to the recordings afterward, many of the answers truly surprised me and would often fly in the face of what I thought I knew. It is quite likely that some of the answers will surprise, shock or offend the readers as well; especially in the areas of religion, extraterrestrials and ancient history. Nevertheless, all of the questions and answers are printed here exactly as asked of my guide. If answers are not in accord with your belief system, please do not judge me for the responses. I am only the messenger. I find that there are some responses that may appear to contradict other responses or seem not to make any sense or appear not to be relevant to the question. Nevertheless, I have included them anyway. I sometimes find that understanding comes later.

Although my husband and our group members formulated the questions, by no means can they be considered experts in the areas of the content in this book. Therefore, to those who are more knowledgeable or enlightened in such areas, many of the questions will undoubtedly appear amateurish. On the other hand, to those who are less knowledgeable, many of the questions may be "off-the-wall", the work of delusional people.

I strongly stress that in no way am I trying to establish any kind of cult-like following. My intent is simply to provide information for the readers to ponder and make their own decisions regarding the worth of the responses.

Please keep in mind that the answers to the following questions are from the perspective of someone who dwells in the world of spirits and the content reflects his experience, his knowledge and his viewpoint. Sometimes when answering questions, he receives assistance from sources above the level where he is. He often confers with other entities in his realm. You will note that the guide usually gives short answers direct to the point. At times the responses may seem enigmatic and require further thought on the part of the listener or reader. Sometimes the answers contain content that seems not relevant to the question. As a dweller in the astral realm, he still maintains his personality. This often comes through in the humor noted in some answers.

Since the questions have been organized under several topics, the same question may appear in two or even three sections if the question or the answer contains information relevant to the topic. If a question appears in more than one topic, the letter(s) in parentheses after the underlined question indicate the other topics in which the question appears. So if you are reading this book page by page and you see a question with a letter after it that is closer to the beginning of the alphabet than the letter of the section you are reading, this indicates that you have already read the question.

Words in brackets [] are editorial comments or words that were added for possible clarification. If [?] appears after a word, it usually means that the word could not be clearly heard in the recording and that the word is what seemed to be heard.

A. DEATH: THE TRANSITION TO A NEW LIFE IN THE SPIRIT WORLD

1.The process of dying

Would you describe what the majority of individuals experience in the process of transitioning from the physical world to the spirit world? For example, is dying easy or difficult, pleasant or painful etc.? Going from the physical world to the spirit world is as easy as going from one room to another. People will be there to assist and bring you comfort. The living experience can be much more painful. The death process is not painful. It is what occurs before you die where the pain is. Life can be more painful. It has been to many others. Dying is as easy as falling asleep and then waking up in a different place. There is absolutely no pain in death.

Is the transition from the physical world to the spirit world easier if you are knowledgeable about the spirit world before you die? I cannot tell you the disposition of every single person, how people will accept their fate. I think it will somewhat because it will be familiar to you. We greet you depending on how you arrive. It is easier to show you your familiarities.

When we cross over to the spirit world do we see what we expect to see or do we see something different from what we thought we would see? G) You see what you want to see.

When we cross over to your world, is our spirit guide there to meet us? Your guide is there to meet you just when you come home. Preferably your family is there. They love you.

There are humans who see auras emanating around the physical bodies of people. They say that often before a person dies, sometimes days or even weeks before they die, the person has no aura when death is eminent. Can you explain why this occurs? No, I cannot explain at this moment, sir. If there is no aura at the time, you are correct. If there is no aura, then the person is going to die. I have also said that every living thing, whether they be animal, vegetable or whatever, everything that is alive, has this field of aura energy around them.

If a person is in a state of mind where they expect to die soon or consciously want to die, does that make their transition to the spirit world easier? That is not necessarily true. The same is true when a person has no fear of dying. The transition from your world to my world is like going through one door [room] to another.

When death is imminent, do people sometimes wait for certain conditions to be right before they die; conditions such as loved relatives or friends being present at the time of departure? Indeed, sir. Human nature is able to greet and say goodbye and say hello to our old friends. You make the decision about when to go at the subconscious level but you are not aware at the conscious level.

Is the transition to the spirit world any different for those who have Alzheimer's Disease than it is for others? It is not different. They are not aware. They are in a different element.

2. What we take with us when we cross over

When we die and discard our physical bodies, do we retain the same attitudes, emotions, and desires when we cross over to the world of spirits? No, my dear sir, you do not take along the itchiness that life has created for you. If they are angry when they die, they will take over that same emotion for the moment, sir. It is not lasting. It is for the moment. The attitudes, emotions, and desires that you have in the physical dissipate gradually when you enter the spirit world. Those that are based on physical appetites such as food, alcohol, drugs and sex cannot be satisfied in this world. This is not one of the concepts of hell but is torture.

If you are in an angry mood right before you cross over, do you maintain that angry mood after you have crossed over? Indeed, sir. If you are angry, sir, please relax. Do not be angry.

Do those entities on this plateau who have mental or emotional disorders carry over those same disorders when they arrive on your plateau? Can they overcome them on your plateau? (BG) Indeed, sir. There are times they do. Anything is possible. It depends upon the individual.

Does the level of intelligence carry over with people when they cross over from this world to yours? Is the same true when they return to this world from yours? 'Tis not true. The level of intelligence, the level of anxiety and fears and beliefs are not cultivated and do not turn over. They are dropped with the new life ahead [when we come back into the physical]. When your newborn is born and reflects on the past is that intelligence to you? Is that intelligence if they are piano players or artists?

When we pass over into the spirit world while in a coma or heavily drugged with pain medication, are our souls immediately alert or is there a period of recuperation first? Sometimes some people are immediately alert and some are not. I cannot tell you how long it will take them to become alert because time is up to you. I cannot give you a specific answer.

When souls cross over to your world, do some need long periods of rest while others need very little or practically none at all? Some need more time.

Do people sometimes continue to feel physical pain for a while after they die? If they wish [at their higher level]. That pain occurs when the etheric body has not fully separated. As I have said, that is why you should not be cremated right away. The etheric body is never needed [after death].

If I remember what you have told us about life in the spirit world and about the transition to that world, will I retain that information when I arrive in the spirit world? If you wish, sir. It is very difficult for me to tell each individuality what they will retain in life in the spirit [world]. It is questionable. The transition to the spirit world varies with the individual. Some of us do not remember.

Since you have said that people lose their religious beliefs when they enter the spirit world, do the attitudes of the terrorists who have killed in the name of their religion change after they cross over? (I) Never, sir. They still have the same attitudes but they don't have their religious beliefs. As I have said, there is no such thing as religion in the spirit world and God didn't create any religions.

3. Effects of the living on those who have crossed over

Can those in the physical impede the progress of those who have recently crossed over by excessively mourning them and by not letting go of their personal possessions? Yes.

When people die do those that are alive keep them earthbound and prevent them from moving on to the spirit world? Unfortunately, sir, yes. Sometimes those that are alive keep them earthbound by mourning them. It is best not to mourn them. Let them go. Let them be well. Let them follow their path. Let them go like a bird has to fly and our children have to grow. People who are alive do help in keeping those earthbound. They do help in a negative fashion. They help and do not let us go on. Those that are earthbound continue to be earthbound because of people that continue to call them. You will not let them go. You do not relieve them. You keep them for your own personal business. Sometimes they continue for many, many centuries to be earthbound.

Do we hold back those who have passed on when we think happy memories of them? Indeed not. Happy thoughts make us joyous. It is fine to have memories of happiness but do not hold them back or restrain them from moving on [by mourning them]. We hold them back, dear lady, when we mourn for them. Be grateful for your cherished memories and your moments of pleasure. You can help them by telling them to follow the light.

Is it possible for humans to help earthbound spirits to make the transition to the spirit world? What is the best way to do that? In some ways, yes [it is possible]. I know of no answer to give you [about the best way], sir, except comfort.

4. Remaining earthbound after we cross over

After a person dies, are there sometimes occasions when at least part of that person's consciousness remains with the body at the gravesite? Is the part that remains earthbound what we call a "ghost" as contrasted with a "spirit", that part that moves to your plateau? (C) It is not for me to give you an example. The answer to your question would simply be yes.

There are times that our consciousness does not dissolve. We are aware. If you wish to give names, that would be correct if you want to call it such. Call it what you will.

When a person dies and becomes a spirit, must he enter the spirit world immediately or as we say "follow the light" or can he remain under the sphere of the earth influence for a while before moving on? Each individual is different and there are many different individuals as you well see. There are many different flowers to make a bouquet. A person does not have to enter the spirit world immediately after they die. As a nurse will tell you there will be a difference in the passing of different souls. A medical doctor will tell you so too.

When it is time for individuals to leave this plateau, can they get trapped on this plateau if they remain longer than they should? (C) Indeed, sir. They are referred to as ghosts in your language. I cannot say how long a soul can stay before becoming trapped.

Are there any measures that a person could take while they are alive that would assure that they do not become earthbound when they die? They can be very strong willed. I do not wish to be earthbound. If you die and want to go directly into the spirit world and not be in the in-between world, you can prevent yourself from being earthbound by eating the right food; that is, think the right thoughts.

5 Adjusting to the new life

What are the most important factors that determine how easily a person will adjust to the transition to your world? Each individual is individual. The adjustment is individual. There is no one factor that is more prevalent than others.

Some people believe that there are many levels in the spirit world and that when you cross over to that world, you reside at the level which matches your actions when you were in this world. Is that correct? (B) Indeed, sir, and I am at one of the higher levels in the spirit world.

If you were well-known but hated by many people because of your evil deeds while in the physical, would that make your transition to the spirit world or your life in the spirit world more difficult? Indeed, sir. It would be more difficult for a negative personality to appear for our culture. Indeed sir.

When a person crosses over to the spirit world, is he able to recall all the events of his recent lifetime with clarity if he so chooses? If he so chooses; even recall events that he could not recall while in the physical.

If you unexpectedly die instantly such as by murder or in an accident, does that have an effect on your entry and adjustment into the spirit world? Indeed, sir. When you go to sleep at night and you wake up alarmed, does that not have an effect on your feelings for the day? If you die after a long illness and are sort of expecting to die, it is easier to adjust to the spirit world than if you die unexpectedly.

When they enter the spirit world, do people who were very religious have difficulty in accepting the fact that religion is manmade and does not exist in the spirit world? They certainly do, sir. Religion is manmade. Those in the spirit world eventually get over the idea of religion. There is no such thing as religion in the spirit world as we encase [?] it to be.

6. Funerals and cremation

Is there sometimes a danger if a person is cremated too soon after dying because there is a possibility that the etheric body may not have fully separated from the physical body, thus causing the entity to feel pain? (S) It is absolutely true. It is painful, sir. You must wait two days before being cremated.

If we are cremated will it hurt the soul? Absolutely, no. It does not hurt the soul to be cremated.

When one passes over, is it important to have a funeral with a priest or rabbi or minister to assure the safe passing? It's like having a party, my dear lady. If you wish to have a party on your birthday, it is up to you. A funeral is having a farewell party. If you wish to have a farewell party with a band or orchestra then I will be happy to attend.

When a person passes on, does having a funeral or a memorial service help that soul to get on the other side more comfortably? No, but it helps the people that are going to the funeral. When you come into this world, you come in alone. When you go out, you also go out alone. So it doesn't matter who is saying goodbye because who is with you will always be with you.

7. Miscellaneous

Does someone who has committed an atrocious crime, such as a mass murder suicide bomber, that they feel they were justified in doing, continue to feel justified for what they did after they have crossed over into your world? Indeed. Why should they change? When you step on ants and see nothing wrong with stepping on ants, there is no such thing as right or wrong.

Many religions teach us that when we die we go immediately to either heaven or to hell but they say nothing about our going to the world of spirits. Are heaven and hell actual places or are they states of mind? What is your view of heaven and hell? (I) (Laughing) Indeed sir. Heaven and hell are not actual places but I would say they are states of mind. I ask if there is such a thing as a heaven or hell. I am not saying that we make our own heaven or hell. I am saying that we go on from there and we learn or we come back again. When we cease to exist we go on or we reincarnate, or we go on from there.

Does a person's age at the time of passing into the spirit world have any effect on his transition to the spirit world or his life in the spirit world? (B) It makes no difference how old you are when you enter into a new regime. Age does not matter.

When people die, do their pets in the spirit world sometimes appear to help their transition to the spirit world? Indeed, sir. They are part of the family. It is a very great possibility that your [i.e. the Zechers'] dog who died twenty years ago will be there to greet you but your dog needs to rest.

When we pass over to the next dimension, will we all speak one universal language or will we still be separated? There will be no language, sir. There is no language. We can read thoughts. A language isn't necessary.

Do people sometimes die at a time that was not in their life's plan to die, such as when there are catastrophic events such as war, typhoons, mass murders, etc.? People die only when their higher self wants them to die. If there is a mass murder and hundreds of people are killed, all of those people were meant to die at that time. A person's life cannot be cut short if that person's higher self does not want to leave the physical.

When we reincarnate is the length of our life predestined at that time? Indeed. Indeed.

After a person dies, should there be a waiting period before any actions are taken that might shock the departed soul that might bring them to the reality that they have died, such as not having their name on a tombstone visible? You should be careful not to shock the departed souls that they are dead because they don't realize it in most cases. That is why in some religions they choose not to put the name on the tombstone.

From my observations of my wife's communications with recently crossed over souls, it seems that some souls are immediately aware that they are in your world but others do not realize they have crossed over even though they are communicating with her. Is this observation correct? (D) Correct sir, very correct.

Also from my observations of my wife, it seems that many souls are able to communicate immediately after they cross over but then must spend a long period of no communication before they begin communicating again. Is this frequently the way it happens or are my observations incorrect? (D) Sometimes that is correct. Sometimes those that pass over can aid you but then they have to move on.

At the soul level, do husbands or wives sometimes choose when to die in order to allow their spouse to evolve in a direction that they were unable to go if the marriage continued? Sometimes a husband chooses to die in order to allow his wife to go in a different direction. Rarely, sir. Sometimes the same is true of friends or other relatives.

B. LIFE IN THE SPIRIT WORLD

1. Personality traits of the spirits

Do people in the spirit world have the same kinds of emotions as those in our world? Oh dear, yes. Some are happy, sad, grouchy. Same kind of emotions as on your plateau.

Do those in your world sometimes have memory problems and forget things they would normally be expected to remember, just as do people in our world? (E) Me, myself, no. I have no memory problems. Some do.

Do those entities on this plateau who have mental or emotional disorders carry over those same disorders when they arrive on your plateau? Can they overcome them on your plateau? (AG) Indeed, sir. There are times they do. Anything is possible. It depends upon the individual.

Just as there are people in the physical whose thinking process is distorted, do some entities in the spirit world not think logically? Indeed, sir. We do not always think properly at the proper time. Time is an issue. Time is manmade. So we cannot proceed as proper.

Just as many humans can be quite egotistical and not much concerned for other people, is the same true after they enter the spirit world? Indeed, sir. One's crossing over does not mean there's going to be a change. There can be an awareness but that does not mean there's going to be a change. If one is a nincompoop one is going to remain such. If you are ignorant you will remain that way. You can grow after you cross over if you wish.

Since you have said that there are no rules or no such thing as right or wrong in your world, can you energy beings still be judgmental? Indeed. 'Tis fun, you know, to be in judgment of nonsense. I know nothing.

Since time does not exist where you are, do spirits generally have a greater degree of patience than those in our world? Do spirits experience boredom or impatience, especially when dealing with those in our world? We have more patience. I do not experience boredom, not even when dealing with those in your world. I can become impatient at times.

23

Does jealousy exist in your realm? Can one spirit be envious of another? Indeed, sir. Just as in your world one human is envious of another.

In our world some individuals are very lazy and others are very ambitious. Is the same true in the spirit world? There are lazy spirits and there are ambitious spirits and spirits that are not aware. High energy spirits such as I are more ambitious.

Some humans have very strong will power but others have weak will power. Is the same true of spirits? Indeed. Some spirits are stronger willed than other spirits.

2. Spirits' Capabilities

When you said that people see what they want to see when they cross over to the spirit world, does that mean we can create our own personal unique world when we are there? I have said that when people cross over to the spirit world they see what they want to see. You can create your own personal world when in the spirit world if you wish to. Most are so miserable and are so unhappy that they don't think clearly. You can create whatever you wish. We eat, sleep, and fornicate just as you do but with our minds.

Are there animals in your world? Since in your world entities can create what they want with their mind, is it possible to create one of the person's animal pets who was on this plateau when they were here? (T) Yes.

Since time and space do not exist where you are, does that mean that you can instantaneously be in the presence of or be in contact with any other entities that you so choose? Immediately, sir. Spirits can be in more than one place at the same time. Most of us can do that. Spirits can also be in different time periods simultaneously, past and future.

Since time does not exist in the spirit world, are spirits able to witness or become aware of the past thoughts and actions of humans? Indeed. We can be aware of things you did in the past. The same about thoughts in the past. All spirits can do such, not just those in the higher level. As soon as someone adjusts to life in my world they can see your thoughts and actions if they are interested, sir. If we wish, we are able to go back and witness or re-experience past events such as President Kennedy's assassination. May I say to you, my dear gentleman, you can do the same, more than with just your memory.

Are those in your world often able to recall events of their most recent physical life more vividly and with greater clarity than they can with their memories while they are in the physical? Indeed, sir, very much so. Entities in the spirit world can recall events from many of their lifetimes in the physical if they so choose. That is why I am not coming back. I do not want to recall. They are not all pleasant.

Is it easier for those in the spirit world to become knowledgeable about their previous incarnations than it is for those in the physical world to do so? (G) My dear sir, your memory is just as well as our memory. It is up to the individual and up to the memory to realize and recognize their past lives. It is not especially easier for spirits to know about their past lives. It is the same. You don't remember your lives past and sometimes that is good.

When individuals are in your world are they better able to see and understand themselves more accurately than when they were in this world? At times, yes.

From where you are, how do you perceive the Akashic Realm? Entities from my realm can go to that plane of information. We can create miracles you know. Every ingredient of nature [and] of awareness is right, is true, is real. Every word that is said is right even when it's wrong; even the wrong is correct. By studying the Akashic record for each individual, if you wish it to benefit your current life it will be of assistance to your current life.

Can people in your world be knowledgeable about technologies they never knew during their lifetimes in the physical? (V) Correct, sir, correct. Not all of us are advanced but we are aware. We have been knowledgeable about the future, have we not?

Are there things that an earthbound spirit can experience that a soul which has entered the spirit world cannot experience? (C) Yes. An earthbound spirit is not fully in my realm. They do not wish to leave the earth. They wish to stay on the earth and cause problems. That spirit is partially in my world also.

How do entities in the spirit world attain a high level of energy? Can spirits perceive the level of energy of other spirits? Are there entities with a level of energy similar to that of Jesus? Resting and seeking and helping those that are in need. We have energy high levels as you stated. Spirits can perceive the level of energy of other spirits. Indeed we help each other as you well know. There are entities with a level of energy similar to that of Jesus, and much more.

If a person has never had a physical incarnation in a certain star system, is that person still able to go to the spirit realm of that star system after he disincarnates? Indeed, sir. They [other spirits who are assisting the guide with the answers] tell me to say yes.

If my grandfather were to reincarnate into the physical world as another personality, would my other relatives in the spirit world still have contact with him as the personality of my grandfather? Would they be aware of his new incarnation identity? God forbid! No sir, this is not possible. I do not believe that they would be aware of the new personality.

Are spirits able to communicate with more than one person or spirit, on totally different matters, simultaneously? Indeed, sir. Do you not have two hands?

Can spirits in your realm be instrumental in exorcising evil spirits from places or people in our realm? (C) It is not important sir. It is more important for you to exorcise them.

Do those in your world have the ability to hear, see, and read the minds of those in our world as soon as they cross over, or is this an ability which develops later? This is an ability that is there that is given at birth. Are you not aware? Be aware. They can read your minds if you wish that.

Are some guides more competent than others? Indeed yes. Some people are better than others. It's like some people play the piano better than others. Some people mislead and we do too. Just because we passed on does not mean we are correct. Yes, as in life, we are not all guided properly.

Is it easier for spirits to accurately predict events in the near future than it is to predict events in the far future? It makes no difference if it is in the near future or the far future.

Are spirits able to fully communicate with other spirits as soon as they cross over or is there a period of adjustment or learning first? It is an individual answer. What I am saying is that sometimes when a person passes over they are able to communicate and sometimes they have to wait a while until they are ready.

3. Spirits' connection with other spirits

On your plateau can you perceive the personality of the spirits you encounter? Indeed. We can perceive different personalities. We have the same five senses but in a different way. We can perceive past life personalities of the spirits we encounter but only past lives, not future lives.

Are you able to perceive the emotions of others in your realm or can they, as people on our plateau, hide or disguise their emotions? In our realm our emotions are open. We can see and feel each other. We do not hide feelings like you people on Earth. You look in the mirror and you lie.

On your plateau, can you choose which personality you wish to show to other spirits or mediums on this plateau? I like to show the best [of my personalities]. I'm [the personality now showing] the nicest. I'm the happiest. We all have different sides. We show what we want to show. Yes indeed, we can show different sides.

Do entities in your world always know when another entity is lying to them or trying to deceive them? We do not always tell the truth. We know when we are deceiving. We lie to each other like you do but we [the guide and his group] will tell you the truth.

When a spirit creates something with his mind, such as a reproduction of his physical home, is that creation perceivable by other spirits? Indeed there are times that it is correct. We go different ways you know.

In your realm is it possible to utilize all of your senses when recalling past events? That is, can you virtually relive past events? Wouldn't that be a wonderful situation to go back and relive all my lifetimes and all my past times? If I were a notable murderer person, wouldn't that be wonderful? I do not think that is so. We learn a little from each lifetime. Such a little we remember of things that seem familiar to you. What would be the sensibility and possibility of observing past events? What will it achieve for me? I am not curious. I am not sensitive to the past. I am looking forward to helping you for your future and for what you can gain ahead. Your past is what you learned.

Do spirits sometime combine their energies so that they can create enough energy to create an apparition dense enough for humans who are not mediums to see? Indeed, sir. A spirit may not have enough energy to create an apparition that you can see but they can get other spirits to combine their energies. And then they can disappear or evaporate, just like you think you are seeing something for a moment and then look again and it is not [visible] to your eyes. That is not the same as what a medium can see.
A medium can actually see the spirits in their true forms.

Other than the physical aspects and the means of communication, is there much difference between interpersonal relationships in the physical world and interpersonal relationships in the spirit world? We in the spirit world need not verbalize. We can read each other. We just feel each other. We can see each other. We know each other without verbalizing. There are some spirits we like and some we dislike. Some we trust and some we distrust. We pick our own friends.

Can a spirit hide from another spirit? Why would one wish to? What is there to hide? We don't have dirty bloomers.

Do spirits communicate with other spirits with language? Indeed, sir. We all are spirits and we all speak the same language. We do not need to speak verbally. We can adjust so emotionally. We are reading the mind of each other's soul. We all get together.

Do spirits have names in the spirit world; that is, names by which other spirits can make contact with them or refer to them? Indeed, sir. We certainly do have identification as you well know. We can call a spirit by name. It is important that I can call Jesus. Many of us call him all the time. Time and time again. We say it in vain. We say it in happiness. We say it in prayer. We call his name. Not just people calling on him but spirits also. He is in my world.

Do spirits who have similar interests sometimes band together to work toward a common goal? No, my dear sir. Once we are human we continue as a spirit to be human too and so we console each other and we correct each other and we argue with each other. When I come to your group to answer questions I sometimes have other spirits with me to help.

As in the physical world, are there leaders in the spirit world? If we wish. We select those that we put on a pedestal if we wish to put a person or someone on a pedestal. We have no rules like you have on Earth. It is not completely true that there is no one in charge. The only person that is in charge is self. Each spirit is in charge. We have no rules, sir.

Do spirits feel more connected with each other than humans feel toward each other? They blend much more, sir. They don't disagree. Spirits cooperate much more with each other than you do. They are eager to cooperate. They are not simple minded as you souls are.

When a person here is officially made a saint by a church on Earth, is that person clearly perceptible to you when that soul reaches your plateau? In other words is the stamp of "official sanctity" of a soul clearly perceptible to you and other spirits on your plateau? (I) We make up our own rules. Indeed I perceive their presence. They huddle around me.

4. Evolution of spirits

Do entities not ready to reincarnate remain on your plateau or go elsewhere? They go on to another satellite. There are many different worlds out there. There are many different plateaus.

29

When a soul has learned or experienced all that can be learned or experienced on your plateau, does that soul remain on your plateau or move to a different realm? We have different levels; don't you know? At this time I am not able to tell you about levels above me. They do not channel answers through me. I speak quite well.

Is it necessary to reach a certain level of perfection before those on your level can move on to a higher level? Indeed sir, if you wish to call it a level of perfection.

If you are no longer required to reincarnate, do most energy beings remain on the astral plane indefinitely or must you eventually move to a higher realm? (K) Or to a lower realm. Wherever you wish. Wherever you feel comfort and solace. A lower realm is other star systems. The earth is not the only place for us to arrive in. Not only Earth.

Since you have said that an entity can dwell both in the physical world and the astral world simultaneously, is it also possible that a soul can dwell in the astral realm and the realm above that, which some call the mental world, simultaneously? Indeed, sir, indeed. My answer to you, they [the other spirits with the guide] said, tell him yes. I myself am able to visit the mental world. The mental world is a private world. Since this is a personal world, there are times that individuals do not communicate with others. That is true. That is very true.

Can a soul reside in your realm and simultaneously have physical incarnations? (B) Indeed. Many incarnations at the same time.

In order for a spirit to serve as a guide, must the spirit have completed the required reincarnation cycle? No. No one is perfect.

Does serving as a guide to physical humans help the personal growth or advancement of those on your plateau? Service to others helps us to achieve, sir. Yes indeed. We all feel better by serving others and make it proper. Others have their own free will and don't always hear what we suggest.

In both your world and our world, are individuals who have a good sense of humor usually more highly evolved than those with very little sense of humor? (K) Indeed. Those who have more humor have more strength. Those who have no humor do not know their ass from their elbow. Those with very little sense of humor are not as evolved.

Is it correct that what resides in your plateau are spirits and what we idealize as souls reach for higher reality? That is true, dear lady. So true. We confer with others such as I [do].

Are there higher powers to whom those in your realm are held accountable, or are spirits held accountable only to themselves? Only to themselves and the God within us. We are responsible.

When a person who has had incarnation on several different planets dies, does that spirit necessarily reside in the astral realm of the planet of his most recent lifetime? Yes, sir.

5. Spirits' connection with humans and other entities

Do angels play a role in your plane of existence? (J) Indeed. Angels are there to guide and administer, as you well know. Angels are with you.

Is there more overt communication with those on your plateau with angels than there is with them in our world? (J) Absolutely, dear sir, but they hear you too. They don't want to be known or seen but they do exist. Angels hear you when they want to hear you.

Are you able to communicate with entities in realms above or beyond the plateau on which you are? Indeed if they wish to communicate with us, we can confer with them. They are on a much higher realm and can see more than we do. Sometimes we can see more from the lower realms.

Do those in your world communicate with animals on both your plateau and ours? (T) Some do, sir. We can communicate with physical animals as well as with animals in our realm. Influence animals too.

Can highly evolved spirits manifest themselves as physical human beings that anyone can see? They are not angels but they can manifest themselves for a brief moment with their energy. They wish for more [energy].

Are spirits aware of the karma of those individuals in our dimension? (H) Indeed. Even though you may not be aware of your own karma, they are aware.

When a person is about to cross over, do those on your side know this in advance? Indeed we are aware and ready to welcome and assist them.

Do friendships sometimes originate when souls are in your world and then continued when they incarnate into the physical? (G) Relationships don't always continue and thank God for that. Sometimes relationships can start where I am and can continue but don't always appear to be so. It is possible. Sometimes it is rejected.

On your plateau do some spirits learn from those in the physical? Indeed sir. My answer to you is yes.

In your world are there times that an individual can like another person and other times dislike that person? Do those in your world have similar reactions to individuals in our world? To others in your world? Indeed, sir. Is it not true in your world and in our realm we like and we dislike? I can like a person in your world but not like what he does or what the person is thinking of doing. Some are negative you know, and we do pick up your thoughts. You can keep your thoughts to yourself and not talk about them.

When spirits see the future of humans, is that always a definite future or is it a strong possibility of a future? It will occur, sir. It will occur. What time it will occur is not endured but it will occur.

When people cross over to the spirit world and then discover that a trusted friend had been dishonest with them when they were together in the physical, do spirits sometimes become vengeful toward those in the physical world? Sometimes, sir, we are like humans. We don't forgive, nor do we forget. We feel vengeful and sometimes we love to step on your tongues.

<u>Do some spirits seek to have humans worship them?</u> Some do, sir. They are not bad spirits. Whatever worship means, I do not suggest that you do that. I do not suggest that you be easily manipulated. I think you should listen to your own inner self.

<u>When a spirit manifests itself to someone in our dimension, can that spirit appear in whatever form he so chooses, similar to how the angels manifest themselves?</u> Indeed. A spirit could manifest itself as both a living object or an inanimate object. Like an angel, a spirit could manifest itself as lightning.

<u>Can humans learn to know when spirits are reading their minds?</u> No one can read your mind, sir. Your mind cannot be read. It is not existing but it is mental telepathy that will go into this organization properly. When I said that spirits could read your minds, that was your emotions, not the actual words you were thinking because your word thinking can change. You can suggest and think and then come out with something completely different. [It appears that the guide is making a distinction between reading our minds and reading our thoughts.]

<u>Do demons exist in your world; that is, negative energies that attach themselves to spirits? (D)</u> They do not exist in my world; only for humans. They cannot attach themselves to anyone or anything that does not want it. They are fearful too. Demons are people or humans that are ignored. A person on Earth, through the use of their will, can avoid having demons attach themselves. You can absolutely be stronger than demons. You should not fear them because you are stronger. Even though they come across as being strong, they are really weak. They show fear and that is control. So if you do not wish to be controlled you must set the demon [free]. That is a negative thought. You will not have fear.

6. Spirits' attitudes, emotions and desires

<u>Do all the spirits in your realm have the form of a physical human being?</u> We are not human. We were once sitting and suffering with illness and disease as you. We have no particular form, unless you see electricity. Many shapes per individual. We can get any shape we want.

Do entities in your world have differing amounts of energy? If so, does the amount of energy they possess determine the extent to which they can help people in our world? Indeed we do! Again they [those with the guide] say "yes". We all stand around and say "yes". They all shake their heads and say "yes".

Since you said that you were not humans but rather energy beings, do more highly evolved souls in your world have a greater amount of energy than less evolved souls? (F) Indeed, some have more energy and assistance as well. Jesus is called most often and he has the energy for that.

Some people believe that there are many levels in the spirit world and that when you cross over to that world, you reside at the level which matches your actions when you were in this world. Is that correct? (A) Indeed, sir. and I am at one of the higher levels in the spirit world.

As in our world, are more advanced souls at your level less influenced by their emotions than are the less advanced souls? We have emotions and feelings too, you know, and we love to give advice.

If a person was obsessed with sex while in the physical, after they cross over do they take pleasure in observing the sexual activities of humans? They take pleasure in participating indeed. They wish for themselves to have sex. Differences among spirits.

When a spirit serves as a guide to a human, is that considered a noble endeavor? What other kinds of work do spirits do? My dear sir, for me to be here and take these nonsensical questions and answer to the best of my ability, am I not noble? Other than serving as guides, there are many ways of serving. We travel and we do help. There is so much to be helped; to give you peace of mind. Many of you are here and suffer and are tortured inwardly. Work is a pleasure.

Do guides sometimes feel relieved when we cross over and they don't have to guide us anymore? Some of us don't always like you, you know, but we succeed in being there for you. You don't always like us either.

In our world some people are gregarious and enjoy being with others but there are also people who are not very sociable and prefer being alone or having very little contact with others. Is the same true in your world? (E) Are they not boring? People are people in my world too, I would say, "Oh, yes." And I am one that is gregarious. I like to talk. I do not like to hear [listen]. There are also people in my world that tend to be loners and like being alone more. They are fearful people.

Just as we have what we call liberal thinkers or conservative thinkers in our world, do you have something comparable on your plateau? On our plateau we have combinations of thinkers, some more liberal and some more conservative in thinking. Some are more intelligent and some are just stupid. There is a wide range of intelligence among the entities in this world just as there is in your world.

Just as there are people here who are nosy and like to pry into everyone's else's business, are there spirits who enjoy reading our minds solely because they are curious? We can read minds. They mean to be helpful. Some are not helpful. Some are too busy. Correct. We don't read minds for our entertainment.

After a person crosses over into your world, does the time ever come when religion is no longer important to him? (I) Religion is manmade. We have no religion where we are. No spirit has any affinity with the religion they had when they were in the physical. It is left behind on Earth. Religion is rules. We are too intelligent to take rules or guidance from religion. When did it [religion] start killing? Adam and Eve had no religion. [Here] they look back and smile and realize what a joke it was. So they lose their religious beliefs.

If a person does not believe that there is such a thing as reincarnation, does that person continue to hold that belief after they have crossed over to your world? Indeed not, because they wake up and say, "Here I am." If a person leaves the earth world and comes into our world, that is not what they think any more. It has dissolved in their thinking.

Just as in our world, do entities in your world have different opinions about situations or how to answer a question, or what to do? Indeed, sir, indeed. We do not all agree. Just as in your world as you wish to state it.

Are there varying opinions in your world regarding the social issues of Earth people, such as gay marriages in our world? We all have opinions which make no value. It is not necessary to have an opinion.

Is the use of numerology by humans an effective device for providing answers, explanations or predictions? Is numerology used in your realm? (D) Indeed, sir. Definitely, sir. There is numerology in my realm also. We make use of it. We often do. They are important because they are fun and helpful to be fun. Doesn't a certain number hit you well sometimes? Can I just say sir, "one one one one".

If people like to travel and explore various cultures and places throughout the world, is it likely that they will still derive pleasure from doing that when they are in the spirit world? Indeed, sir. People who are inquisitive will remain inquisitive. People in the spirit world actually do like to visit places in the physical world. Certainly, I have come from a big place.

When a person is in the spirit world, does that person have any emotional attachments to the dates of his birth or his death from when he was in the physical? Ridiculous, sir.

Does the place where a person died have any significance to them or purpose for them after they have crossed over? It is just another place to be put at rest. It has no meaning; [it is] not where they have lived. The meaning of where they have lived is much more important than the place where they have perished.

In your realm, how would you define love? When I care about someone else more than I care about myself, that is true love.

Like humans, do spirits sometimes do or say things that they later regret? Indeed, sir. That is why pencils have erasers.

7. Spirits' activities

Is it possible for an individual to overcome physical addictions while in the spirit world? Does this include alcohol, drugs, gambling, sex. food? If they realize, sir, that it is an issue. Most of us do not realize that we have issues. It does not necessarily have to reoccur in a subsequent lifetime as karma.

What do souls on your plane do for entertainment? We are here to assist you, which is entertainment for us.

In your world, in addition to helping those on this plateau and helping those when they cross over, what kind of work do you do? Do music and visual arts play a role in your world? I am aiding and assisting you. Is that not work? Not all are able to assist. Music and art are manmade. Beauty is in the eye of the beholder. Do you not agree?

Do spirits sometimes need to restore their energy? If so, how? Yes, my dear sir. We do that. We do not sleep in a physical sense. We withdraw unto ourselves and do not communicate with others.

When there is a major disaster such as an earthquake or a tsunami in our world in which many people are killed, does that cause repercussions in your world? (W) We are aware of what is to be and we are always there to welcome those who are coming into our world.

Are there places in the universe where spirits cannot or are forbidden to go? I never heard of a place that is forbidden. All systems are available to all. I have full freedom to go anywhere in the universe and can do that instantaneously.

When there are spirits in a house, can electrical appliances be activated by spirits? Indeed, sir. We cannot control this but have fun doing this nonsense. They can sometimes be activated even when they are not connected to an electrical outlet. (Note: At this point during the channeling session there was a very loud clap of thunder.) You hear the thunder? It is your electricity answering you, sir.

Can spirits in your world wreak havoc or manipulate objects in the physical world much the same as earthbound poltergeists do? Indeed. In other words they don't have to be an earthbound spirit. They do it for harassment as you harass on your plateau.

Like earthbound spirits, do spirits in your world have the ability, for example, to sit in a rocking chair and make the chair rock back and forth so that anyone could see it rocking without actually seeing the spirit? Indeed, sir, and I am not an earthbound spirit.

If someone dies with unfinished business, do they try to finish it, or help a problem after they die or do they just let it go. In most cases, they will just let it go but in the case that you [the person who asked this question] are talking about, he will try to complete it. By that, he means to help you.

8. Miscellaneous

Is life in the spirit world easier or more pleasurable than it is in the physical world or is it just different? It depends on the route you take, sir. If you wish to take a difficult route, then life would be difficult. I have said that I do not want to reincarnate. That implies that I prefer my existence in the spirit world rather than in the physical world. Life in the spirit world can be more pleasant than life in the physical world. Indeed, sir, indeed. Indeed. It's very simple and easier. On Earth you proceed to dominate each other as you well know. It's a possibility that many of the religions developed the concept of heaven because life is so much easier here. Only heaven knows that. I am not aware of such a place as hell. It is not on our map or chart, you know.

Is life in your world where the concept of heaven and hell originated for us? (H) My answer, sir, what is heaven or what is hell? When people arrive [on this plateau] we are here to greet them and console them. They will feel comfort and ease and happiness in arriving when they come on our plateau. Heaven and hell is purely a religious concept. It's another way to have control. You have control with your religion. You make your own heaven, what you call heaven, and you make your own hell as you well know. Heaven and hell is a state of judgment.

Does a person's age at the time of passing into the spirit world have any effect on their transition to the spirit world or his life in the spirit world? (A) It makes no difference how old you are when you enter into a new regime. Age does not matter.

Do high energy evil entities exist in the spirit realm? Indeed, sir, indeed. A spirit at the same level as I am could be evil. If I don't agree with them they are evil. Is evil not knowledgeable? Evil is ignorance.

Since stars, planets and other celestial bodies exist in the physical world, do they also exist in the spirit world? Indeed, sir.

Does astrology have influence in the spirit world as it does in the physical world? Indeed, sir, and astrology has influence in the spirit world as it does in your world. Astrology always existed and always was helpful. Those in my realm do not make use of astrology. It exists in my world but we don't use it. Not all of us are interested in stars or planets. It is actually effective in your world.

Are there parasites in the spirit realm that feed off of the negative energy created by humans? No. There is nothing in the spirit world. No, we don't allow it. We just reject it from the very beginning. We do not have that in our world.

Does prayer play a role in the spirit world much the same as it does in the physical world? To whom do you pray? What is prayer? It helps, sir, to a degree. We pray to ourselves, sir, to the god that is within ourselves. I define prayer as wishing. I have said that even better than prayer is to visualize something. It is more productive than prayer. Undoubtedly so.

What aspect or aspects of life on your plateau do some entities find difficult? Having to change the environment. Sometimes it is difficult, sometimes not; sometimes familiar and sometimes not. We don't always come back to America.

Although spirits do not experience physical pain, do they experience emotional pain? I myself do not experience physical pain because I am not in the physical but I experience emotional pain when people do not listen to me. It is painful when I am here to assist you and my assistance is ignored. So it does hurt, not me individually, but it is hurtful when you are not reaching your hand out for help and help is given for you.

Even though time does not exist in the spirit dimension, is there a distinction between the past, present and future? It is all together now. It is always now. As your wife has said many times, "How do you spell NOW? Turn it around and you have WON. You are living the present, past and future all at once.

If there is no such thing as time in your dimension, can an action and the consequences of the action occur simultaneously? Indeed.

Although there is no gender, race or religious distinction in your world, are there any other kinds of class groupings of spirits other than higher or lower levels? We are sitting here adjusting and we're saying yes and no and yes and no. That is the truth. It does not matter.

C. EARTHBOUND SPIRITS, GHOSTS, POLTERGEISTS, DEMONS

1. The world of earthbound spirits

From your perspective, what are earthbound spirits? How would you define or describe them? [They are] people that cannot leave [the physical world] because they are seeking your assistance on Earth here and you do not let them go and continue on their journey. They are in a very much confused state of mind and they will continue to be so until you let them go. Most of the time individuals are not aware that they are deceased but they will move on once they realize they have passed.

When a person dies, is it sometimes more advantageous or desirable to that person to knowingly remain earthbound for a while before crossing over before entering the spirit world? Indeed, sir. That is sometimes questionable. At times it is possible that the person might want to oversee, for example, the work on a project he had be working on until it is completed by others. It depends upon the individual.

Do some spirits remain earthbound because they fear that they will go to hell if they follow the light, perhaps because of their religious upbringing? Who is to judge and what is hell? There is always fear. The unknown is always fearful. Fear could be a reason why they remain earthbound. My answer to your question is yes.

When we use the term ghost to refer to a spirit that is earthbound, can that entity be simultaneously in the spirit world? Indeed, sir. Sometimes it is only the etheric body that is earthbound. Sometimes it is the full spirit. It can be both.

Are there things than an earthbound spirit can experience that a soul which has entered the spirit world cannot experience? (B) Yes. An earthbound spirit is not fully in my realm. They do not wish to leave the earth. They wish to stay on the earth and cause problems. That spirit is partially in my world also.

When there has been extreme suffering in a place, do earthbound spirits often hold themselves to that place? It is certainly not the cemetery, sir, because we do not suffer on the grounds that you make for us to be sheltered. We do not suffer in the cemetery but that is where you place us. They are not attracted to places like prisons where they have suffered.

Are earthbound spirits often attracted to the place where they died? At times, sir, that is possible. The same cannot be said of the place where they are buried. Where they are buried is not a place where they have selected. You do not have to fear cemeteries.

If someone died many years ago and at that time their house was a small cabin and now it has been rebuilt as a large house, will the earthbound spirit see that home as a small cabin or as the newer house? They will see the house as it was.

Are the spirits of children who experienced a tragic death often likely to remain earthbound longer than other earthbound spirits? Yes, and they are likely to show themselves to other children.

Putting together some of the answers you have given us in the past, we have learned that spirits can remain earthbound for several reasons. You have mentioned that a person can remain earthbound intentionally in order to conduct unfinished business. You have also indicated that the person is lost and cannot find his way to the world of spirits and, third, that the emotions of Earth people are holding him back Are there any other reasons for remaining earthbound rather than going directly into the world of spirits? They do not know better. Their ignorance keeps them back.

Can earthbound spirits who have not fully crossed over into the spirit realm foresee the future the same as those in the spirit world do? Sometimes they do, sir, and sometimes they don't. It is correct to say that everyone in the spirit world can see the future to some extent. Everyone does not like chopped liver. I mean that some are not interested in seeing the future.

2. Earthbound spirits' interaction with the human world

Can an earthbound spirit who has not yet fully crossed over to the spirit world influence a person's thinking to help them? Indeed, sir, and they can help them be fearful too. That earthbound spirit is not a ghost but has just not fully moved over yet. They are not fully dressed.

It seems that earthbound spirits can manifest themselves so that many people can see or sense their presence but when spirits in your realm manifest themselves, only a few people can see them. Is that correct? That is not correct. If they can see earthbound spirits, they can see spirits from my world.

Can the use of tarot cards provide an entry for an earthbound spirit to communicate or in some way make its presence known to those on this plateau? Indeed, sir. They can be given positive energy. There could be danger in using tarot cards in regard to calling in negative spirits, depending on what they are used for. If they are wishing for control, it helps. It's like going to your psychic. Does she wish to control you? Does she wish to harm you? Ouija boards are definitely more harmful than tarot cards.

Do earthbound spirits sometimes materialize to ask for help from those in the physical world? They not only do ask for help, they plead and they beg for help. They also ask to control. So that can be good and it can be bad.

Are children's imaginary friends usually earthbound spirits? Can they be destructive spirits? Indeed, sir. They are not imaginary. They are real friends. They are playful usually, not destructive.

When earthbound spirits repeatedly do the same thing, such as moving the same object again and again, is that action usually to let people know of their presence? Indeed, sir.

It appears that earthbound spirits must follow physical laws, such as turning a doorknob and pushing the door in order to enter a room? Is that correct? That is correct. And they need energy, a great deal of energy to do that. They like to move chairs also. Spirits in my world can just appear and we do need energy.

Can an earthbound spirit that is not a demon inflict physical injury, such as scratches, on a person? Indeed they can. You are asking for the scratch. We take power over our own[selves]. It is a form of karma if you wish to call it that. Give it whatever name you wish to give it.

Do animals, especially dogs, have an innate ability to perceive the presence of earthbound spirits? Indeed, sir. Indeed they are aware, sir. They are very sensitive. They are not touched like humans are touched or confused.

Why does the room temperature drop when an earthbound spirit is present? Because it is easier for us to communicate in coolness. When it is cooler and not heated temperature, it is easier.

Eastern Airlines flight 401 crashed in the Florida Everglades in 1972. Did the pilot and the engineer actually appear as earthbound entities on other airplanes which used parts that were salvaged from that crashed plane? Yes, 'tis true. The parts that were used in other airplanes attracted them to the airplane and they were actually seen on a number of airplanes that used those parts. They were shadows that were seen. The equipment was seen also.

Is there usually a disturbance in electromagnetic energy in the vicinity of earthbound spirits? Indeed. They can and will be measured by equipment that you have.

Is there such a thing as physical entryways to the earthbound spirit world for humans who have a sensitivity to such? Indeed, sir.

When spirits attach themselves to a person, are those spirits able to experience the world through the senses of that person? Indeed, sir. All six senses.

3. Ghosts

Is it true that there are ghosts on this earth? I am not a ghost. Ghosts are people who are stranded and they cannot be moved. To be unstranded they have to release their thoughts, their garments, their impressions. Release them. Please release them.

When it is time for individuals to leave this plateau, can they get trapped on this plateau if they remain longer than they should? (A) Indeed, sir. They are referred to as ghosts in your language. I cannot say how long a soul can stay before becoming trapped.

Are ghosts people who have passed away but do not want to make the transition? Or cannot make the transition because you hold them back. Do not hold a deceased person back. Wish them well to go on. Don't mourn. Let them go. Let them be free and you will be free too. If a person has committed suicide they are not at rest. They are hurting not only themselves but their inner being. There are many people in every one of us. There is not just one person. That is why we don't know which way to go. That is why we have to listen to our first answer [thought].

After a person dies, are there sometimes occasions when at least part of that person's consciousness remains with the body at the gravesite? Is the part that remains earthbound what we call a "ghost" as contrasted with a "spirit", that part that moves to your plateau? (A) It is not for me to give you an example. The answer to your question would simply be yes. There are times that our consciousness does not dissolve. We are aware. If you wish to give names, that would be correct if you want to call it such. Call it what you will.

Are ghosts always earthbound spirits or can they sometimes be something else? They can be elsewhere [something else] too, sir. There are many kinds of spirits and issues when we leave this plateau.

Would you say that the majority of ghosts are harmless to humans? Indeed, sir. If poltergeists wish to frighten you, they can frighten you. If you wish not to pay attention, then they will not frighten you.

Are there any rules that ghosts must play by? Is there a limit to how far they can go? Can we bar the door? Indeed. No one will have control over us that we do not allow. The more education we have in this area, the better off we are. The more knowledge we have that we are in control and no one or nothing can control us unless we wish to be controlled; unless we have a higher regard for someone else's ridiculous opinion over our opinion. We can say that the wanting or not wanting comes from the unconscious level rather than the conscious level.

People say that is ghostly spirits that are the cause of so many people committing suicide at Aokigahara located at the base of Mount Fuji in Japan. Is that correct? (W) Japan, sir, has its own influence and has been inundated by much water. The concern there in Japan is the water, the overflow. There is very little truth in ghostly influence. They are committing suicide because they are mentally disturbed and they are in fear.

Can a ghost pass through a person's body and that person feel the energy pass through him even if the ghost is not seen? Indeed, sir, it is often like a cold energy.

4. Demons

What are demons? Is it their intent to take possession of humans? A demon is miserable, negative. A demon is a scorpion that clamps onto you; a soul that wishes misery to join misery. A demon is a negative spirit. All earthbound entities are not demons. There are people that eat meat today. People that eat flesh are demons. The intent of demons is to harm humans, or frighten or control. Demons can be removed through exorcism.

Do demons sometimes attach themselves to a person and then remain dormant until many years later when something arouses them? Indeed, sir. That is very possible. If a person becomes religious, that is not the cause of awakening the demon. Fear within the person is the action that will bring the action out. If you believe in demons, you will have demons. If you don't believe, then the demons will not harm you. Demons will only harm you only if you believe in them.

Regarding demons that attach themselves to people, are they usually something other than earthbound humans? Were they ever members of the spirit world in which you dwell? Do they have gender? Indeed, sir. Some are of alien origin. They are not fallen angels. They were members of the spirit world in which I dwell. They are amongst you also. Demons have gender even though in my world we don't have gender. They can be either male or female. Most of you are both.

Are demons that attach themselves to humans always entities in the spirit world who performed nefarious deeds when they were in the physical world? Indeed, sir. They were negative and continue to be negative until they learn to be positive. Their basic home is in the astral realm. They are bugs in the attic.

Do demons sometimes attach themselves to the individual while they are still in the womb? Can they attach themselves at any time? Do they attach themselves to specific organs? Demons attach at different cycles. There are different cycles that demons attach themselves. They attach themselves to specific organs sometimes.

Can a person be simultaneously possessed by multiple demons? Indeed, sir.

Some people believe that demons are created by Satan. Is that true? Demons are a state of mind, sir. Whether they exist or no longer exist depends on your mind. As I have said in the past, demons are negative energies. The source of those negative energies is a negative mind. You attract demons to yourselves by your thoughts.

When a demon is perceived by people in the physical world is that always the manifestation of an evil earthbound spirit? Not necessarily. Not true. It is their own being that is evil.

Can demons attach themselves to objects and places as well as to people? Indeed, sir, if you believe in demons. Demons exist but you can tell them to go away. Tell them to leave and go in peace. You don't have to listen to them. Demons cannot force anyone to do anything they don't want to do.

Can demons show themselves to humans in whatever form they choose? Why do demons not show their faces when they materialize? Indeed sir. That is how demons are demons because they deceive you. They don't show their faces because that is pleasure for them because they are scaring the person more. They are devious. They are controlling. They wish to control. They are evil. Anything evil that wishes to control should not control. Some demons have been physical humans before becoming demons; some have not.

Are there people who can sense the presence of demons in other people? Do demons have names? At times that is possible. Demons have names. They do not want their names to be known. Most are idiots.

5. Poltergeists

Would you say that poltergeists are ghosts that have enough energy to make noises and make objects move? Indeed, sir. They can do anything they wish to scare the hell out of you. Some poltergeists can be negative and others not negative. They can be negative when they wish to have control. They are there to control and have their way.

Are poltergeists always evil entities? Mostly. Mostly or just children or pranksters. They sometimes make things move just to get your attention because they need help from you.

From what source do poltergeists get their energy to move physical objects and cause various kinds of havoc and damage in our world? Drawing on their own anger or other strong emotions, poltergeists can become energized to the point that they can be heard or move physical objects. Their energy is so strong in what they want to say to you. They want to say it over and over and repeat it over and over. They want you to hear them. They want you to listen to them. They want to control you. You do not wish for any other entity to control you. You do not want to be controlled. Fear or other negative emotions of people make it easier for poltergeists to perform their activities. If they do not control, they get angry.

Can poltergeists attach themselves to people as well as to places? Indeed, sir. They can attach themselves to people.

Are poltergeists frequently the victims of a violent death, such as a murder or tragic accident? Can be, sir. Can be if they wish to be. If it has not been solved and has not been equalized.

Can places, such as a house, prison or hospital serve as entrances for multiple poltergeists to enter the physical world? 'Tis possible, sir, but not probable.

Can a poltergeist's actions result directly in the death of a person? Not directly sir, indirectly but they can cause fear when one is not aware.

Do poltergeists ever show themselves when they are making objects move? Indeed, sir. Some people can actually see the spirit and the results of the spirit's actions.

Can poltergeists' voices be heard by people who are not mediums? Indeed. sir. You would be able to hear a poltergeist's voice if you wished to but you do not wish to.

Can poltergeists which haunt a place make things, such as blood, appear in the physical world? If they wish, they can actually make things appear.

Do poltergeists often follow people when they move from one home to another rather than remaining in the original home? Indeed that is possible but rare. They do not always want to harm and hinder. They more often remain in the place but they can move.

Do teenagers often provide an easier entryway for poltergeists or demons than do other people? Indeed, sir, because teenagers are more easily influenced. Those that are in adulthood, they are easily influenced also.

Can babies become poltergeists when they die? Indeed, sir.

6. Negative Spirits

Can malevolent spirits attach themselves to a person and influence them to perform evil deeds? Indeed so. It is true. Depends on what you consider evil. Do you kill unless you want to kill? It is your willingness to do many things. You can't be forced by malevolent spirits.

Can evil earthbound spirits lie dormant for long periods of time and then become active when someone disturbs their resting place or comes in the vicinity of where they are? Indeed, sir. That is true. That is enabling.

Can the use of Ouija boards unleash evil spirits that can take possession of a person or bring about negative happenings? Indeed. Definitely.

Can animals be possessed by evil spirits? (T) Indeed. And they can be earthbound and not cross over.

When a person has been hypnotized, is it easier for an evil entity to take possession of that person? No, sir. They cannot take over when a person does not wish to be taken. They cannot take over one who does not wish to be controlled. The same can be said about a person who is influenced by drugs. The drugs will take over. Taking drugs does not make it easier for an evil spirit to take over a person. If the person does not wish to be so, it cannot do so.

Can an evil spirit take over a person and make the person's facial features appear different or endow him with supernatural strength? Indeed, sir.

Are there certain specific words or phrases, which when spoken, have the power to remove negative spirits? Indeed. "No" is one [such] word. There are also certain specific words or phrases that can be uttered to bring about change that the speaker desires. Your phraseology is very important. An example of one phrase [to get a spirit to go away] is "Leave in peace." That has power.

Can ancient Egyptian mummies or artifacts from their tombs bring negative energy to people? Can the spirit of the mummy take possession of a person? It depends, my dear sir, on the energy of the person you are talking about. If conditions are right they can affect people. [Regarding the mummy taking possession], that is nonsense. It depends on the weakness of the individual that you are referring to.

Are there books that exist that give effective instructions for conjuring up evil spirits? There is always a book for anything, sir. If a person follows the instructions in a book and it is their desire, which is nonsense, they can actually conjure up an evil spirit. There are those that seek out nonsense.

Is there power in the use of the pentagram to evoke evil forces if the user believes in it? If the user believes in it, it will be for the user. The user that is doubtful should not be a user.

Is it dangerous for a person to imbibe large quantities of alcohol or to take mind altering drugs because doing so makes it easier for negative spirits to influence or attach themselves to people when they are in a weakened condition? It is easier for any spirit to enter when the person is not in control. The danger in taking drugs or alcohol is more than just a physical danger.

Can diabolical entities that attack or attach themselves to humans sometimes be something other than disembodied Earth humans? Indeed.

Can a single diabolical entity simultaneously manifest itself as multiple diabolical entities? Indeed, sir. I also can manifest myself as different entities simultaneously but not diabolical.

Can dark forces that affect humans emanate from anywhere in the universe or are they always of Earth origin? Anywhere in the universe.

7. Haunting

Can objects, such as a car, be possessed or haunted by earthbound spirits? Are the spirits who do so usually evil? Indeed. sir. If you wish to call them evil, yes. There are all kinds of spirits and people. Some are evil. It depends from which end of the road we wish to see them.

When a place is haunted by earthbound spirits, do people often become depressed and withdrawn? Or frightened. It can affect the person's personality.

If an earthbound spirit haunts a house and then that house is torn down and replaced by a new house, will that entity haunt the new house? The entity will haunt the earth until it finds peace. It is often the land, rather than the building, to which the entity is attracted. The land is essential. The building doesn't really matter.

Can the presence of a specific person living in a home be the only reason that an earthbound entity haunts a house? It is possible but not probable.

8. Exorcism and cleansing

Are religious articles or religious scriptures read aloud useful in exorcisms of poltergeists and demons? Indeed, even though it is nonsense, it does work. A means of exorcizing an evil spirit is to pick up a cross and hold it close to you. That will work even though you don't believe in the cross. The same is true even if the user is doubtful of its potential. It does have power. You don't necessarily have to believe in something in order for it to become effective.

Can evoking the name of Jesus Christ help exorcise an evil spirit who possesses a person or cleanse a place that is haunted? It is absolutely effective in cleansing a place, and powerful. If you were to use that name, or any other name that has power, it would have the same effect as a priest using it.

Is sage actually functional for the cleansing of a house from earthbound spirits? Water itself is also good for cleansing. It does not have to be holy water. What makes it holy?

Can spirits in your realm be instrumental in exorcising evil spirits from places or people in our realm? It is not important sir. It is more important for you to exorcise them.

Can demons be exorcised trough the rituals of the Catholic Church? My dear sir, it is helpful. This church is very strong and so it can be done. It can be helped. It depends upon the belief. Do not put the Catholic Church in the Jewish church. I am not saying that if you are Jewish and have a demon attached to you that you should not have a Catholic priest exorcise the demon. It really doesn't matter.

9. Miscellaneous

When a person has a near death experience, is there an increased likelihood that the person will pick up a spirit attachment? Indeed, sir. That is at times because the person does not have full control. It is easier for a spirit to attach under those circumstances. Sometimes that attachment will remain with the person after the near death experience, sometimes not, either way.

Can ordinary cameras sometimes photograph earthbound spirits that the human eyes cannot see? Can ordinary sound recorders pick up sounds from them that humans cannot hear? Are thermal imaging cameras an effective means of detecting earthbound spirits? Indeed they can. Thermal imaging cameras definitely.

Do spirits on your side try to enlighten earthbound spirits and encourage them to move on? It is important for you to encourage them to move on.

D. COMMUNICATION AND INFLUENCE FROM SPIRITS AND OTHER UNSEEN SOURCES

1. Spirit influence and assistance

Do all people have a spirit guide who stays with them throughout their life? Yes, indeed. Each person has a spirit guide through their entire life. Some even have two or three. At times other guides will come for specific occasions. We will stay with a person as much as needed and we will guide as much as needed.

Since you already have stated that angels do not choose whom they protect, is the same true regarding spirits and the humans for whom they serve as guides? Indeed sir. A guide has no choice in whom they want to be a guide for.

Is it true that what we call intuition is often the influence of our spirit guides? Indeed. Intuition should be taken seriously and must be followed through. Intuition is influenced by you. Remember your first thought [when confronted with an issue to be solved].

Does a person's good luck often come from the influence of a very attentive spirit guide? Indeed.

Can those in your realm bring protection to humans directly or do you act as intermediaries between humans and angels or other higher level entities? Both are available to us. We conference with our elders.

Is it true that each person engaged in intellectual activity (i.e. scientist, medical doctor, writer, teacher) is always assisted by one or several spirits? Yes. At times assisted by several of us. Most of the time, yes, it is true. People are sometimes assisted by other people just like on this plateau. Some of us need assistance, good or bad. On our plateau we at times get assistance of other spirits.

Is it true that all modern communication technologies (e.g. computers or wi-fi) are inspired to humans by spirits who previously experienced embodiment on more advanced worlds? (V) Yes. This is true. It was all here before you simple souls appeared. My good friend Plato had all of these advanced capabilities like your electricity.

Do entities in your world sometimes seek to harm people in our world who wronged them while they were together in the physical? Can the harm be real? In answer to your question, yes. We try to show you we do not forget. We do not forgive either. So be careful. sometimes the mere facts can make a person deranged.

Can people in your world have malevolent influence over people in our world? Over those in your world? On your plateau can a spirit be hurtful to another? A simple answer to you will be yes. They can be misleading to the living and to the passed on. Some of us are tricky.

Do spirits sometimes show themselves as another person we know in order to fool us? Not to fool but to help you interpret things. Sometimes you see us from the corners of your eyes. Indeed, spirits can show themselves as another person to manipulate you.

Some people say that they feel more energized after a channeling session with you. What is the source of that energizing? Do you have anything to do with that? [The source is] being relieved and freed. We are here to aid and help others. I would say that you are picking up energy from me. If you wish to state it that way, you will be stronger and more assertive to go ahead full force with kindness.

When we know people on Earth who have transitioned into the spirit world, do they keep in contact with us and do they want to help us? At times some wish to help you and care about you. Some are not able to but some are able to. You can tell who are the helpers and who just want to go on their own voyage.

Are the questions I [Charles Zecher] ask you sometimes sent to my mind by nonphysical entities or can I take credit for the origin of all the questions I ask you? You can take credit and you are being influenced and you have a very intelligent quick mind. Some of the questions come into your mind from other sources and some you create from your own mind. You have a wonderful mind, sir.

2. Spirit communications

When we sleep and travel to the spirit realm, do we sometimes meet directly with our spirit guides? Indeed.

Do spirits on your side enter our dreams? If they wish to.

Can individuals who are in a coma or vegetative state communicate actively in your realm? Indeed, sir. Indeed. Most of you are [in a coma or vegetative state]. Is that not true?

It seems that more high energy entities in your world who channel to humans are of male energy rather than of female energy. Is that correct? Both are equal sir. Equal. Does not matter what gender you select. Both are equal. We have no gender here, neither male or female. We have fun either way. When we show ourselves to others we can show as either male or female.

From my observations of my wife's communications with recently crossed over souls, it seems that some souls are immediately aware that they are in your world but others do not realize they have crossed over even though they are communicating with her. Is this observation correct? (A) Correct sir, very correct.

Also from my observations of my wife, it seems that many souls are able to communicate immediately after they cross over but then must spend a long period of no communication before they begin communicating again. Is this frequently the way it happens or are my observations incorrect? (A) Sometimes that is correct. Sometimes those that pass over can aid you but then they have to move on.

Why do some spirits channel in rhyme? That is their way to express themselves. We at the beginning spoke in rhyme, you forget?

When a soul is on an interplanetary or interstellar sojourn between physical incarnations on Earth, it seems that the entity is unable or reluctant to communicate to mediums in this world? Is that observation correct? I would like to answer you with a pure yes.

<u>What are the orbs that often appear in photographs?</u> They are people that have messages. They are entities probably from your world. In our world we have so many plateaus. We have a star system. We don't have just one system like your Earth system.

<u>Are there any writers of poetry or prose who have transitioned who still want to write and are looking for someone to write or receive their words?</u> Indeed. You can get in touch with them. If you are interested, you can think of them and call them but not all will answer. Keep thinking of it and it will come to you and it will bring you comfort and aid.

3. Influence and assistance from other entities

<u>Do angels channel information to humans as the spirits do? (J)</u> Indeed, sir. Angels are more apparent. Sometimes they show themselves and they don't show themselves for all. Mediums can tell the difference of an angel and a spirit. Angels are dear souls. Spirits are not always that. Angels are always honest, truthful and sincere but spirits are not always.

<u>Are the butterflies that often appear to people after a loved one has died sometimes manifestations of angels or some sort of communication from the one who has just passed over? (J)</u> Indeed, sir. They should be cherished.

<u>Do spirit guides sometimes request assistance from angels to help the person whom they are serving as a guide?</u> Indeed, sir.

<u>Do entities from realms other than that of the angels or your plateau communicate directly with humans?</u> Some do. Some are able to and some humans are very stubborn. They don't listen.

<u>Are there individuals in the physical world who channel entities from realms above the spirit realm?</u> Indeed, sir. That would be above what you call the mental world.

<u>Is it possible for us to tell the difference between an angel manifesting as a physical human and a spirit manifesting as a physical human?</u> If they wish and they seek an answer, yes. They can tell the difference. Most of

the time, my dear sir, is it not what we wish or we ask for advice. Someone negative can also respond and give negative advice.

Do we receive information from extraterrestrials when we are in the dream state? Indeed.

Are animal totems that are said to hover over each person's head a reality? What is the purpose of a totem? (T) Indeed. Part of a composition. A build-up of strength to help the individual gain strength.

Are conscious entities present at the time of conception ready to aid in the process of bringing life to the human body? Indeed so, my dear sir, but we each have our own free will. The free will will make its own choice.

In regard to the original Star Trek television series, were the authors influenced by something other than their imagination: either past life memories or some outside source? Is the same often true of other writers of science fiction? Just as your Dick Tracey, just as your cartoons, it was their imagination. Science fiction authors are often influenced by outside sources and they will become more known. The better science fiction writers will be those of the future.

Did Gene Rodenberry, author of the television program Star Trek, receive information from extraterrestrials that influenced his writings? And his imagination. His thinking was influenced partly by extraterrestrials and partly by his imagination. The part that was influenced by extraterrestrials was real. It actually existed.

Throughout history has the majority of great scientists been influenced by extraterrestrials? (V) Indeed, sir. Their creations are not necessarily emanating from their own minds but their minds are being influenced by the external and being controlled. Thomas Edison, for example, received a lot of his information from other sources. He had information on what we call electricity. He channeled the information from extraterrestrials.

Was there extraterrestrial or angel involvement in aiding the Americans in the fight against the British in the War of 1812 in regard to the manipulation of weather conditions? (Q) Ridiculous, but angels and extraterrestrials were always there to help the Americans.

Do the Illuminati exert a strong influence on the Hollywood entertainment industry? On the media in our country? On politics and political parties in our country? Indeed, sir [pronounced very emphatically]. They own it. That is the music industry. They have a strong influence on the media also, all of it, sir. They control it. They control your political situation. I would like to think that they are more influential on one political party rather than the other. There will be a third party. The third party will arise as an offshoot of one of the current parties.

Did the Nordic race of extraterrestrials aid the Germans in World War II. Is that correct? (D) Indeed. They are disliked by other extraterrestrials.

Is it possible for a person to cast spells on other people without their knowledge? They [the one casting the spell] will feel better. It is ridiculous that casting spells will be more effective if devices such as a lock of their hair or a voodoo doll are used. Spells cannot be cast if the affected person does not believe that spells can be cast on them. You can always avoid what you may relate as a spell. You yourself may be pointing the gun and remember where the trigger finger is. [It] can backfire.

Brad Johnson channels an entity named Adronis from the star system Sirius. Are the messages from him credible? He knows a lot of friends, you know. People know people and take people's advice and they do not take their own advice. It is always good to listen, sir, to the messages that he channels but the advice of jumping off the bridge isn't always right. The messages from Adronis are not always accurate.

Can spirits, as well as angels, put thoughts or ideas into the minds of humans? (J) Indeed, sir. Humans usually think that those thoughts are their own thoughts. Physical extraterrestrials, not just spirits, can also put thoughts into your minds. Our minds are wonderful attractions.

Does any entity, other than oneself, have the power to take control of a person's will? If a person lets their control go, they will listen to whatever they choose. You are the masters of the control of your free will. If you wish to relinquish that control, you can. No matter how brilliant you are, there is someone who is even smarter.

Is the Dogon tribe in Mali Africa a descendant of or influenced by the inhabitants of the Sirius B star system? Indeed, sir. They are strange people. They love to play around.

When a person prays for assistance, does it help if more than one person prays for the assistance? It always helps. It can be heard. It is a stronger signal for the request. When everyone cries out for rain, more rain will come.

If I were to meet you or other extraterrestrials in the physical could you be able to project thoughts into my mind without saying anything aloud as just spirits and angels do? If we were to meet in the physical, we could put ideas into your mind the same as spirits and angels put ideas into your mind. This would be easy, sir.

4. Influence and assistance from objects

Can physical objects such as a statue of St. Jude placed on the dashboard of your car or a mezuzah placed at the doorway of your home or amulets be imbued with special powers, such as for protection or healing? (S) It only comforts those who believe. It is a comfort to believe in nonsense.

Can symbols, incantations or physical objects such as voodoo dolls be used to bring harm to people or put a curse on them? If it makes you feel better to put a pin in someone's behind. It is much better to be able to forgive. A person who wishes to do that to someone might receive it themselves.

In using a pendulum to douse answers to questions evoking a yes or no response, where does the force come to move the pendulum come from? The pendulum gives you comfort. The energy comes from within one's self. We as individuals when we are on this earth make things happen. We do things to make things happen. We walk away from things to make them not happen. We plan and do whatever we perceive ourselves as I have mentioned. We go for the brass ring and pull it if we wish it. How many are fearful in going for chances?

5. Humans seeking and providing assistance

If you want something to occur, are any of the following more effective than the others: to think it, to say it aloud, to visualize it, or to pray for it? Saying it aloud will bring it to you. Visualizing will definitely help. It is the best way, better than praying.

Is there a best way to pray and does it matter whom you pray to? Whatever feels comfortable for you, whatever makes you feel complete, whatever makes you feel good and resourceful, that is the best way. And you needn't pray aloud. You can keep your thoughts within you. Praying is thoughts. When we pray to God or whomever we wish to pray to, we are asking for help. Most of the time when we need to ask, we are pleading for help. We have different planets that we pray to or pray for. When you pray you say that you are praying to God but you are actually like broadcasting out to any entity that wants to pick it up. There are many gods. You always think of prayer as something going directly to God but sometimes it is an angel that will hear us or a spirit that will pick up that broadcast. You can be helped from various sources. That is what God is if you wish to call it God. Maybe an angel is what you call God and maybe God is one's self; the god within you. I have said that you can pray to yourselves, meaning the god within yourself.

Religions teach us to get down on our knees when we pray. Does bowing down when we pray make our prayers more effective? Indeed, not. It does help to say them out loud.

Are our prayers or calls to spirits or angels more likely to be answered if we promise to do or stop doing something in return? It will not help your prayers but it will help you. Your prayers go into the wind [i.e. broadcast everywhere].

Who answers our prayers? You do. Your soul connection brings the energy. It makes you feel better when you feel there is a mommy or a daddy watching over you that can fulfill your dreams. Is that not true? In reality you are self-dependent. It's like the Theosophists who believe that thoughts can be manifested into reality. Prayers are thoughts.

Would you say that for humans prayer could be defined as submitting a request to any higher level force above that of the human kingdom? Prayer to me is very interesting, a really waste of time. I do not understand what prayer is. [It is] wishing for something. We don't have such things. I am trying to figure out what God is.

Will talking lovingly to household plants and other forms of vegetation help them to grow more healthy? Indeed. A plant or anything that is perfection will blossom.

Will talking lovingly to inanimate objects, such as your car, have a positive effect on them or their functioning? Why not? Talking positively, it is very necessary for a person to think positive and be positive. It is very important for your existence, not only for you and what ails you.

Is the use of numerology by humans an effective device for providing answers, explanations or predictions? Is numerology used in your realm? (B) Indeed, sir. Definitely, sir. There is numerology in my realm also. We make use of it. We often do. They are important because they are fun and helpful to be fun. Doesn't a certain number hit you well sometimes? Can I just say sir, "one one one one".

6. Miscellaneous

What is the force that enables a person to perform automatic writing? The force that causes automatic writing is mental. It is the same force that causes the pendulum to operate.

Are what we consider the laws of science, such as the Law of Gravity, implemented automatically or are there conscious forces overseeing the implementation of those laws? (V) At times there are conscious entities overseeing that that occurs. With all of what you call the laws of science you can say that conscious entities, whether they be angels or some other kind of entities, see that those laws occur [are implemented].

You have said that there is power in sound. Is there power to raise our level of consciousness in the aum chant? Is the same true of the Buddhist chant Nam-mythoi-renge-kayo? Indeed, sir. It would be of your benefit to practice these sounds in a group situation. And in speaking to me the voices are able to protect and tell me about your future as you speak.

Since you have told us of the importance of numerology, would you say that there is significant negativity in the number 666 or is that something without meaning that religion has invented? There is a reason for that. There is a negative with 666. It is not just something that religion has invented.

You have said that the number 666 actually is a very negative number. Conversely, would you say that the number 7 is a very positive number? Indeed, sir.

Are what appear to be weird, unrealistic dreams just the meaningless products of our minds or are those dreams some sort of coded or disguised information that comes from our higher self? That depends on your dream. You could have a weird, unrealistic dream. It is not necessarily some disguised coded message.

Can a person cause physical or emotional harm to another person from a distance simply by the thoughts they project about that person? Can they bring harm to a person by performing certain rituals such as sticking a pin in a doll that is intended to represent that person? Wouldn't that be wonderful? If you think evil about a person or wish them harm it will go back to you. When you point an arrow and aim at a person with your arrow, that arrow will boomerang. You cannot either physically or emotionally harm another person. It is your thoughts that hurt you. If you had a doll that represented another person and stuck a pin in it, the thoughts or actions only hurt those that have it. The one that has the evil thoughts will have the evil. No one can hurt anyone. We only hurt ourselves with our thoughts. Thoughts help ourselves, praise ourselves. Our thoughts are very important and very useful. Think positive and be positive.

Is there such a thing as random events or outcomes or is everything that occurs the direct result of specific actions or influences of conscious entities? That is, is there such a thing a toss of the coin? It is the way we toss the coin. Everything that occurs is the result of specific actions. There is no such thing as random results. It is already achieved who is going to win the lottery.

E. MY GUIDE

1. Incarnations

If you were to tell us your names in one or more of your incarnations would we probably have heard of those personalities? Yes.

Would you be able to tell us if you were one of the major personages portrayed in the Old Testament of our Bible? (I) Indeed I am him, her, them. I was also incarnate at the time of Jesus. I was more than one person mentioned in the Bible. I have incarnated in many [star] systems.

Is your current personality the same as your last life? Indeed not. I have been here sooo many times before, so many times. It took me a while to learn what I needed to learn.

Do you remember all your previous lifetimes? Not all, my dear sir, and thank God for that. Some I wish I remembered. Some I don't. I remember drowning in Ireland. I didn't like that. I don't wish to tell you [my names in my incarnations] for fear you would be calling me.

Should we consider you to be an extraterrestrial? You have not seen me but my form is different from the human form. Indeed, very different. I am not as ugly as you are. I can display a human form to your wife because I have had Earth incarnations. I can also display myself in other forms.

When you yourself incarnated in other star systems did your physical bodies always need air, water and food? At that time, yes, my dear sir. They were different [from human bodies]. Since I have had incarnations in other star systems you could consider me an extraterrestrial if you wish my dear sir, and human also. In other star systems our bodies were always carbon based. It was easier for you to see through a carbon based [body].

You have said that you yourself no longer have a need to reincarnate. Does that mean that you will remain on the astral plane forever? I don't want life in the physical again. Indeed it is correct that I will move eventually beyond the spirit world.

Since you have said that you no longer need to reincarnate, how was that determined? I do not wish to come back to the nonsense you people put on yourselves. I decided not to come back. The community agrees. They are those who make regulations above and beyond our plateau. They help us. It seems I am a trouble maker. I have lived on Earth many times before. I do not wish to return. I am administering a good deed and working and helping and assisting those that need assistance and pleasure. That is why I am here with my friends to assist you. I have had other physical lifetimes on other planets in your star system as well as Earth. My head is always in the clouds anyway.

Was there a soul connection between Jesus and John the Baptist? (F) Indeed, but they are two different entities. Jesus was a dear friend. John started trouble in our realm. I was incarnated there at that time. It was difficult times. You wouldn't recognize the clothes I wore.

Who masterminded the construction of Stonehenge? (P) Many of us masterminded the construction. We had what you call architects. The extraterrestrials, the name you have selected to call us, are here now too. We are the bright ones, you know. You can call me an extraterrestrial also but I have had many lifetimes on Earth. I'm not coming back. No way! I do not like to live on Earth. Too many rules. I have been here many, many times.

What was the cause of the destruction of Sodom and Gomorrah as portrayed in the Bible? (I) 'Tis your Bible that made up the story. It really didn't occur. I remember not exactly as it was given down to you. When I was there, we had long black hair, curls. It was beautiful black. I cannot go further.

Is there such a thing as an intergalactic federation composed of various extraterrestrial groups? (MN) Yes, there are many. Human hybrids are placed on Earth to help humans to connect with extraterrestrials to the point that Earth may become part of the federation. Indeed just as the young lady that I have just spoken to, there are a number of you in this room who are hybrids. I do not wish to offend you but you all look so strange. Where I am from, my physical appearance is not the same as the appearance of the earth people. We do not have male or female. There is no such thing as division into sexes. We have more fun than you have. We are able to please ourselves. We don't rely on others to please us. I would say that we are what you might call hermaphrodite. We're just like a bug that reproduces. They're [those with the guide]showing me a white bug that reproduces itself. Some of it would be like a starfish where you cut of part of and a new entity [appears]. There are other ways of reproduction. I prefer my own physical appearance over yours.

2. Personal characteristics

Did you have the same level of intelligence or awareness when you were in the physical as you have now? If not, what brought you to this higher level of understanding? Indeed no. I arrived at this level of understanding by the view. I am now on a very high view. I can oversee much. It comes automatically at my level. It was not easy you know.

Do those in your world sometimes have memory problems and forget things they would normally be expected to remember, just as do people in our world? (B) Me, myself, no. I have no memory problems. Some do.

You have said that English is not your language and often ask us if you have said things correctly. With what language are you most comfortable speaking? There are many languages. We don't have to speak in Tongues. Probably my best language is Tongues.

Using spoken language, you have shown to us that you have a good sense of humor. How are you able to show your sense of humor on your plateau without spoken language? Just look at me and you will see. They sense my sense of humor. I had a good sense of humor in my previous lifetime.

In our world some people are gregarious and enjoy being with others but there are also people who are not very sociable and prefer being alone or having very little contact with others. Is the same true in your world? (B) Are they not boring? People are people in my world too, I would say, "Oh, yes." And I am one that is gregarious. I like to talk. I do not like to hear [listen]. There are also people in my world that tend to be loners and like being alone more. They are fearful people.

Since you mentioned that we looked like birds without wings and since we don't see ourselves as such, the implication is that you can identify yourself with a physical form that does not resemble us. Is that correct? Indeed, if you wish. I do not always see myself as a physical human being but rather as something else. In my lifetimes in other systems I did not look like human beings.

Is it appropriate to say that you are of a high level of energy in the astral world? How else can we refer to you that distinguishes you from lesser advanced souls in your realm? I consider myself to be more advanced than most people because I've been to your earth many, many times and I'm not coming back. I do enjoy coming and being in your presence and giving advice.

If we were able to see you in the physical form of your native planet, would some of us be fearful of your appearance? Not fearful, sir, hysterical. I have said that, even though I have had many incarnations on Earth, to my way of thinking humans are ugly. Therefore you can assume that I like my natural appearance better than my human appearance. The reason I show myself to your wife as I was when I was incarnate as a human is so that she will accept me more. She will also recognize me more. She loves the sandals I wear. That is the incarnation I choose to show myself to her. That was one of the incarnations as a character in your Bible.

3. As a guide and channeler

Since you have had many lifetimes in the physical, do you have a choice in which personality you will use in your work as a guide? Yes, I do. [This seems to contradict a previous answer.]

As you said you were the guide for several people, can you communicate with them simultaneously? At times and sometimes collectively. Simultaneously we reach out and they can hear us.

What led you to becoming my wife's guide? She is so sweet, such a nice person. She is very kind and thoughtful. We enjoy working with her. She has a good sense of humor.

Are you a guide to other people as well as to my wife? Indeed yes. We are very busy with her too, you know. And we are enjoying the pleasure of aiding and assisting. We are usually right. You know that, right?

When you answer our questions, do you often have a favorite group of friends assisting you? Some are not here with me [now]. They don't always agree with me. I am so always right. I have others assisting me but they don't know any better.

Are there questions or topics that you are not permitted to answer or talk about by those in charge? We are gathered here to explain to you. Sometimes that is true. A simple answer and direct is most important.

Would you say that you understand our questions not so much by our words but rather by the vibrations of our voice? When you answer us, it is sometimes difficult for you to formulate your response in our language for us to be able to understand what you are saying? Your vibrations, my dear sir, tell me much more than your words. Indeed, the voices, the feeling of the body, the feeling within, we know. We pick it up by the vibrations of your voice. When I answer you it is sometimes difficult, especially for those who do not speak [Tongues?] but I am reading peoples' minds if you want to call it that.

When we ask you questions do you receive information from levels above you or from the angels? Indeed, from both angels and levels above me. It depends on how I administer the answer. There are times I consult with others from my realm.

Although you said that those in your world can take any form they choose, from some of your answers to previous questions, it appears that you often visualize yourselves as physical humans. Is that correct? Indeed sir. I wish to adapt myself as an equal to you when I address you.

From your own experiences, what is the most important piece of advice that you could give to the people of Earth? Do not look for an enemy. You fight each other and argue with each other and slaughter each other. You disagree with each other.

Very often when you come to us you say that it was a long journey. At the same time you have said that in the world of spirits there is no such thing as time or space. Can we assume that by a long journey it means that transferring from where you are to here takes a lot of your energy? Indeed, sir. I am not talking about distance. I am talking about the amount of energy. When you travel does it not take energy for you? Even though there is no time or space, it takes energy. I have to get dressed for you. That is indeed a pleasure for me. I am an extraterrestrial. When I say I have to get dressed that means that I have to put myself in an Earth human being form rather than my native state. You hear me but cannot see me. Only your wife sees me as an Earthling not as an extraterrestrial.

You have said that the high degree of accuracy of your predictions is based on considering the past actions of people but are there also occasions where you actually foresee the future as it definitely will occur? Definitely, sir, and the future is very bright and not alarming and full of gaiety.

When we ask you questions, most often you give an answer immediately. Sometimes you pause for a while before answering. Do you pause because you are conferring with others? Indeed, sir. I am asking for advice from others who can help and give me advice to help you to become more successful.

4. Contacts with other sources of information

Do you have contact with human beings in other star systems? (M) Indeed I do. They are all the same or similar, just different systems.

According to the Blavatsky materials, there are, I believe, 63 entities which we call the masters who dwell in the mental realm? Do you have contact with these entities? Indeed we do, sir. We do not necessarily get advice from them, just their thoughts.

Do you visit the plateau above your plateau much the same as we visit your plateau when we sleep? Do you get help and guidance from those above you? Indeed, sir. We get interference and annoyance but sometimes they are correct. It is still interfering.

You have said that when helping humans, you sometimes confer with your elders. How would you define "elders"? Elders are people who are superior to our thinking. They are spirits who are more intelligent and have more insight.

5. Miscellaneous

A long time ago you said you would help my wife write a second book. Are the questions I am asking and the answers you are giving a means to the development of the book to which you were referring? I promised her I would stand by her and I do because she is kind.

Do elementals such as gnomes, fairies, leprechauns etc. really exist? Can you perceive them? Indeed they do! I do not like them.

Are there areas of knowledge or information that you are forbidden or otherwise unable to access, either directly or indirectly? Correct.

Do you show yourself differently to various other spirits depending on which lifetime you were associated with them in the physical? Indeed, sir. Do not we all have different appearances for different people? Some make us happy and some make us sad. Some make us hide. I do not want to be with [them]. Is that not true, sir?

Although you have said that you cannot predict the timing of future events, are you better able to state when events occurred in the past? It is of no issue, sir. The past is the past. The future is coming up, looking forward for you. We can foresee future events but not always when they will occur.

Do you have a companion? I do not need a companion. I need my strength and myself. Here on this plateau we do not have companions. That is not necessary. We are all strong.

Are there multiple spirit worlds just as there are multiple physical worlds or is there just one world of spirits? (L) Indeed, there are also multiple spirit worlds. Spirits such as I can instantaneously travel from one spirit world to another. My origin is not on this earth. Thank goodness for that. That is why it takes me a lot of energy to travel to you, from one spirit world to another.

Does the spirit world that is your home consist of only entities who were once physical entities on your home planet, or does it also contain entities whose origin was in other star systems? Sir, we are all here and we help each other. Each physical world has its own spirit world. Spirits from different worlds can be in the same spirit world.

Have you yourself traveled in the physical form from one place to another in the universe through wormholes or has your travel been in the spirit form only? In the spirit form. You don't need wormholes when you travel from one place to another in the spirit world.

When you are in a group and answering questions, do you like answering some questions better than others? My dear lady, it is my pleasure to be here and be of use to aid you and comfort you as best as possible. It is a pleasure that we get from our world to come here and help you as far as comfort is concerned. We do receive pleasure when we give pleasure.

Although you have told us many things about yourself, you have told our group that you do not want to reveal your identity to us. Why is that? That is because if many people were to call on me, that would be a drain on my energy level. That is one of many reasons. I do not have the energy that Jesus and Hitler have to be called on. Jesus has so much energy that he can be called on and that doesn't sap his energy. Hitler is an extremely negative energy. His name was negative. The person was not negative. They made him into a negative. In the spirit world where I am, the entity that was Hitler has a great deal of energy.

F. JESUS AND OTHER PERSONALITIES IN THE SPIRIT WORLD

1. Jesus the man

Would you describe the physical appearance of Jesus when he was on Earth, such as his hair, skin color, stature, facial features etc.? My dear people, many of you may not like it but Jesus was black, as black as his curly hair would allow him to be, a lovely man indeed.

How did Jesus' family pronounce his name? Yaho. Many different languages there. That was the Aramaic pronunciation.

Did Jesus travel to far off lands such as Egypt, Persia or India for the purpose of study in his lifetime? Correct. Yes, he went to all those places. All those places are so close and Jesus visited them. Very bright man you know. I dare not say anything negative about him.

While in the physical was Jesus what you might call in today's terminology a psychic? A medium? Indeed, sir, as all of you are psychic in many different areas. We all are psychic. He was also a medium to a point but his feelings were more to what you call psychic as he could see the future of people who can get well.

Is it correct to say that Jesus the man was a healer but did not perform miracles but that Jesus the Christ did perform miracles? Jesus the man was a man that was caring and loving and giving. Jesus that you call the Christ Almighty was a powerful one that was able to make peace within you. Jesus the man was a healer. The people who agreed with him and saw him and selected him to be a healer, he healed. Both Jesus the man and Jesus the Christ performed miracles.

Did Jesus perform all the miracles that are attributed to him in the Bible? Did he heal the sick? A lot of the information in the Bible about the miracles is imaginary. He healed the sick. Wouldn't it be wonderful if he turned water into wine? Wouldn't that be wonderful and we would all be drinking more water?

73

Although you have said that Jesus actually died on the cross, did he ever marry? Did he have children? Indeed sir, he did marry and have children. He was not a surgeon, my dear sir. He enjoyed his life.

Was Mary Magdalene Jesus' wife? I'm not going to tell. I already told you that Jesus had children so you can assume he was married if you wish to. He had a good time when he was here.

There is an increasing number of children born today who can do things that far exceed the abilities of other children. We call them star children. Was Jesus a star child? (K) So was Mohammad. So was Confucius. So is your wife.

I will read a list of seven miracles that are attributed to Jesus in the Bible. Tell us if each was really performed by him, or was fiction, or was performed by the Christ.

1. Changing water to wine	Fiction
2. Raising the dead	Fiction
3. Calming the stormy sea	Jesus the man
4. Casting out demons	Jesus the man
5. Feeding thousands of people with just a few loaves of bread and two fish	Exaggerated, but there was some truth in that.
6. Walking on water	Exaggerated
7. Catching a fish with a gold coin in its mouth	(laughing) Poor fish. Just a story.

You mentioned some time ago, "a split soul". Was Jesus a split soul? All humans are split souls. Jesus was a human. Was he not? When the Christ spirit entered, there were two spirits in the same body. So we would call him a split soul.

Was Jesus "Jesus the Christ" his entire lifetime or did he become the Christ later in his life? He voluntarily incarnated knowing that he would serve as the Christ and be crucified. He wanted to help humanity. He loved people. He loved to be of assistance. He loved to help others. Jesus the man spent most of his lifetime preparing to be the Christ but it was not intentional. It was his growth. He did not want to be of the status that he later became in life. I have said before that he was a split soul, meaning that Jesus the man was in that body and then the Christ entered also. So there were two entities in that body. There are two entities in most everyone's soul. There is good and there is evil.

Is what is written about Jesus closer to reality as portrayed in the Bible or as portrayed in the Koran? (I) You may not like to hear my answer to that question but Jesus as portrayed in the Koran is more likely. He was a very different kind of man than what is portrayed. He was not blond haired with blue eyes. He did not exist that way.

Did Jesus voluntarily give up his life? Indeed, sir. He was aware of what was about to happen. He was not ready to argue or fight. He was under restraint and overrun by his enemies and his friends too but there were no such friends. They were not friends.

Did Jesus have a human mother and an extraterrestrial father? Joseph was his father and Joseph was completely human. He was very human, as you well know. Look at his lifestyle. He had nine children before he had Jesus but not with the same wife. He had a great influence on the education and upbringing of Jesus. He took him to many different countries throughout the known world at that time.

2 Jesus the Christ

Although you have said that Jesus did not perform all of the miracles attributed to him, did Jesus the Christ perform miracles? Indeed sir. Jesus the Christ performed wonderful miracles and a great amount of happiness and security. It was not the Jesus that is my friend. It was Jesus the Christ.

Is what we call the Christ or the Christ Spirit a soul that has evolved to the point of completion? (K) If you wish to say it that way. Jesus is not fictitious. He is in the spirit world with me. The Christ spirit is manmade but faithful [?] for you to believe and have hope with the Christ spirit. Throughout history there have been many Christ spirits. Many spirits, sir. Christs are highly evolved spirits that have helped mankind to evolve.

Jesus and Buddha and other such people are considered Christs. There will be future Christs. There are Christs sitting here now. The Christ spirit is one that gives hope and peace.

<u>Is Jesus going to make a second coming as they predict in the Bible?</u> Isn't that interesting? He and Moses will appear at the same time.

<u>In response to one of our earlier questions, you said that Jesus is going to make a second coming as they predict in the Bible. Is it Jesus reincarnated in the physical or the return of the Christ Spirit that you are referring to?</u> Even though I have said that religion is manmade and that religion does not exist in the spirit world where I am, I have said that Jesus is going to make a second coming. Jesus the man will be reincarnated. Jesus the Christ was manmade. Jesus in my world now will reincarnate and he will also be a high level savior.

3. Jesus' Birth, Crucifixion and Resurrection

<u>Is the Biblical account of Jesus' crucifixion and resurrection mostly accurate or is it to a great extent fiction or concepts taken from the lore of other ancient civilizations?</u> In your Bible, Jesus was portrayed as a fairytale. The physical birth of my friend Jesus is very simple. There are many accounts of that birth. There were no palm trees there, I assure you, in the desert. Palm Sunday did not exist. He was not born in a manger and did not ride on a donkey. He was in a comfortable family and Joseph loved his son, all his children. A good father. Both Joseph and Mary influenced Jesus. Joseph went with Jesus to India to study while Mary was busy with the children. She kept kosher. The Biblical account of the crucifixion tore my heart out. Where is my heart? It is ridiculous. Nonsense. Nonsense. I hate to see pain and suffering. Pain and suffering was not necessary.

<u>If Jesus did rise from the grave, as the Christian scriptures say, was it his physical body that people saw or was it a projection of his astral body?</u> Those that saw, saw what they wanted to see. However, you could see the plasma of his body rising, the ethereal body. Those in the medical field could tell you about plasmas.

Some people say that Jesus did not die on the cross but recovered, married and was the father of children when he was on this plateau. Is there any truth in this? Somewhat. Whatever you wish to believe. Jesus was a good soul. Indeed he died on the cross but he was very strong. That was [for] criminals and that was the way of his execution at that time. They had no other way. Today we use guns and we use a knife.

Is the shroud of Turin actually something that was used to cover Jesus' body? The shroud to cover my dear friend was very uncomfortable you know. It was not made for him but was used on him. It was very annoying for him.

Was there an unusually bright star about the time of Jesus' birth? That is ridiculous. He was born a Jew. He was a wonderful man and he was black. Everything that they portrayed was not true. A good deal of the information about the birth of Jesus in the Bible was more fiction than fact.

Is the account of Jesus as being born of a virgin true or is it modeled after older traditions? If you wish to call Joseph a virgin, that would be nice. Virgin birth actually exists but not in this case, for other children followed. Am I not correct?

Is there truth in what Tom Harpur says about the Pagan roots of Christianity (i.e. such as the details about Jesus birth, miracles and crucifixion) being based on ancient Egyptian traditions? Is there not some fact of truth in every story we hear and then we embellish the truth? Is that not true? Tom Harpur tries to uncover that. What he says is true. He tries to reveal the truth.

4. Jesus and the archangel Michael, John the Baptist and the disciples

What is the connection between Jesus and the archangel Michael? (J) There is a special bond. The choices and love that they have very deep within themselves. They are very loving. At times Michael influenced Jesus' thinking. Michael is not in my realm.

Did Jesus have an incarnation as the Archangel Michael? (J) Jesus Christ was Jesus Christ. He was the Christ. He was not Jesus. There is a difference between Christ and Jesus. Jesus was not the incarnation of the Archangel Michael. He was too busy being himself. He was Jesus and he became the Christ which is very powerful and very noble and very dear and very loving. He thanks me gratefully. I thank him too.

Was there a soul connection between Jesus and John the Baptist? (E) Indeed, but they are two different entities. Jesus was a dear friend. John started trouble in our realm. I was incarnated there at that time. It was difficult times. You wouldn't recognize the clothes I wore.

Do Jesus' disciples do healing from the other side as Jesus does now? My dear lady, there is no comparison as to the work that dear Jesus has. It [the disciples' healing] does not have the same empowerment.

5. Jesus in the spirit world

How would you describe Jesus and the role he played? Jesus, my dear souls, is a very gentle man. He is here with us and is shocked at what is happening on Earth with his name. He had no idea he would be worshipped like this. He is very grateful.

Since, as you said, religion does not exist in your realm, how do you energy beings view Jesus? Are there others of the same stature as Jesus? He is a nice guy. He is right here tapping on my shoulder. He speaks Hebrew, you know. There are others of the same stature as Jesus.

Since you said that you were not humans but rather energy beings, do more highly evolved souls in your world have a greater amount of energy than less evolved souls? (B) Indeed, some have more energy and assistance as well. Jesus is called most often and he has the energy for that.

If you say "Help me Jesus." is it Jesus the spirit entity in your world who actually helps you? It brings on the assistance of angels or Mohammad or any other name. It is not necessarily the Jesus that is in my realm, in your realm. In your very limited realm. Jesus will answer your prayers because why don't you ask for Mohammad?

You have said that Jesus resides in the realm where you are. Does Jesus channel information to many humans the same way that you are channeling to humans? Indeed, sir. Many people call Jesus. Jesus dwells currently in both the spirit world and the physical world and has simultaneous multiple incarnations on Earth. I have said that Jesus the man was black and beautiful and Jewish. He is very interested in the welfare of people.

6. Jesus and reincarnation

Is Jesus reincarnated at this time? Indeed. Indeed, yes. Many parts of his heart and his soul have reincarnated and have been here many a year. Jesus is both on my plateau and on your plateau. He has multiple simultaneous incarnations.

Although Christians believe that Jesus will be there to greet them when they cross over, in reality does Jesus actually greet some souls when they cross over? If the soul wishes and very strongly wishes my answer to you is yes.

In his book *Lives of the Master* Glen Sanderfur talks about the previous incarnations that Jesus had according to Edgar Cayce. Is that information correct? Partially so, sir. There is always some truth in every lie. Jesus did have many incarnations.

7. Other personalities in the spirit world

Do the readings given by Edgar Cayce provide knowledge we should consider important? Edgar Cayce's readings are somewhat important. He, like me, has lived many times and wishes to reincarnate again. He has not reincarnated at this time.

Was Edgar Cayce the reincarnation of Ra Ta, the ancient Egyptian high priest? Indeed, yes. Indeed, he was.

Are the writings of Zachariah Sitchin substantially factual or can they, to a considerable extent, be attributed to his imagination? He will smack me in my face if I do not tell you he is factual. That's what he wants me to say. At times he is factual.

Is the entity Seth who channeled information through Jane Roberts several years ago on your plane? He is here a lovely kind gentleman, appreciative to be remembered.

Is Plato a friend of yours? Plato is a friend to everyone. Plato is a lovely man. He is at a knowledgeable level. He is with his friend who is also his teacher, and very bonded to his friend. By friend I mean Socrates. They were very close you know and Socrates did suffer quite a bit. It is true that they gave him hemlock.

Since his arrival in your world, what has Adolf Hitler experienced? What he experienced is other people that have done evil things. He is just evil. At this point in time he is not sleeping. He is aware. He is no longer in control. You can step on him.

When you said that what Hitler has experienced in the spirit world "is other people that have done evil things", does that imply that a person's place in your world is where people of a similar level of consciousness are? Indeed, sir, and I am not saying or advocating that Hitler was wrong or that he was bad. He was doing his thing. He was playing a predestined role. It wasn't him. He was giving the orders but he was being given orders too, playing a role in Earth's history. He himself was not necessarily evil. He doesn't want me to say it but he was given orders to do what he did. He was not knowledgeable. He was a simple man. He was helped by extraterrestrials.

Did Leonardo DaVinci receive information from extraterrestrials? Indeed, sir. Quite intelligent, sir. Was he not intelligent? He is with me in my world now. There are many hidden messages in his works of art. He has reincarnated since then, not as a scientist but he has reincarnated in many different volumes. You got information from his drawings about how to invent the helicopter. You could say that Leonardo DaVinci provided your scientists or engineers with some of the information.

Was the boy that Pythagoras adopted a star child that provided him with much information regarding mathematics, religion and philosophy? Is it from this source that Pythagoras developed his knowledge of mathematics? Indeed, sir. It is from this source that Pythagoras developed his knowledge of mathematics.

Is Mahatma Gandhi in your realm or has he reincarnated? He is in my realm. He exerts influence on, or provides assistance to the people of Earth. He is your [Charles Zecher's] friend.

G. REINCARNATION

1. Reincarnation in human evolution

What would you consider to be a high number of lifetimes for a soul to have reincarnated on Earth? Six hundred. That's a good number. People do not learn. So they come back again.

Using our measurement of time, what would you estimate to be the average range of the number of years between incarnations into the physical? I cannot give you an element of time. We do not have the element of time here.

Are there many entities on your plateau who have never experienced life in the physical? Some people have not lived in the physical. Mostly yes. Some are not long-lived so they will come back and recapture.

Are there people on Earth who are now experiencing their first incarnation as a human? Are there some who will never be required to incarnate? Indeed, sir. There are some spirits who have not yet experienced a physical incarnation. There are some spirits who do not wish to incarnate. There are some who will never reincarnate.

Is life in the physical a necessary experience for all souls in your realm? (K) We all must suffer to be in the physical. The past is the past. Sooner or later. Indeed, sir. Many do incarnate as a physical human. All souls have to go through this at least once.

Do we choose to incarnate or is it not a choice? Most of us choose to incarnate. Correct. We wish to come back and be a baby again and grow. We select our parents as you know. You selected your parents.

From what you have said about reincarnation, is it correct to assume that when to reincarnate or whether to reincarnate is completely up to the decision of the individual? Indeed. We do have a little push. We do have some say. Not everyone is welcome. Basically it is the decision of the individual involved.

Must all spirits who have chosen to be part of the reincarnation cycle remain in that cycle until they have reached a level that entitles them to forego future incarnations? Future incarnations are not available until we decide in which direction we should proceed.

When souls cross over can they come back immediately or do they stay on the other side or can they decide if they want to come back into the physical or stay and relax on the other side? Either way, dear lady. Souls can do whatever they are comfortable in doing. Every individual soul is very different.

Do people have different lifetime experiences in all of the human races? Are there significant evolutionary differences among the races? Indeed, sir. There are absolutely no differences among the different races.

If a person's personality is still very annoying to others or appears to be in need of substantial improvement, can that person nevertheless reach the state where further reincarnation is not necessary? That person will grow when one is aware and one is more knowledgeable. When one loses the fear of losing knowledge then one cannot grow. If someone in my realm is very annoying to spirits, that person still has the need to reincarnate. What is annoying to one is not annoying to others.

With each incarnation does a person advance forward in his evolution or does he sometimes regress in his progress, although not back to the animal state? That is, are our latest incarnations our most highly evolved? Sometimes the clock stops; and what happens when the clock stops? Your current incarnation is not necessarily your most highly evolved.

Do spirits sometimes choose to reincarnate after they have reached the status that reincarnation is no longer needed for them? I have said that I have reached the status where I no longer have the need to reincarnate. There are some spirits who choose to reincarnate to help humanity.

In the far distant future will the necessity for physical incarnations of any Earth human or spirit cease to exist? It will be over and over and over. Reincarnation. It is a continuing process forever.

Do miscarried children reincarnate? Indeed they do.

Could I reincarnate to a prior time? Why would you want to do that, my dear lady? Would you not wish to go ahead and lead to progression? It is not likely that you could go back in history.

Is it unusual for a person to be the reincarnation of one of his ancestors? No, this is absolutely true. In some cases it happens rather frequently. You know you [Charles Zecher]are the reincarnation of one of your ancestors.

2. Incarnation in places other than the earth

Is it true that many souls must have interplanetary sojourns [in spirit form]for specific purposes before they are able to reincarnate? Does each planet in our solar system serve us for a different purpose in the evolution of our soul? (K) Yes, indeed.

When we retire from Earth, can the soul inhabit other planets in other forms? Indeed. Very much indeed. Are they not in progress immediately?

Do most souls have a particular star system into which they prefer to incarnate? Indeed, sir. They tend to go back to the same star system. It is not incorrect to assume that they can from time to time incarnate in a different star system. They only incarnate in the same star system because they are familiar and feel at home. They feel safe in the same system. They will learn to go to other systems.

Must humans complete a series of incarnations on Earth before they incarnate in other star systems or can they incarnate intermittently among star systems? Many times it is easier for a soul to create over and over and over in one system than going to different systems because sometimes you are not well mentally. In other words we are not allowed to use the word dumb.

Some people believe that highly advanced entities that were once on this plateau can eventually evolve to the state in which they can become a planet or a star. Is that true? (KL) Indeed, sir. That is at a higher level. Souls can evolve into the sun or things like that. These are highly advanced souls. There are many stars. You can always be a star. So we can say that all the billions of stars out there are souls. It's hard to believe. That's why we wish upon a star. Do we not? Planets and stars have a level of consciousness that is above the level of that of humans. I will not start up with a star. To become a star you must be knowledgeable. Humans have the potential of someday becoming a star. Indeed if you are good in school, you will become a star. I will not tangle with a star because they are more knowledgeable.

Since you have said that Earth is the most difficult planet on which to incarnate, why do so many souls continue to incarnate there? The souls on Earth are not the most intelligent souls in the universe. The physical beings on Earth are less evolved than the physical beings on other planets. The more advanced souls incarnate elsewhere rather than on Earth.

Is there a major reason why souls incarnate on Earth rather than on some more comfortable planets? Souls do not have to reincarnate on Earth. They reincarnate where they are more comfortable, sir. It is the people on Earth that make it the most difficult planet for physical life. They reincarnate on Earth because of their level of stupidity. So all you Earthlings, be aware of how limited you are.

Do all souls who no longer need to reincarnate remain where you are or can they move on to a higher level? We move on to different levels like you people. We embrace more. There is more to do.

3. Entering a new life experience

When we cross over to the spirit world do we see what we expect to see or do we see something different from what we thought we would see? (A) You see what you want to see.

Do those entities on this plateau who have mental or emotional disorders carry over those same disorders when they arrive on your plateau? Can they overcome them on your plateau? (AB) Indeed, sir. There are times they do [overcome them]. Anything is possible. It depends upon the individual.

The knowledge we gain in this lifetime, can we take it to the next lifetime? Well, it is what you call knowledge and sometimes it is called stupidity. So sometimes it takes up with us to another lifetime.

Can our attitudes, emotions and desires change from one incarnation to another as a result of our experiences in the spirit world between lifetimes? Indeed, sir.

Does the extent of an individual's ability to remember things increase from lifetime to lifetime? Somewhat. In some cases indeed and in some cases it does not succeed. What you call déjà vu.

Are certain incarnation event destinies determined between lives and then are the outcomes of those destinies determined by the use of our free will during the physical lifetime experience? In answer to your question, your free will can be used at any time. When you get to a corner, you make up your mind whether you want to proceed straight ahead or go left or right. If you wish, certain destinies are determined between lifetimes. Whatever you wish.

Some belief systems hold that the length of a person's life is predetermined before birth. Is that correct? At times, yes. And the person can achieve what they wish after birth. The length of time is predetermined but is not cast in stone.

Do people sometimes make the choice at the soul level to have a particular disease or physical problem so that they can advance more rapidly in their spiritual evolution? (S) My answer to you would be yes. People before they incarnate can choose to have an infirmity so they can advance more rapidly.

Is it true that birthmarks are often vestiges of fatal wounds in previous incarnations? I will answer you briefly by saying the word yes.

Is it true that homosexuality often occurs when a person reincarnates in the opposite gender from that of the previous life? Not true. It's what you choose. It depends on how many times they have been male or female.

If a person becomes knowledgeable in a certain field of study in this lifetime, will that knowledge become easily retrievable in future lifetimes? Some of it, sir. Only those that interest you. If you were a physician in this lifetime, you will remember some details but not all. The learning of that content will come more easily if you had learned it in a previous lifetime, more easily or more acceptable; more of interest to you. You may not do well with it but you will be interested.

Some men have an intense attraction to fishing or hunting. Is this usually the result of past life experiences? That interest didn't necessarily emanate from previous lifetimes.

4. Multiple incarnations and split souls

What is one or some of the major reasons that souls choose to have multiple simultaneous incarnations? (K) Some souls have multiple simultaneous incarnations because they want to progress more rapidly. It is especially true when a new era on Earth is approaching. In time a new era on Earth will approach. Some souls choose to have several lives, several goings on, several interests. Some people eat the same thing every day. They advance more rapidly when they have several simultaneous incarnations. Very much so. You have choices to do as such if you wish.

Can a soul have multiple simultaneous incarnations in several different star systems? Indeed, sir. It doesn't matter whether it's on Earth or a [different] star system. The soul can have a physical entity on Earth and a physical entity on other planets at the same time.

Since souls can have multiple simultaneous incarnations, do those individuals have some special bonding or recognition if they come into contact with each other? Some do have special contact. Some are not so happy about it. The contact may not be happy or good. They may dislike the others profusely.

Can a soul reside in your realm and simultaneously have physical incarnations? (B) Indeed. Many incarnations at the same time.

When we reincarnate is it just one soul or many lives that come into the next existence? It would be many lives that come into the existence, not one soul. And sometimes in many instances it would be a split soul. And that is why we come into this life with so much confusion because of the split soul. We remember a lot of things from the other existences. We don't remember them but we are confused by them. That is why it is simply referred to as "I can't make up my mind."

5. Before a new incarnation

Is there a time before a soul reincarnates that memories of lifetimes before the most recent lifetime are brought to mind? There are flickers of moments that you have in your lifetime that you recall but don't recall completely. In our lifetime we don't forget but we remember what we want to, just as you do. I was on your plateau being there and knowing things that exist.

Before we enter the physical life, do we have some kind of preview of the new life in the physical that we are about to enter? At times there are some individuals who have that choice. Indeed, sir, yes.

Prior to reincarnation, does the individual choose the level of intelligence he will have, or does he maintain the level of intelligence he had previously attained? He always wishes to be more intelligent, a little brighter but once a cook, always a cook. You cannot come into your next lifetime more intelligent than in this lifetime but you can choose to be less intelligent.

Before an incarnation is the spirit of every newborn human baby imbued with the language or dialect of its future parents; like English, Tagalog, French, Mandarin etc.? Indeed, it is decided. Upon arrival they have already decided the language.

When a person is born deaf, or blind or in some way deformed, is the reason for that condition something the person has chosen at the soul level? Not necessarily. It could be the result of karma or something that was chosen for their own advancement. It is very similar with animals.

When we choose to reincarnate, do we really have a plan for our new life? Somewhat. Sometimes. Some people do and some people don't.

Do we have a choice to never reincarnate with certain people again? Yes, but you know that what we choose will happen. You will reincarnate again and again until you learn not to come back. You have much learning to achieve.

6. Relationships

When we are in your world do we tend to associate mostly with people we were close to in previous incarnations? Heaven forbid! People like you may not want to associate with people in your lifetime. You may not like people here, so why take them with you into the next lifetime? You like to suffer.

When individuals reincarnate into a race different from that of the previous lifetime, are they likely to feel greater affinity to people of that race rather than to people of other races? That question is not necessary to answer because it depends on the individual and the amount of prejudice in that individual.

Do friendships sometimes originate when souls are in your world and then continued when they incarnate into the physical? (B) Relationships don't always continue and thank God for that. Sometimes relationships can start where I am and can continue but don't always appear to be so. It is possible. Sometimes it is rejected.

Are people whom we consider to be our enemies in reality often friends who, prior to reincarnation, agreed to help us with certain lessons that we needed to learn? Indeed, sir. When we dislike a person it is easy to look into a mirror and see ourselves. Why is this person disliked to a point that you dislike this person? Our enemies are often our friends at the soul level. Our enemies are often ourselves because we are our own worst enemies as you well know. Do you not look into a mirror and smile?

You do not look into a mirror and growl. You show your finest feature in the mirror.

7. Animals

Note: All of these questions also appear in Chapter T: Animals.

Are domestic animals who have bonded with their human masters more likely to reincarnate as a human than are wild animals? (T) The answer to your question is yes. Are they not more like humans? You have a cat that is like a human. You have a dog that is like a human. They understand the human race.

Which species of animals are more likely than others to incarnate as a human rather than as an animal in their next incarnation? (T) Certain kinds of animals are not more likely to reincarnate as humans than other kinds. Domestic animals are more likely to reincarnate as humans. Aren't you happy?

Since you have previously said that humans often first incarnate as animals before incarnating as a human, is it possible for a human to reincarnate as an animal? (T) Can a person become a dog? No, it is impossible.

Do animals reincarnate as members of their former species until they finally incarnate as a human, or do they reincarnate in different species? (T) They reincarnate differently. A cat won't always reincarnate as a cat but a human will always reincarnate as a human. It is not completely true that there is no going backwards. Humans can act like animals.

Must all humans incarnate as an animal before becoming a human? (T) Not all, sir. Not all. Some never outgrow being an animal. They can be human but act like an animal. Many of you are pigs, snakes or elephants.

If an animal died in a fire, is it likely that the entity might have fear of fire when it incarnates as a human? (T) Indeed, sir. That is very possible and likely such as one drowning. It can transfer from the animal to the human if it was a fear.

Is it possible for a soul to have two or more simultaneous incarnations? (T) Yes. True. Animals also reincarnate same as us and live in parallel lives.

You mentioned that animals also reincarnate the same as us and live in parallel lives. Can you tell us what you mean by "parallel lives"? (T) They live in many lives like you do. People live many lives simultaneously.

8. Miscellaneous

After a soul has had several difficult or unpleasant incarnations, do they sometimes choose to have a pleasurable incarnation of enjoyment? They choose but they do not get it. They have to learn. They are on this plateau to learn. Make sure you learn while you are here. The learning while you're here is much easier.

Can an individual be the reincarnation of one of his own ancestors? Indeed. Lots of luck!

Are more Atlanteans currently reincarnated in the yellow race than in other races? Indeed. That is why that race is so bright. Are they not bright and knowledgeable? The yellow race will inhabit [inherit] the earth, you know my dear sir.

If you are hypnotized and regressed to a past life, is what you experience really episodes from one of your own past lives or is it sometimes pieces of past life experiences of other people that are relevant to your own situation? It is still your own past life. Is it not? No matter how you seek it, it still points to you. When your are hypnotized it is a suggestion that is made that is deep within you.

Are those individuals who have transgender operations working against their predetermined plan for that incarnation? Individuals are individuals. Each individual is individual. It really doesn't matter whether or not they have an operation for this life. I'm not sure that the purpose of the changing of one's sexual habits will change a person.

It seems that an increasing number of people are covering themselves almost entirely with tattoos. This gives them a reptile like appearance. Is this in any way connected with their physical forms in previous lifetimes? Indeed, sir. That is another way to cover up who they truly are. I have said that on other planets humanoid forms are not all like you. Some are covered in feathers, scales, and things like that but they are all basically the same inside as I myself am. When people tend to cover their whole bodies with tattoos it is a hidden memory of a previous incarnation on a different planet, another way of what they consider art work.

Are the Delhi lamas actually the reincarnation of the previous Delhi lama? (I) Indeed. It is true that the current Delhi lama is the reincarnation of the previous Delhi lama, like your kings and queens. A blood inheritance.

H. KARMA

Before reincarnating does a person have a choice regarding which aspects of his karma should be addressed in the new lifetime? No, sir. He brings all of his karma from all of his previous lifetimes together into the new incarnation at times. Each one is individual. I am saying that he can bring it all in or sometimes not bring all of his karma in.

Is an entity's entire karma part of his being in every incarnation or dimension he is in? From your vantage point, how would you define karma?
No. Part of it will be, yes. In this incarnation you do not have to deal with all of your karma. Karma is what your future will be [or] is to be. Nothing threatening. Nothing to be afraid of. It is the dealing of cards. Which hand you are given and how you play your hand of cards.

Does karma relate only to the physical world or can some aspects of karma be resolved in the astral realm? Indeed, yes. That can be done. We can learn and grow just as much in our world as in your world and such is taking place.

Can an individual still have what might be called karmic debts or still have much to learn and yet not be required to ever reincarnate? In my realm there are some entities who do not need to reincarnate. In my opinion they still have a lot to learn and karmic debts to pay back. Yes, but in their opinion, no, but my opinion is always worthwhile.

In some circumstances can individuals be absolved of paying back karmic debts and the slate swept clean, so to speak? You wish! There is no way of getting around it. No such thing as a state of grace.

Do individuals sometimes reincarnate for the purpose of working toward a noble goal for the betterment of others or mankind? Indeed, sir. That is one way to become successful if you wish.

Can a person's will be so strong that it can be used to override or negate the effects of predetermined karma in a lifetime? Even if something is predetermined, it can be changed. You can override it by your will. Absolutely, sir.

Is there a point in an individual's evolution where they become aware of the karmic cause of why seemingly negative things occurred to them while in the physical? Indeed sir, yes. Not after they are in the spirit world. You will be able to relate to things that seemed negative to the karmic cause and you are not being, as you say in your life, punished. You are not being punished.

If a person commits a crime and consequently sentenced to a term in prison, will his karma be different than if he had not been apprehended and imprisoned while in the physical? If a person commits a wrong and is punished while in the physical that does not affect his karma differently than if he had not been punished.

Are people sometimes confronted with problems or negative situations that are not the result of their actions either in this lifetime or in previous lifetimes or decisions made between lifetimes? Indeed. sir. Not the result of karma. Not the result of decisions made between lifetimes. They are learning points, opportunities.

Are spirits aware of the karma of those individuals in our dimension? (B) Indeed. Even though you may not be aware of your own karma, they are aware.

Is it possible for an advanced soul to remove someone's negative karma? Not remove but help to remove. Remove is the same as forgive. Who are we to make judgments? We do not judge. You make judgments.

Is it possible to take on someone else's karma? It is possible to take negative karma, indeed.

Does the language a person speaks in any way influence or reflect his character, personality or karma? In your world of existence it does because you people have likes and dislikes [prejudice].

Do nations or other large groups of people have group karma?

Somewhat. Some do and some do not. Some are strange.

Since you seemed to have indicated that countries may have karma, does karma play a role in the numerous natural disasters that have affected the country of Haiti? Ignorance has affected Haiti. Ignorance, not being knowledgeable. Making their homes out of straw but they will learn and they are wonderful people. The Haitians are misunderstood people. It has nothing to do with karma of things that occurred in the past. They are kind people. They are gracious people. They have not been educated.

Can an individual be held accountable in a karmic sense for the actions of his ancestors, as Jesus was asked in the Bible? Each individual is responsible for himself. Each individual has an individual will, either he will or they won't.

Does karma play a role in the world of animals? (T) At times, yes. Poor souls.

Can a long painful death, such as from cancer, help resolve karmic debts? (S) If you wish.

If a person is born blind or in some way what we might call physically defective, is that always the result of karma? No, it is not always the result of karma. It is not the result of mistakes by the intelligent entities that create you. It can be to teach you to grow faster. To gain further results.

When a person is born malformed, conjoined or crippled in some way and then doctors fix the problem, have the doctors interfered with their karma? Absolutely not.

Is there a cosmic system of justice? That is, if someone wrongs us or behaves evilly in this life, will they be eventually punished or get their "just desserts"? Indeed. It goes on and on. On and on. Do not force anyone.

Is there such a thing as harmless lies; that is, lies that have absolutely no consequences in a person's lifetime or future lifetimes? On the person creating these fabrications, there is no difference. Who is in judgment? You are your own judge.

If a person repeatedly tells many lies about himself that have no negative impact on others, does this have a negative impact on his karma? It is his karma that is affected.

If a person's actions are the result of demonic possession, do those actions affect the karma of that person? It does not affect the karma of the individual that is achieving what they wish to achieve.

Does a soul ever reach the level of evolution where karma no longer plays a role? When they are not interested they are disinterested. It is not important if they do not wish to come back again. Karma plays a role in my realm, the astral realm, and it plays a role in the realms above that.

Do extraterrestrials have karma? Indeed, sir. There is a mixture similar to your color. Color goes on and on and on and karma goes on and on and on.

Is the United States now experiencing what some may call negative national karma payback because of its history with slavery? Indeed, sir. You are paying back. Slavery still exists, sir. It should be abolished because you all have the same blood. You have the same sweat. You have the same tears. You are the same.

I. RELIGION

1. Religion as viewed by the spirits

After a person crosses over into your world, does the time ever come when religion is no longer important to him? (B) Religion is manmade. We have no religion where we are. Religion is rules. We are too intelligent to take rules or guidance from religion. When did it [religion] start killing? Adam and Eve had no religion. [Here] they look back and smile and realize what a joke it was. So they lose their religious beliefs.

Do all entities in the spirit realm, for the most part, have attitudes similar to yours regarding religion? (B) Do all of us? No sir, but most think religion is nonsense. We are not religious sir. We do not have any religion or any rules. We do not have rules. Religion is rules.

Will there come a time when religion will no longer play a significant role in the lives of those in this world? 'Tis coming so soon. Religion is manmade. It is made for different benefits of man. Some are needed and some are not. Like you have a police force where you are and we do not.

Was the Bible written by God or by man? Was it inspired by God? By man, my dear lady. I do not know what or who God is. Man has been behind everything that has been created. I am God. You are God. We all are God.

Can you explain the meaning of the Trinity: The Father, the Son and the Holy Spirit? Nonsense! That is religion, you know. Religious belief only. Man made. The Holy Spirit is something that is manmade for comfort. And it is important for one to believe in one's faith.

When a person here is officially made a saint by a church on Earth, is that person clearly perceptible to you when that soul reaches your plateau? In other words is the stamp of "official sanctity" of a soul clearly perceptible to you and other spirits on your plateau? (B) We make up our own rules. Indeed I perceive their presence. They huddle around me.

From the point of view of those in the spirit realm, is there such a thing as sin or is that purely a religious concept? (B) Again, that relates to religion. That is so ridiculous. That is manmade. What is sin, sir?

Is there any basis in reality, even though it may be distorted, for what some religions call purgatory? Is not life purgatory, sir?

Since you have said that people lose their religious beliefs when they enter the spirit world, do the attitudes of the terrorists who have killed in the name of their religion change after they cross over? (A) Never, sir. They still have the same attitudes but they don't have their religious beliefs. As I have said, there is no such thing as religion in the spirit world and God didn't create any religions.

2. The Bible

Are many events portrayed in the Old Testament of the Bible actually a recounting of encounters with entities from other worlds? (M) Some are precisely that situation. Some are true but not all.

Is it correct to assume that many of the events portrayed in the Bible actually did occur or were allegories and that there are other events that could be termed as made up stories? Events did occur but [were] interpreted in a different way. Jonah being in the big fish? Ridiculous! It's interpreted differently. Your interpretation is very different. It is possible that he was in an extraterrestrial submarine.

Did the creator of Adam also create a first wife, before Eve, for him named Lilith? Who created Adam or where did he come from? (P) Indeed. From Earth. The Biblical story was a story. We make up stories to please ourselves.

Who were Adam and Eve? What was the Garden of Eden? (Q) Your mother and father. A name you derived for a peaceful habitat for people. A "Pleasantville" in your dimension. Adam and Eve come from people who make up names.

Where on the present day Earth was the Biblical Garden of Eden? Wherever we place it, it will survive. Everybody wishes it was a specific place on the planet. There were several places, different Gardens of Eden in China, in Japan, in Italy. Everyone has their own Garden of Eden.

Did the Biblical characters from Adam to Noah actually live very long lifetimes? (Q) May I ask you what do you consider a lengthy lifetime? More than one hundred twenty years is not considered a lengthy lifetime.

Is some of the ancient history portrayed in the Bible, including that of the Great Flood, a recounting of earlier Sumerian legends? (Q) All is recounting of interesting stories. Some happened and some did not happen. Some of what is in the Bible is taken from earlier civilizations and embellished.

Did Noah in the Bible and humans who lived on Earth before him have physical features different from ours, such as webbed fingers? Was Noah the founder of city of Zion which later became the city of Jerusalem? Indeed, sir. [In regard to founding Zion] there is no foundation for that answer. That is a fallacy. He was not the founder of the city of Zion.

Are there remains of Noah's Ark that still exist? (T) There are no physical remains that archeologists will ever find because it never existed. What we call Noah's ark was an extraterrestrial vehicle. I would prefer to call it a spaceship. It was not a real Noah's ark. They were able to save not animals but the sperm [perhaps DNA] of the animals. That's how they got the thousands of animals into the ark.

What was the major source of the food that provided nourishment for the Israelites during their forty years in crossing the desert? They were able to eat many, many different foods and seeds that they grew. The desert is not all desert. There are plants in the desert. It did not take forty years. It took them time. It was not as long as was interpreted [to] you, sir.

Did the ancient Israelites intentionally prolong their stay in the desert, one reason for which was to amass a large army for battling the various Canaanite groups in the reconquest of the land of Canaan? (P)
Indeed.

In the Biblical account of the Israelites crossing the Jordan River on the way to the promised land, what caused the river to become dry land to allow their passage. It was always dry, sir; all full of pebbles underneath the sea.

Were the ten plagues of Egypt in the Bible actually the result of a sequence of events of natural causes? (Q) Indeed, sir.

Can you tell us about Moses' physical appearance in his Biblical lifetime? My dear friend Moses was black. Cheerful man. Funny humor. Very humorous. Black skin you know. Dark curly hair, a little on the kinky side but he liked it long you know and I must admit, a little bit sexy.

It appears that Moses was more than what we might call an ordinary human. Was he a star child, Christ, an extraterrestrial or what? He was a Jew. He was more than an ordinary human. He was an extraterrestrial hybrid. I knew him. Such a nice man. A gentleman.

What was the role of or the importance of the Ark of the Covenant in the Bible? (V) It produced energy. It still exists today in your head. There is an Ark of the Covenant. Indeed, it will comfort you and you need to have that. It is hearsay that it is in Israel.

Did the Ark of the Covenant, as described in the Bible, actually exist? Did it contain alien technology? Were there several Arks of the Covenant in Biblical times? Yes, sir. It contained alien technology, energy producing technology. There were several Arks of the Covenant. They were all used as weapons.

In Biblical times, did the Philistines steal the Ark of the Covenant and then suffer the serious consequences of its effects? Indeed, sir. After the return of the Ark of the Covenant from the Philistines, many people, perhaps as many as seventy, actually died when they looked at it.

Was the technology encased within the Ark of the Covenant in the Bible instrumental in bringing down the walls of Jericho? Indeed, sir. It was amplified sound waves of the blowing of the trumpets that caused the walls to fall. Loud noises can jar anything. The Biblical account of this event is accurate for the most part, and you know how interpretations get misconstrued.

Did the ancient temple of Solomon that was reported to have been built in the ninth century B.C. house the Ark of the Covenant that was described in the Bible? Isn't that ridiculous? No, it did not hold it.

What was the cause of the destruction of Sodom and Gomorrah as portrayed in the Bible? (E) 'Tis your Bible that made up the story. It really didn't occur. What happened to Lot's wife is a made up story. I remember not exactly as it was given down to you. When I was there, we had long black hair, curls. It was beautiful black. I cannot go further.

In the Bible, what did Jacob's ladder represent? It represented strength.

What is the origin of the historical significance of the Stone of Scone that is placed under the throne of the British monarchy? (Q) Nonsense. It is not the pillow that Jacob slept on in the Bible. Jacob took his pillow with him and it has since disintegrated. The stone is of meaningless significance.

What was Solomon's ring? It was believed to have magic powers. Magic powers? Nonsense!

Was the original purpose of male circumcision to identify those men who were descendants of Adam or the superhuman race created, at least in part, by aliens? (Q) Indeed the answer to your question was [that] it was to be part of a tribe purely identification reasons. They were not knowledgeable at that time about health reasons. This was for purely identification reasons.

Were some people knowledgeable about the creation of and the use of electricity in Biblical times? (V) Indeed, what you call electricity. Was there not lightening at that time? They were able to harness that. The pyramids were used to create electricity.

Would you be able to tell us if you were one of the major personages portrayed in the Old Testament of our Bible? (E) Indeed I am him, her, them. I was also incarnate at the time of Jesus. I was more than one person mentioned in the Bible. I have incarnated in many [star] systems.

Are the people who call themselves the Lemba in Zimbabwe actually descendants of one of what we call the lost tribes of Israel? Yes. They are the priestly tribe of the Cohens. They are black and they are slaves.

Even though you have said that much of the material in the New Testament of the Bible is not entirely factual, did Christianity nevertheless serve the purpose of helping to raise the level of consciousness of the believers? Indeed. In that aspect Christianity was a positive thing for those that get benefit.

You have said that religions were the inventions of humans and they do not exist in the spirit world. Some people say that Christianity is one of the great hoaxes played on mankind. Is that true? Indeed sir. It is also true, so they tell me, that the creation of Christianity was part of a master plan to raise the level of consciousness of humans. It keeps people together. Those that are falling apart, it helps keep them together.

It is said that the most cherished object in Christianity is the Holy Grail. Did such an object exist? (I) Sir, I do not know if it did exist. If it did, I did not see it. It does not exist today. Religion is manmade. It is what the intellects taught you. It is all imagination. It is like Noah's ark? It is like your Bible.

The Bible says "With thanksgiving let your requests be made known unto God." Could that be correctly interpreted as that it is to our benefit to express our gratitude to our spirit guides and the angels? It is control. If you come before someone that is [giving them] control. There is no harm to give one peace within. We are giving ourselves peaceful thoughts. Even though you may not be consciously aware of your spirit guides, it will make you feel better and that does not hurt. It is important to show your gratitude to the angels. The same is true of showing gratitude to the spirits.

In our Bible, was the pillar of fire that guided the Jews through the desert a UFO? There was something in the sky guiding them. It was manipulated by extraterrestrials.

Our Bible tells us that the prophet Elijah descended into the heavens in a fiery chariot. Was that chariot a UFO? Indeed, sir.

3. Extraterrestrials in the Bible

What was the cause of the Great Flood that is mentioned in the Bible and in the lore of other ancient civilizations throughout the world?(Q) The accumulation of weather that had formed was not an accident you know. It was precisely planned. It was planned by aliens and to be helpful.

I will read seven events portrayed in the Bible. After each one would you tell us if there was any involvement of aliens or their technology? (M)

1. Moses receiving the ten commandments   Indeed
2. The Israelites crossing the Red Sea   Natural
3. The manna provided to the Jews in the wilderness   Natural
4. Enoch's ascension into the heavens   Ridiculous! Indeed not!
5. Ezekiel's account of a wheel within a wheel   Indeed
6. Jonah in the belly of a big fish   Ridiculous, fairy tales
7. The walls of Jericho that crumbled   It was sounds
                    The power of sound will crumble anything.

Were some of the people in the Bible actually extraterrestrial beings disguised as humans with the intent of the betterment of humankind? (M) If you want an answer, some of it would be yes.

Did the Nephilim, often considered as the race of giants that existed in Biblical times really exist? Was Goliath one of them? Were they extraterrestrial in origin? (MQ) Indeed. Indeed. They were not the offspring of fallen angels. They were not fallen angels. They were extraterrestrial in nature. Goliath in the Bible was one of them.

Are the accounts of angels in various cultures, including the Bible, often references to extraterrestrial beings? (M) On some occasions. Not all occasions.

Did many of the world's great religions today come about as the result of encounters with extraterrestrials? (M) Indeed. Many of the confusions. It could be said that Jehovah was an extraterrestrial.

Since you have already said that Jehovah was extraterrestrial being, does he still guide the Jews in modern times? Is Jehovah in your realm? (M) Some of the Jews. He is here now. I am speaking [telling] some of your questions for him to aid me in guiding you. In answering your questions now, I have assistance from Jehovah. I am not alone, sir.

Regarding the source of the information that came from the prophets in our Bible, was it from extraterrestrials? (M) Sir, there is some that came from extraterrestrials. Some of that information came from those in my world. The information did not come from their own access to the Akashic records.

Were the Ten Commandments in the Bible given to Moses by the extraterrestrial Jehovah? Indeed, sir. Jehovah gave the ten commandments directly to Moses.

Is the origin of some of the rites and rituals of the Catholic Church connected with ancient extraterrestrial encounters with humans? Is the same true of the Jewish religion? Yes and some of the rituals of the Jewish religion started with extraterrestrials. They started it. All religions were initiated or in some way connected with extraterrestrials.

4. Non-Biblical Religions

Does the Prophet Mohammad dwell in your realm? Is he among those entities of very high energy? How does he react to what is happening with the radical element of Islam? Indeed sir. He is among those of very high energy if you wish to consider that. That is not of your consideration, sir. He reacts to what is happening with humor and fear. There are some instances where we want control and he wants control and [we] fear that he will get control. He is mainly positive creation but everything positive does have a negative. I do not see a time in the future when the radical movement will cease. It is not showing any recession there but it is growing to amount in abundance. Your fear of what will happen in the future has no basis. The fear is still there but it is not taken in the abundance that it should be.

Is what is generally portrayed or known about the life of Mohammad more consistent with reality than what is generally portrayed or known about the life of Jesus? Mohammad is not known about but more cherished than people are aware. What you generally believe about the life of Jesus is not always true but what is publicized or known about the life of Mohammad is more accurate.

Is what is written about Jesus closer to reality as portrayed in the Bible or as portrayed in the Koran? (F) You may not like to hear my answer to that question but Jesus as portrayed in the Koran is more likely. He was a very different kind of man than what is portrayed. He was not blond haired with blue eyes. He did not exist that way.

Is the murdering of those whom the Moslems call infidels in the current movement of Jihadism fulfilling the intent of Mohammad? Indeed not, sir. It is not what Mohammad wants. It is ridiculous. They are killers.

What is the cause for the recent rise in radical Islam? They blame the Jews, sir, as you well know. I have previously said that many of the current radical Moslems are reincarnated Nazis. That is why they are reacting in such ignorance. The same hatred of the Jews that the Nazis had. The same entities have reincarnated against the Jews.

Will the radical Muslim movement become less of a serious threat to us in this generation? (R) It is making a good point of its generation and more radicals will prove with time. It will still be here in twenty years and it will progress to be more of a threat. This will not come to an end soon. It was always there. It is a very serious situation with Syria. Eventually there will be an end to the threat. Fifty years from now there will be more peace on Earth after more destruction.

Did the angel Gabriel dictate the Koran to Mohammad? (J) No, sir. The Koran is manmade. Is that not true? There were non-physical conscious entities involved in the writing of the Koran like spirits or angels or extraterrestrials but it was not the angel Gabriel.

Was the Hindu god Vishnu a Christ? In every circuit there is always one that we look up to. We pick our different religions and they are all the same. I have said that there have been many Christs throughout history and that the Jewish Christ was the most despised. Many of the religions began because of the appearance of a Christ on Earth. You will believe anything on Earth that is given to you.

Did various religions exist among Earth people before the time of the Great Flood? Indeed, sir. Ridiculous religions. There were religions at the time of Atlantis. There was always something to make you fear and [be] controlled. There are many kinds of gods, sir. It could be an evil god, too. Sometimes in the past, Earth people saw extraterrestrials as gods.

Are the Delhi lamas actually the reincarnation of the previous Delhi lama? (G) Indeed. It is true that the current Delhi lama is the reincarnation of the previous Delhi lama, like your kings and queens. A blood inheritance.

5. Mary the mother of Jesus

When people reportedly have seen the Virgin Mary, is that often the manifestation of an angel instead? (J) Indeed, sir, indeed. Our angels are gathered all over the place. They are there to assist you and help you. Very often people think they are seeing the Virgin Mary but it is really an angel. An angel comes forward to greet you and assist you.

Who was the entity seen by the three children in Fatima Portugal in 1917? [Jesus'] mother Mary. She came down and sometimes she visits other planets too. She is very loving.

Does the person referred to as the Virgin Mary in the Fatima visions in 1917 have a stature similar to that of Jesus on your plateau? I am holding back from laughter, you know. She is not a he. She is there as she is. She, as most, has the same energy level as Jesus. Different directions.

Since the Catholic Church has never released the third prophecy that the spirit called Mother Mary gave at Fatima, can you tell us anything about the content of that prophecy? No. I wish not to.

6. Christs and antichrists

You have said that there have been many Christs but what is the Christ Consciousness? Indeed [there have been many Christs]. The Christ consciousness is from your soul. (Laughing) Jesus was not the last Christ to appear on Earth. There have been more recent ones. There are many. There are many different religions, many different races, many different cultures. In your race, there are one limited [?] but there are many in many different races. All of the religions are started from a Christ-like. There is not one that is more upholding than any other. Jesus was the most controversial in your knowledge, in your lack of knowledge. If you were a different color or in a different country, it would be someone else.

Were Napoleon Bonaparte and Adolf Hitler the first two of the three antichrists that Nostradamus predicted? Has the third one been born yet? (Q) Yes. The third one has been born.

Just as various antichrists have appeared throughout history, have various Christs appeared also? Indeed sir. The Buddha was a Christ. Krishna was a Christ. There were many Christs but the Jewish Christ was disliked most of all. He is a friend of mine. All my friends are of different faiths. We are all one and we all have the same beliefs. We are all equal, the same. We lose our religious connection on this side. Religion is manmade. You made religion. Religion only exists in the physical world but it is necessary for controlling. It is controlling and it is a comfort to others that wish to be controlled. Religions will cease to exist within the next couple of centuries. There is no need for that nonsense.

Regarding the discussion about the Christ, could it be said that the Christ could be described as a job? You can put any name that you put on it. If you want to call it a job, then it does its job well because it does give comfort to those who are not knowledgeable.

7. Miscellaneous

What is it that causes people to speak in Tongues? When people speak in Tongues on your plateau it is the same language I speak. There are times they don't know what they mean. The inspiration for speaking in Tongues comes from the mind, the brain, you know. It is a fantastic way of expressing oneself. It is something that is built into the system of everyone who has a brain.

When people speak in Tongues are they actually channeling non-physical entities? Indeed, sir. In the charismatic church services, where they speak in Tongues, they are actually allowing an extraterrestrial to speak through them which they themselves do not understand. I have said that my most comfortable language is Tongues.

Is life in your world where the concept of heaven and hell originated for us? (B) My answer, sir, what is heaven or what is hell? When people arrive [on this plateau] we are here to greet them and console them. They will feel comfort and ease and happiness in arriving when they come on our plateau. Heaven and hell is purely a religious concept. It's another way to have control. You have control with your religion. You make your own heaven, what you call heaven, and you make your own control and make your own hell as you well know. Heaven and hell is a state of judgment.

Many religions teach us that when we die we go immediately to either heaven or to hell but they say nothing about our going to the world of spirits. Are heaven and hell actual places or are they states of mind? What is your view of heaven and hell? (A) (Laughing) Indeed sir. Heaven and hell are not actual places but I would say they are states of mind. I ask if there is such a thing as a heaven or hell. I am not saying that we make our own heaven or hell. I am saying that we go on from there and we learn or we come back again. When we cease to exist we go on or we reincarnate, or we go on from there.

Can the acceleration of the demise of religion to some extent be attributed to what we refer to as the New Age movement that was purportedly begun by Helena Blavatsky and the Theosophical movement which followed? She is here with us. She doesn't want me to say a thing against her. They would wish to be a major factor in pushing religion aside. She channeled information from both those in our dimension and the angels. Some of the angels try to help us or me. We have been able to help many people on Earth.

Will Christians, Jews and Moslems ever coexist peace fully without confrontations or warfare? Without warfare? They love warfare. The time will come when they won't have warfare but you won't be existing. In your lifetime you will still have wars. Religion causes wars. Religion is very good for those who are not knowledgeable. It is a safety guard. It is very strong for those that are [not knowledgeable]. They take advantage of religion.

Years from now, will we still have Christians, Jews and Moslems or will we be all one? (R) In many times there will be one bank, there will be one car, there will be one time. Is that understood? So your religious beliefs will continue to be one. One religion after many, many, many failures and many deaths. Fighting over religion is ridiculous. It does not matter what you believe. It's all one.

Do you see an end to religious beliefs? (R) It will no longer exist centuries from now. It will slowly dissolve and it is coming about showing you now very slightly how it is dissolving. The big churches that you perceive will become less and less.

Is there such a thing as the devil? The devil is in the eyes of the beholder. There is a person Lucifer but that is not an evil person. If you are looking for an evil person, that is not an evil person.

Was the entity that we refer to as Satan instrumental in giving us the tools for civilization? Do Satan and Lucifer refer to the same entity? In a way, yes, my sir. Lucifer and Satan refer to the same entity. That is your refer[reference] to the same entity. The names are interchangeable.

What, if anything, did the angel Lucifer do to cause him to have a negative reputation in the physical world? What was his intent in doing so? (J) People like us who give names out and determine whether they are good or bad or evil. His intent was to bring both good and evil. It depends on what side of the street you are on. It depends how you view things, whether it is good or bad or evil. He brought knowledge to mankind that he shouldn't have given. Lucifer was not competing with higher authorities. Lucifer was competing with Lucifer. Did you not have conflict within yourself?

<u>Is it important for us to give special respect to cemeteries as "hallowed ground"?</u> If you wish. All Earth is full of cemeteries, sir. Every place you step on, there is a burial and even in your ocean you have burial grounds. You do not have to treat cemeteries any different from any other area of Earth. That is not where we go. It is for you a comfort to go to where you believe the person is buried. It is all in your heads.

<u>Does the widespread prejudice that many people have against the Jews emanate from something embedded within their souls arising from events from the distant past?</u> There is prejudice in every color, every religion. There is always some interference.

<u>Does the Vatican secretly accept the fact that they believe in the possibility that extraterrestrials may exist on Earth?</u> Indeed, sir. That is why we are here. I am saying that the Catholic church does know it but they're keeping it secret. They do not want to [make you] aware you and scare you. Aware and scare. That is not the main reason they are keeping it a secret. The main reason is control.

<u>Are there secret files in the Vatican that support the existence of UFO's and extraterrestrials? (M)</u> Indeed, sir. Indeed. Files and rows of books. They are in control. They are keeping it secret so they can keep control.

<u>Is there truth in the belief that there was once a Catholic pope who was a woman disguised as a man and who was later referred to as Pope Joan?</u> Indeed, sir, that is true. She was quite a lesbian, you know. That person is still in the spirit world, not reincarnated.

<u>Throughout history a number of men have had stigmatas appear on the palms of their hands which were believed to represent the wounds made in the crucifixion of Jesus. What is the cause or significance of the stigmatas?</u> And on their foreheads. They actually represented disease.

<u>Do religions exist in any star systems in addition to ours? (O)</u> Religion, sir, is manmade. You make up rules. You make up your art. Your theater is manmade. Your music is manmade. Religion does not exist elsewhere,

only on Earth. Art, theater, music etc. is individual. It is what is perceived by the individual. That occurs in other star systems.

Will a major crisis or scandal occur in the Catholic church within the next decade? (R) It is now, sir. That scandal will be the cause of the demise of the papacy. It is on its way out, sir.

There have been various predictions over the years about the end of the papacy. Do you see a final Pope within the lifetime of anyone alive today? Yes. This is your final Pope. Pope Francis will be the last Pope.

Many religions condemn gay marriages as being against the word of God. Are those marriages an indication of a decadent society or can they be considered as natural as a marriage between a man and a woman? A gay marriage, what you call gay, is loving a person's soul. It is not what you appear to think as loving a gay. No condemnation should be made of gay. It was always there, sir, and not always of visual service. Religions condemn gay marriages because religion is manmade. It is for the purpose of controlling and having children.

Was it solely because of his health or age as he stated, that Pope Benedict resigned? (Q) Anything that would cause health [problems] would be the reason he was resigning. It was only for health reasons and for gallbladder. It was because of differences of opinion. That can cause a gallbladder [problem].That is why he resigned but he is there and will be of assistance. He is a dear, darling person, kind and genuine.

In response to one of our earlier questions, you said that Jesus is going to make a second coming as they predict in the Bible. Is it Jesus reincarnated in the physical or the return of the Christ Spirit that you are referring to? (F) Even though I have said that religion is manmade and that religion does not exist in the spirit world where I am, I have said that Jesus is going to make a second coming. Jesus the man will be reincarnated. Jesus the Christ was manmade. Jesus in my world now will reincarnate and he will also be a high level savior.

Is there a connection between the Catholic Inquisition many centuries ago in which great numbers of infidels were killed and the current radical Moslem movement in which the infidels are killed? (Q) They are disassociated occurrences. It is not the same group reincarnating. They are similar but not the same but I have said that the current group of Moslem terrorists is the reincarnation of the Nazis. That is a fact.

J. ANGELS

1. Manifestations

<u>Can angels manifest themselves as physical human beings that anyone can see?</u> Yes, that is easy.

<u>Do angels often manifest themselves to humans as butterflies or dragonflies?</u> Indeed, sir, they do. They wish to show themselves to you as what you picture as beautiful. They can be anything that flies. It is very interesting.

<u>Are the butterflies that often appear to people after a loved one has died sometimes manifestations of angels or some sort of communication from the one who has just passed over? (D)</u> Indeed, sir. They should be cherished., They should be cherished.

<u>Do angels sometimes manifest themselves as our pets that remain with us until they die? Do they sometimes manifest themselves as extraterrestrials? (T)</u> Indeed. Sir. They can manifest themselves as bolts of lightning, flies, butterflies.

<u>When people reportedly have seen the Virgin Mary, is that often the manifestation of an angel instead? (I)</u> Indeed, sir, indeed. Our angels are gathered all over the place. They are there to assist you and help you. Very often people think they are seeing the Virgin Mary but it is really an angel. An angel comes forward to greet you and assist you.

<u>In the answer to one of our previous questions, you used a term that was puzzling to us: *extraterrestrial angels*. Does this mean that the beings were extraterrestrials but were thought to be angels?</u> Indeed, sir. Frequently in the Bible they were extraterrestrials manifesting themselves as angels. Extraterrestrials and angels are always two distinct types of entities. They appear separately, sir.

2. Characteristics and abilities

Since you said that angels hear us when they want to hear us, does this imply that angels have free will? Do they have attitudes, emotions and desires? Indeed, sir. Angels select and approve their questions. They also have attitudes, emotions, and desires such as we have. Indeed sir, even a butterfly knows when to fly away. They are here to assist you. I have said that angels are here to assist you whether they like you or not. They might not like what you do, sir. It is your actions that they do not like.

Is the nature of angels such that they are programmed to help others? Do they assist those in the spirit world as well as those in the physical world? Indeed. They are interested in assisting abiding and helping those that need it. They help the spirits as well as humans. Angels are there and they are there to guide and administer, as you well know. Angels are with you.

Do angels have the capability to create, much the same way as spirits do with their minds? Indeed, sir, indeed. They do not have to verbally communicate as you well know. 'Tis not necessary. Angels can create physical things. They can manifest easily whatever they wish.

Can angels manipulate physical laws when they assist humans in the physical world? Is the same true of highly advanced humans? Absolutely! Angels sometimes manipulate the weather or physical laws, such as gravity, to prevent physical harm to humans. Also special humans too, if one wishes to. You can have different things occur but not like an angel. An angel will act immediately.

Do angels have the ability to help us change our attitudes, emotions or desires? Indeed, sir. Angels are here to help us. If we seek their help they can absolutely help us change our desires. They care, sir. By caring they love you. They mean well among you. At times angels will be there with you but whether you will be there with them is another question. Indeed they will help you if you are needing help. You must ask for their influence but sometimes they take the initiative to do so.

In addition to working with humans and spirits, do angels also work with animals? Do they work with the vegetable kingdom? (T) At times, sir. They do not work with the vegetable kingdom. The nature spirits take care of the vegetable kingdom.

Since you have said to us that all spirit guides are not equally competent, can the same be said of angels? In other words, does the extent of ability of angels depend on what kind of angel they are? They are just like people. Some people are more competent than others. The same is true of spirits and the same is true of angels. That is true of everything, sir.

3. Assistance to humans

Just as we have a spirit guide who stays with us through our physical life, do we also have a specific angel to help and protect us? Indeed. Some of us are fortunate to have more than one angel. Some of us need more than one angel. The angel you have is related to the month and day you were born. They are there to greet you and assist you.

Is the construction, growth and maintenance of our physical bodies controlled by numerous entities from other realms related to the angelic or other kingdoms? 'Tis true. Not one type but many types. Your heart does not beat automatically. Several of us are involved in that situation.

Do angels help us when we pray to God to answer our prayers? Do angels come to our aid? Indeed. They are there to embrace you, to help you, to teach you. They are there for you to benefit and they will be very beneficial for you. That is why it is always so nice to have an angel by my side and that is why some people react like an angel. They are so good and positive because they are angels.

When we wish to seek help from someone in your world or from the angels, does it make any difference whether we just think what we want or whether we say it out loud? In other words you are asking if we can read your mind. Spirits and angels can read your mind. Correct, you can be silent or say it out loud.

If you are having difficulty doing something, will angels sometimes assist you even if you don't ask for assistance? Indeed, sir.

Can angels exercise their free will to assist people without having received instruction from a higher level to do so? Indeed. They do receive instructions or they receive messages but whether they may give you the message or whether you may not take the message is up to you. When you pray to God or what you think is God, it is the angels who answer your prayers. Spirits where I am also respond to your prayers. When you pray, it is not just Big Daddy up there in the sky who directly helps you. It can be spirits or other non-physical entities and also, my dear sir, it can be yourself. By yourself, I mean the God that is within you. In other words [it is] your higher self or your soul. That is the important one. You should go within yourself first, even in preference to praying. Go along with your first thought, which is not easy to connect. It is hard to catch on to that first thought.

Can angels influence the thoughts of those people who want to bring harm to a person? Can spirit guides do the same thing? Indeed, sir. Spirits also can influence the thoughts of someone who wants to harm you. That is a form of protection.

4. Communication

Do angels channel information to humans as the spirits do? (D) Indeed, sir. Angels are more apparent. Sometimes they show themselves and they don't show themselves for all. Mediums can tell the difference of an angel and a spirit. Angels are dear souls. Spirits are not always that. Angels are always honest, truthful and sincere but spirits are not always.

Is there more overt communication with those on your plateau with angels than there is with them in our world? (B) Absolutely, dear sir, but they hear you too. They don't want to be known or seen but they do exist. Angels hear you when they want to hear you.

Does it help to get the attention of angels if you call them by name or do angels prefer to be anonymous? Both. Humans have certain angels assigned to them. Sometimes it would do you good to know the names of the angels assigned to you but sometimes they want to be mysterious. They don't want to be named. They don't want to be called or pressured. In other words, don't wake them up. It is important to show your gratitude to the angels. The same is true of showing gratitude to the spirits. Just broadcast it [your request] and the angels will help.

5. Evolution

Do those in the human or spirit kingdom ever evolve into the angelic kingdom or are the two kingdoms always separate? (K) The kingdoms are separate, my dear sir. No one from the human kingdom or from the spirit kingdom can ever become an angel.

When you said that humans can evolve to a state that they are like angels, were you referring to what is commonly called the "masters"? (K) Some of us are not able to reach that plateau. Some can and will. Very few can and will reach the angel state. [Note: Not "angel" but "angel state"]

Can birds and flying insects evolve into angels? (T) 'Tis so. 'Tis so.

Are nature spirits (such as fairies, elves, leprechauns etc.) on the same line of evolution as angels? Indeed no. Indeed no. Your leprechauns and fairies are very childish you know. They are very immature and childish.

Were angels created before the creations of humans? Well that's who created humans. The angels came first.

If angels created us, who created angels? That's an interesting question. We were here before all creation. I am getting an answer that I am not able to communicate.

Do angels always remain angels or can they evolve beyond the angel state? Angels will remain angels.

Since you have said that angels will not evolve beyond the angel state, is there potential for humans to eventually evolve to a level above that of the angels? (K) Indeed, sir. Don't we call people who are kind an angel?

In the answer to one of your previous questions, you used the term "new angels". Does that mean that angels are continuously in the process of coming into existence? They are trying so hard to be of assistance.

They want to help or make you successful. A new angel is one who is learning to be bright and have experience.

You have said that insects and birds are part of the evolutionary path of angels? Does the type of bird or insect determine what type of angel will evolve? Not necessarily so. There is not a direct line. Let's say, that a duck will become this kind of angel or that a canary will become that kind of angel but flying animals will become angels. I have said that butterflies become angels; but angels, in the reverse, can often manifest themselves as butterflies in your world. You have two kinds of butterflies; butterflies that have not yet become angels and butterflies that are angels manifesting themselves as butterflies.

Do angels evolve through the mineral kingdom, the vegetable kingdom and the animal kingdom as do humans? They go through the same process of evolution as do humans.

6. Specific angels and types of angels

What is the connection between Jesus and the archangel Michael? (F) There is a special bond. The choices and love that they have very deep within themselves. They are very loving. At times Michael influenced Jesus' thinking. Michael is not in my realm.

Did Jesus have an incarnation as the Archangel Michael? (I) I don't like to tattle you know. This is not true. Jesus Christ was Jesus Christ. He was the Christ. He was not Jesus. There is a difference between Christ and Jesus. Jesus was not the incarnation of the Archangel Michael. He was too busy being himself. He was Jesus and he became the Christ which is very powerful and very noble and very dear and very loving. He thanks me gratefully. I thank him too.

Is the account of the fallen angels known as the Watchers portrayed in the Book of Enoch basically accurate? Fallen angels existed. They are angels that did not exist to achieve and so they are called fallen because they did not achieve what they were put [here] for. They intermingled with Earth women and men and bore offspring. Their offspring were sometimes giants.

Did the angels described as the Watchers pass on knowledge to humans? What was their role regarding humans? Indeed, sir. Their role was [for humans] to be aware.

Was the Incan god Viracocha one of the angels described as the Watchers in the book of Enoch? Indeed, sir.

What, if anything, did the angel Lucifer do to cause him to have a negative reputation in the physical world? What was his intent in doing so? (I) People like us who give names out and determine whether they are good or bad or evil. His intent was to bring both good and evil. It depends on what side of the street you are on. It depends how you view things, whether it is good or bad or evil. He brought knowledge to mankind that he shouldn't have given. Lucifer was not competing with higher authorities. Lucifer was competing with Lucifer. Did you not have conflict within yourself.

Is Lucifer an evil entity working toward the corruption of humanity? [Laughing] Or for the wellbeing of humanity also. Lucifer is not all evil. Lucifer and Satan are the same entity.

Was Lucifer involved in the creation or the development of Earth humanity? (K) Indeed, sir. Many of you are here as friends of Lucifer. This was in accord with the universal plan of evolution. There were other angels in a similar process with you. As I have said in the past, Lucifer is not a negative entity.

Did the angel Gabriel actually dictate the Koran to Mohammad? (I) No, sir. The Koran is manmade. Is that not true? There were non-physical conscious entities involved in the writing of the Koran like spirits or angels or extraterrestrials but it was not the angel Gabriel.

Are there many different species of angels that play different roles? Yes. Angels work for the good of mankind but there are times that is not always angelic. You can ask them to do something that is harmful to you or contrary to your karma but that is not always given. It is always possible that they might give you what you want that is harmful to you or contrary to your karma.

7. Miscellaneous

Can humans sometimes perform miracles without the assistance of angels? Indeed sir. If I gave you a million dollars, would I not be an angel?

Are all non-physical beings, such as angels and nature spirits, manifestations of souls? Indeed, sir.

Are events that we consider to be miracles usually the work of angels? At times. There are times that is so. Spirits in my realm can also cause miracles if they wish. We wish to work for you.

What do our angels do when they're not guiding us? Resting. They always find work to do. They are always busy.

Are angels and archangels bonded only to Earth? That is not true, sir. They help others. They travel.

K. HUMANS AND THEIR EVOLUTION

1. The soul and its evolution

What is your definition of the soul? The soul is a complete being. The physical body is used to receive information for the soul and then the physical body passes away. Then the spirit body passes information to the soul. The spirit body eventually passes away and just the soul exists. The physical body is just temporary and the spirit body is just temporary. There is indeed a big difference between the spirit and the soul. The spirit body intervenes between the physical body and the soul. The soul is more controlling than the spirit body.

Could you define the difference between the soul, the ego and the spirit? The ego and the id. You have a mind and you have conscience and you have an id. Your id seems to keep things quiet and to themselves. The dear lady speaking is using her id to give you satisfaction and gratification. She is not aware of her id. I might add that the physical body is not a permanent part of the soul. And likewise the spirit body is also not a permanent part of the soul. There will be a time when humanity will evolve where there will not be physical bodies and there will not be spirit bodies. I myself will eventually evolve where I will not be a spirit. Originally we were the soul and the soul created the physical body so the physical body could have input into the development of the soul. The physical body is like an instrument to make the soul grow and to help you achieve to get where you are going. The same is true of the spirit body where I am, to give input to the development of the soul. The soul is our real self. The physical body is not our real self and the spirit is not our real self. And the brain is not the real self. There will come a time where we will evolve to the point where we will not need a mind.

Is the soul the only permanent thing that distinguishes one individual from another? Yes. The soul is very important and that makes the difference between each individual of mankind. Our souls are dynamic and forever changing by the information that is fed to it [them] through the physical. Indeed, sir, my answer is yes to your question.

121

Do all souls eventually evolve to the state of completion or perfection, or are some souls eventually dissolved because they have become irredeemable? They come back again, again and again. Souls are not totally dissolved. They just have to start over again. They start over from the mineral or the vegetable kingdom.

Since old souls are people who have had many previous incarnations, we tend to think of them as being wiser and more evolved than the others. Is that always correct or is it sometimes that they are old souls simply because they have been slow learners? Some old souls never learn, you know. They are sitting among you. Just because you are an old soul does not mean that you are more highly evolved than newer souls. Some new souls, a young angel can deal with you in a more positive way, a more intelligent, knowledgeable way.

Were all souls created at the same time? All souls were not created at the same time. Old souls, many lifetimes. New souls in your language "purple" They are very advanced souls, the indigo children. Listen to them.

Is there such a thing as living creatures who do not have souls? Indeed. There are human beings without souls. They are among you. They are your neighbor. As Edgar Cayce told of a child who did not have a soul until the age of nineteen. That child did not wake up until the age of nineteen. That is when the soul entered the physical body.

Does a soul evolve more rapidly on this plateau? Some do. Your school is learning. You are repeating. Some repeat and repeat.

What is one or some of the major reasons that souls choose to have multiple simultaneous incarnations? (G) Some souls have multiple simultaneous incarnations because they want to progress more rapidly. It is especially true when a new era on Earth is approaching. In time a new era on Earth will approach. Some souls choose to have several lives, several goings on, several interests. Some people eat the same thing every day. They advance more rapidly when they have several simultaneous incarnations. Very much so. You have choices to do as such if you wish.

Is life in the physical a necessary experience for all souls in your realm?(G) We all must suffer to be in the physical. The past is the past. Sooner or later. Indeed, sir. Many do incarnate as a physical human. All souls have to go through this at least once.

If someone commits suicide, what happens to their soul? [When they commit suicide] they are disappointed with the life that they created. We create our own fears. We must be aware of our fears because our fears become our reality. Their soul will not rest because it was not a natural planned incident. They are uncomfortable and suicide is not always a comfortable but easy way out. If you wish to regard it as a severe detriment to an individual's evolution, please do. Because with suicide we hurt others around us. We make them feel guilty and responsible.

Is it true that a soul can, through agreement with another soul, willingly leave the body permanently and return to your realm so that another soul can take over that body until it dies in order to perform a specific predetermined role? 'Tis true in many aspects. It's what we call walk-ins, a change of personality. It is a change of who they were and no longer wish to be. This can happen and that's how evil gets into progress. It can be good or evil.

You mentioned split soul in one of your previous answers. What is a split soul? Half a walk-in and half not. An individual can be two personalities at the same time, the original and the new personality. Many of us are split personalities, if you wish to term it as such.

Would you agree that the noblest of souls' purposes in both your world and ours is to be of service to others? Indeed, sir. Always helping others, as I am here helping you. My helping you is aiding my own evolution. If it is not I, it will be others who will do the same, as your glorious Ruth [Charles Zecher's mother] wants to do.

If there is such a thing as soul mates, what are they? It is an interesting made-up word. The soul is a heart. The soul should be strong enough to survive by itself and it doesn't need a mate.

Can souls be part of a greater soul, similar to the way that a soul can have multiple simultaneous incarnations? Indeed, sir. Sometimes those in the spirit world are part of this. Not all times but sometimes. It's like a hierarchy of souls. We have groups here, my dear sir, amongst us. They are waiting to answer your predictions [questions].

Is what we call the Christ or the Christ Spirit a soul that has evolved to the point of completion? (F) If you wish to say it that way. Jesus is not fictitious. He is in the spirit world with me. The Christ spirit is manmade but faithful [?] for you to believe and have hope with the Christ spirit. Throughout history there have been many Christ spirits. Many spirits, sir. Christs are highly evolved spirits that have helped mankind to evolve. Jesus and Buddha and other such people are considered Christs. There will be future Christs. There are Christs sitting here now. The Christ spirit is one that gives hope and peace.

Was Lucifer involved in the creation or the development of Earth humanity? (J) Indeed, sir. Many of you are here as friends of Lucifer. This was in accord with the universal plan of evolution. There were other angels in a similar process with you. As I have said in the past, Lucifer is not a negative entity.

Is there a limit to how far a human soul can eventually evolve or do souls keep evolving to higher levels forever and ever? The evolution of a soul does not reach a limit. It just goes on evolving endlessly. There is no end to an answer. You will eventually evolve to the God level if you wish, if it makes you feel better. That is a personal thing.

Does the soul suffer when a fetus is intentionally aborted? At times, sir absolutely, sir. That implies that there are times that abortion could be a negative act. There are different factions in your thinking. Some want abortions and some don't. My view of abortion is that I wish to be loved, sir. I wish to exist as long as I wish to exist. I don't know how to interpret what I am saying but this is what I'm told to tell you. It is not my personal opinion.

Many eons ago when major Earth changes took place in which the great majority of humans died, were all of those souls accepted into the earth's spirit world or did some go to another spirit world? I remember it well, sir. We scattered as you people have scattered. We scattered too. We are like dust in the wind. We go in different directions. I dwell in the spirit world of my home planet. Yet I can visit other spirit worlds.

Does the spirit or soul change when the DNA of humans is modified? No, sir. The spirit stays the same as does the soul.

2. Humans before Homosapiens

Note: All of the questions in this section also appear in Chapter P: The World before Biblical times.

Did we originate in some place other than on Earth? You come from many multiples. There are many places. There are many Earths. Earth is not the only. There are other stars besides yours. You did not originate on Earth. My answer to you is yes, glory be yes.

Did the human race, both the Neanderthals and the Homosapiens, first appear on Earth in Africa? (P) Yes. In Africa.

What is the origin of the different races on Earth? (P) There was only one human race before the Great Flood. We were all here together and we all separated different ways. When we separated we became different races. Until then we were all one. It goes back many, many years even before I was born. Atmosphere changed the color of the skin. The current races are one race that went to different atmospheres or, as you well know, climate. They are becoming more similar. They are blending and blending.

Was there a time when reptilian physical characteristics were prevalent in a large portion of Earth people? Are there still such people on Earth living underground? (P) Indeed, sir, and they are still under the earth too.

Did the early physical humans communicate by telepathy or did spoken language gradually evolve and become their means of communication? (P) Telepathy, probably so. Telepathy is much easier when we would read other people's minds and actions.

Was there a time in the distant past when physical humans were not divided into sexes? (P) Indeed. They were not divided into sexes. They reproduced both ways. They were hermaphroditic.

In our ancient past, were there once several different varieties of human or humanoid beings on Earth at the same time, including Neanderthals and Homosapiens etc.? (P) Indeed sir, and there was a mixture and that is why you are so odd. Many of you are like part Neanderthal.

What was the cause for the apparent leap in human consciousness from the Neanderthal Man to the Homosapiens? (P) An awakening, my dear sir, an awakening. Extraterrestrials were absolutely involved and they are always there. It was an infusion of their DNA into the Neanderthal man.

Did either the Neanderthals or the Homosapiens ever co-exist with the Atlanteans? (P) [The Atlanteans were] before, sir.

Did the Neanderthal humans and Homosapiens ever co-exist peacefully? Was there warfare between them? Were they of equal intelligence? (P) Not peacefully sir. Not warfare as you stated. Different opinions. They were of equal intelligence.

Why did Homosapiens outlast the Neanderthals? (P) It was a time for them to change sir. Every neighborhood changes.

Did the Ice Age affect the development and physical appearance of the Neanderthals? (P) Yes. The skin color changed. That was primarily the many colors you have endured. The climate had an effect on the development of the races today. The races were created by climatic conditions.

Did volcanic ash of approximately 39,000 years ago have an effect on the demise of the Neanderthals? (P) Indeed, sir. If you were being burnt by the ashes wouldn't you say that you would be disappearing?

Was there originally just one language rather than the proliferation of languages that exist in the world today? (P) Yes. And then we separated and went different ways. Language was given by those that were able to communicate by sounds and grunts and sounds of pleasure. We speak many languages on Earth. Your grunts are closest to the original language.

Were the Atlanteans physically different from us to the point that we could easily see that they were not like modern humans? (P) No, sir. The Atlanteans are beautiful human beings. They are beautiful and well cared for. They did not resemble one of the current races more than the others. They covered many races, not only one race. The American Indians were the closest to what the Atlanteans looked like. The brown skin. A mixture, sir. They are beautiful souls.

What were the major ways in which the physical characteristics of the Lemurians were different from Homosapiens? (P) Indeed, sir. They were hermaphrodites, quite different from physical human beings. Before that they reproduced like starfish, cut off a part of themselves.

Were the various types of humanoids such as the Neanderthal man, the Cro-Magnons etc. created by the Anunnaki as prototypes that led to the development of the modern Homosapiens? (MP) Indeed, sir. They were models of humans created as an aid and consistency to continue. The Anunnaki are very much involved in the creation of the next humanoid species after the Homosapiens that some people refer to as the Homonoeticus.

3. Extraterrestrial involvement

From what star system was there the most extraterrestrial intervention in the development of the human race? (M) There are many star systems that we all come from on Earth. There are many inhabitants in your system. Your Earthly beings are so simple. There wasn't one single system that had more influence.

Were our distant ancestors given increased intelligence or intellectual ability by modification of their DNA by extraterrestrial beings? (M) Indeed, sir. This is still going on today. Why not?

Did aliens introduce their DNA to the then developing human race in order to jumpstart it to make it evolve more rapidly which is why there are missing links? (M) It's a mixture. It's an interpretation, a mixture.

Did the Anunnaki create or assist in the creation or modifications of human beings for the purpose of being workers for mining the gold which they needed? (M) Indeed. The Anunnaki did take part in the creation of human beings, and they enjoyed it too. They had a mixture [of animals]. May I add that you can attribute your beings, the way you look now, to the Anunnaki if you wish?

Was the human body designed by the Anunnaki to look like them? In a simple way, yes my dear sir. They modified the bodies of the then existing Earth beings by infusing their DNA into them. That is how they made them to look more like them. When your Bible said that God created man in his own image, that was actually in reference to the Anunnaki creating humans in their image.

Do the Anunnaki continue to play a role protective of mankind on Earth? (M) Indeed, sir. They are in control.

Would you say that all humans were at least once in their existence a hybrid, that is a mixture of their original Earth being and an extraterrestrial being? Indeed, sir. Some humans have become hybrids on repeated occasions. That process is continuing to occur at the present time. Indeed among you.

Can we usually assume that if one of a person's parents was a human and the other an extraterrestrial that his physical appearance would appear somewhat unusual to other humans? (M) There is interbreeding between extraterrestrials and humans. If an extraterrestrial should interbreed with a human, that child will not look completely different from a human. There will be a time that robots will take place. This is already in existence at this time. They are robots and they are people from outer space. There will be robots invented to be sexual partners for humans. That will be in your lifetime. They are right now.

If one of a person's grandparents was an extraterrestrial, would that person be likely to have any noticeable physical extraterrestrial features? After how many generations would an individual appear totally human with no unusual features from the extraterrestrial ancestry? No. It would skip a generation. The next generation. It is recessive.

Has the human mind as well as the human body been expanded with the infusion of DNA of the Anunnaki? In a way, yes. More the body than the mind.

Were humanoid beings introduced to our planet by extraterrestrials or was there a form of a humanoid being that was indigenous to our planet before the intervention of extraterrestrials. There are annoyances. Yes. There were some humanoid beings on your planet before the Anunnaki came and changed them.

4. Planet and interplanetary sojourns

Is it true that many souls must have interplanetary sojourns for specific purposes before they are able to reincarnate? Does each planet in our solar system serve us for a different purpose in the evolution of our soul? (G) Yes, indeed.

Although you have said that the evolution of the soul involves interplanetary sojourns, is the earth's moon also a place for such? The earth's moon is indeed a wonderful place for such decisions. If a soul wishes to go, there are so many atmospheres and options for a soul to select. There are specific lessons that the moon is noted for, as the earth is needed for certain lessons. Many of you don't want to leave the earth and are fearful of leaving the earth.

Some people believe that highly advanced entities that were once on this plateau can eventually evolve to the state that they can become a planet or a star. Is that true? (GL) Indeed, sir. That is at a higher level. Souls can evolve into the sun such things. These are highly advanced souls. There are many stars. You can always be a star. So we can say that all the billions of stars out there are souls. It's hard to believe. That's why we wish upon a star; do we not? Planets and stars have a level of consciousness that is above the level of that of humans. I will not start up with a star. To become a star you must be knowledgeable. Humans have the potential of someday becoming a star. Indeed if you are good in school, you will become a star. I will not tangle with a star because they are more knowledgeable.

5. Humans in the future

Will humans eventually communicate through telepathy rather than by spoken language? They already do. Some people do not speak. In the very far future perhaps telepathy will be used, for your many different nations do not have to but they will be able to draw pictures.

Will women become the dominant gender at some point in the future? (P) Your wife will. Women will take more leadership roles in different areas of the world. Do not fear if it will be in the relative near or distant future.

Will marriage become less significant or popular within the next several generations? It will be less important. Your laws will change. Your bylines will change. People will change. A smaller percentage of the population will be married. Only those who produce will be married. By produce [I mean] bearing children.

Will the genetic manipulation of human DNA to create a more advanced human being by our scientists become a reality in the near future? (R) It is already sir. It is in progress definitely and they are experimenting and this also will come to light in a very short time. The danger in what they will create is another person. It is not being developed for negativity. It is being developed to be used in a harmless way but everything harmless turns out with some negativity.

It is said that we use less than twenty percent of our physical brain. As humans evolve, will we be using a greater part of our brain? Most of you do [use less than twenty percent]. Indeed [as humans evolve, you will be using a greater part of your brain].

Will humans look more like the Greys thousands of years from now; such as the size of the head, eyes, legs, muscles etc.? Are humans gradually evolving into Greys? I will see you there then. You can assume that you will look somewhat more like the Greys. Humans are gradually evolving into Greys in a different way, if you wish to call it that.

Will the average life span of a human being increase by more than twenty years within the next few centuries? Indeed, sir. It is doing that now. Humans will be living more than one hundred twenty years.

Are star children the forerunners of a new race of humans that will eventually replace Homosapiens? Is this the race what is often referred to as Homonoeticus? Isn't such happening at this moment, sir? Humanity is evolving to a higher level through the entry of star children being born on Earth. That is the new race that is often referred to as the Homonoeticus, if you wish to give it a label. The new race will be more evolved. They will be able to see the future without talking. They will be what you would call psychic.

When the Chinese government recently made a study of more than 100,000 children with unusual abilities, were they what we call "star Children"? Indeed, sir. Star children are very bright, intelligent and wise. They are more highly evolved souls than most souls with much confusion.

There is an increasing number of children born today who can do things that far exceed the abilities of other children. We call them star children. Was Jesus a star child? (F) So was Mohammad. So was Confucius. So is your wife.

Is the generation of people that we call the Millennials (Generation Y) for the most part more advanced in their evolution than those in the generations that we call the Baby Boomers and Generation X? The Millennials and those born after the year 2000 are more advanced than the baby boomers. They are also very, very clearly intuitive or as you will, if I may, psychic. As time proceeds a greater percentage of the population will be more psychic than at present.

Can you tell us something about the Indigo children? Indigo children, as you have named such, are brilliant, intelligent and very superior, you know. They are very bright, a bit mystical. They are aware of the past and they are aware of the future. Many of you are mystical children. Indigo children are an increasing percentage of all the babies being born today. Much smarter than you.

You have mentioned several times that human kind is getting more in touch with psychic the capabilities that we have had right along. Are we ever going to get to the stage where people cannot lie to each other or when we can tell when we are being lied to? You can do that now, sir, by just looking at who you are looking at. [Could that be a reference to telling so by the reading of auras, which many people can do?] Most of us are liars, sir. We even lie to ourselves. Well, maybe not lie, fib.

Will the time ever come when we will be able to control tornados by using our technology? Indeed, using your mind sir. Your mind is a wonderful asset and is not being able to be used to control. An example of this would be that you and your wife once knew a person who could make clouds disappear using her mind.

6. After the human state

If you are no longer required to reincarnate, do most energy beings remain on the astral plane indefinitely or must you eventually move to a higher realm? (B) Or to a lower realm. Wherever you wish. Wherever you feel comfort and solace. A lower realm is other star systems. The earth is not the only place for us to arrive in. Not only Earth.

After they have reached the level of evolution where they are no longer required to remain in the spirit realm, do spirits cast off their spirit bodies much the same as we cast off our physical bodies when we enter the spirit world? Indeed sir. After the spirits cast off their spirit body, some go to a higher realm. Some are left back. They have to come back and learn. Above my world, we go on and on and angels take over.

When you said that humans can evolve to a state that they are like angels, were you referring to what is commonly called the "masters"? (J) Some of us are not able to reach that plateau. Some can and will.

Do those in the human or spirit kingdom ever evolve into the angelic kingdom or are the two kingdoms always separate? (J) The kingdoms are separate, my dear sir. No one from the human kingdom or from the spirit kingdom can ever become an angel.

Since you have said that angels will not evolve beyond the angel state, is there potential for humans to eventually evolve to a level above that of the angels? (J) Indeed, sir. Don't we call people who are kind an angel?

Will all humans and spirits eventually evolve to a higher plane of existence, or will some be dissolved or relegated to a lower plane of existence? They will not be dissolved or relegated. The goal of all humans and spirits is to go up to an even higher realm of existence above that of spirits. That is very important for the spiritual aspect.

Do souls manifest themselves in various stages in their upward evolution such as the physical human body, the spirit form as well as various cosmic entities such as planets, moons, stars etc.? It goes on from where you are and manifests itself in heavenly bodies. It is a natural course of events that I and the rest of you will eventually evolve to the point that you become stars. All the billions of stars out there are souls.

Do humans have the potential of eventually evolving to a level much further than we can now conceive, more than even cosmic entities? We are all able to reach a higher level. We all can climb up and do well. Helping people, being with people, being of aid is an asset to people. Help others and you will feel better and be better. That is the best way to evolve; to give, help others. Give and you will receive. When you give, the happiness you receive inside cannot be expressed.

7. Level of consciousness and evolution

Do all things in the physical world, whether they are animal, vegetable or mineral, have some level or form of consciousness? Indeed, yes.

Is the ability of an individual to easily feel love for others (not physical love) an indication of that person's level of evolution? Indeed, sir. The more you can be sensitive and feel love for people, the more spiritual you are.

In both your world and our world, are individuals who have a good sense of humor usually more highly evolved than those with very little sense of humor? (B) Indeed. Those who have more humor have more strength. Those who have no humor do not know their ass from their elbow. Those with very little sense of humor are not as evolved.

It is said that there a relationship between the kind of music we enjoy listening and the functioning of our chakras. Can we actually raise our level of consciousness by listening to classical music? Indeed, if the music doesn't get on your mind [nerves] [and] the music does not tear you apart. If it brings peace to you, you can control it. You advance more spiritually if you listen to classical music rather than rap type music.

Is an important means for raising the level of a person's awareness to spend time in nature and vegetation rather than in metropolitan areas? If you want to think like a bug, go where the bugs are. It is ridiculous that you will raise your level of consciousness if you are in pure nature rather than in the city.

Although you have said that being in the countryside rather than in urban areas will not help you raise your kevel of consciousness, are there any places on Earth where you could help raise your level of consciousness simply by being there? Every individual is an individual. Every stone has a different need. Everyone has a different answer. It depends on the person where it would be best to raise the level of consciousness. Wouldn't it be interesting if all were to gather in one place!

Is eating meat a reflection of lower level consciousness? (S) You can raise your level of consciousness by avoiding red meat. Definitely. Eating red meat is not beneficial to your health.

Does cursing or using foul language have any repercussions on the individual's evolution? Release, sir. I feel better when I don't give a damn what I say.

When a person has a disease such as Alzheimer's, is that person's consciousness more in the spirit world than in this world? Confusion exists in that person. They are not in any world. They are out of this world.

You have said that we humans are stupid; but would you also say that we are more ignorant than stupid? Indeed, sir. You are not knowledgeable.

Both your ignorance and your stupidity are overwhelming. I am being very kind.

What caused the people of Earth to be among the least advanced entities in the various star systems? They are ignorant. They do not spread [?] their own words. They just cannot see ahead. They are more ignorant than stupid. You just don't know but you do have the potential to learn. Some Earth beings need more incarnations than those on other planets. I had many incarnations because I was a slow learner. I am still a slow learner but I can tell you what to do.

8. Validating information from other sources

Is there considerable accuracy in the letters of those individuals in your realm who channeled the Urantia Book? (L) There is some accuracy in some of the Urantia statements.

Is Darwin's theory of evolution mostly correct, somewhat correct, or mostly incorrect? Brilliant man, you know. Somewhat correct.

Is Erich Von Daniken on the right track in his book *Chariots of the Gods*? (M) There is some truth in what he has written.

Is the information about the root races as depicted in the Theosophical belief system basically accurate? Yes, indeed. 'Tis correct. Blavatsky is correct. She is telling me to tell you yes. Homosapiens are gradually evolving into Homonoeticus. You will not have to use your voice in the future. Homonoeticus will be more psychic and telepathic. Most already beginning. Forerunners right now. Beginning slowly amongst your younger children right now. The indigo children are the forerunners. There are many people who can foretell and foresee.

Are the fundamental principles presented in Theosophy correct for the most part? (L) Indeed sir. Indeed sir. You could learn and grow if you looked into Blavatsky's work, the Secret Doctrine and things like that. It is of use to find out where others have failed so you can prevail. You will do so.

9. Homosexuality

Since it seems that you indicated that that homosexuals are so by choice, could you give us a couple of reasons why they might choose to be so? The choice can be made either before birth or after but mainly after birth. Sometimes there are times they cannot finish their gender and come back to finish even though they are in a different gender body. Sometimes you just like the same people. You find it appealing. That's why so many wish to transfer.

It seems that there are a greater percentage of homosexuals today than in the past. Is that more apparent than real? Yes, it is just the way it has always been. More individuals have been acknowledged and more people have been educated and they are not stupid.

Through psychological therapy can homosexuals become heterosexuals? Through psychological therapy they can be both if they wish, you know. They can attain any wish they desire. It is not uncommon. 'Tis very common.

10. Human abilities

Since time does not exist in your dimension is it correct to assume that no medium or psychic on this plateau can accurately predict the dates when future events will occur? If they are good, yes, but accuracy does not exist. The future does exist.

Is instant teleportation of a person from one place to another possible both through the use of technology and also through the use of the human mind? (V) Indeed, sir. Some humans can instantly appear in a different place from where they were before. You can do the same. The answer is yes.

Are there any civilizations on other planets where the inhabitants do not need mechanical means to travel from one place to another but instead are able to use their minds to teleport themselves wherever they wish to go in the physical? Yes, my dear sir. You can do that now. Earth people can learn teleportation.

Would you explain what happens in fire walking events to enable a person to do so without harm? They do not actually walk on fire, sir. They walk on dead coals. You can do it any place you wish to if you can do it fast and run right through it. I've seen many a dumb thing done.

Are mediums the only ones who can see spirits? Many people can see spirits but they do not trust their vision or do not trust their mental abilities.

Since you have no time and space in your dimension, is the closest thing to that we can experience in our dimension is that we can instantaneously take our thoughts to any place or any time? Indeed.

Is it possible that as we age we can, even in this life, begin to live life on the spirits' level? For some this is true; for some a fallacy. For some it is very true. Each person or individual has to know the difference. It is imperative to know the difference.

11. Time Traveling

Has anyone ever been able to time travel? Indeed, my dear lady. We all time travel. We go forward or we go back It is easier for you to go back but you can go forward.

You have already told us that time travelers do exist and that there are some people on Earth right now who are from our future. Can time travelers go back in time and change our history? Indeed sir. They can go back and change themselves; not the world history, but their own history.

Can time travelers travel to the future as well as to the past? Absolutely, sir.

Can a time traveler visit himself in the past? My wife thinks, but is not sure, that she saw me as a time traveler from the future. Is that true? A time traveler can go back in time and visit himself. It is true that your wife saw you as a time traveler from the future.

When a person is having an astral projection is he able to travel anywhere in the universe much the same as the spirits do? Absolutely.

The person is also able to travel in time, both to the past and to the future much the same as do spirits.

Were human encounters with extraterrestrials sometimes not really encounters with extraterrestrials but rather encounters with human time travelers from our future? You thought they were extraterrestrials. They were imposters. They were you from the future.

12. Miscellaneous

Is the theory of the vanishing twin syndrome a reality or the product of imagination? The theory is true. It occurs frequently, you know, but it is not important. Some of it is not digested well. Miscarriages are also part of the vanishing twin.

Regarding the vanishing twin syndrome, before birth do all babies have a twin in the womb with them? Can the twin that disappears, have any influence on whether the surviving twin is heterosexual or homosexual? [All babies have a twin in the womb with them], it is considered so. The surviving twin will be aware. The gender of the surviving twin will be whatever it wishes to be. If it wishes to be female, it will be female. The twin that disappears has no affect on the surviving twin.

Is the desire for humans to become godlike implanted in our DNA? No sir. It is implanted in our mental abilities that we have lacking of.

Is intuition something we have because we have lived before? Do we have the knowledge or is intuition something just for this time and place? Intuition, my dear lady, is like a brain. It is a brain that you had before and is the feeling of the knowledge that you have lived before. Your intuition is another word for being psychic. Everybody has a heart. Everybody has intuition. Everybody, every single soul is psychic.

Is a personal astrological chart a good source for life guidance? 'Tis a good source. It can be helpful if it is interpreted properly, if you are able to interpret it in a proper way.

Does spontaneous combustion of human beings exist? Indeed, sir. A person's body temperature can actually reach three thousand degrees. We can do anything, sir. We can reach a low degree and a high degree. The source of the combustion comes from within.

In regard to good luck, can we say that the good luck is how we enlighten ourselves and how we grow inside and the more light inside the more we can illuminate what is outside for us. Indeed, my dear lady. That is how people have a lot of luck then how it was described. It is know yourself. And that is most difficult, you know.

Some people believe apes are errant genetic descendants of humans rather than the reverse. Is that true? (T) Sometimes it's true.

Does everyone go through an out-of-body experience at least once in a lifetime? In one form or another that is true but it may be misinterpreted what an out-of-body experience is. We have gone through many, many out-of-body experiences. One is [when a person is] asleep.

If a person repeatedly says negative, but untrue, things about himself (such as "My eyesight is poor.") is there an increased possibility that this will eventually become true? Indeed, sir. We know how to make it prevail. We talk ourselves into being good and to be not.

When you see a person's future does that mean that you can tell how that person will exercise his free will? Are the results of a person's exercise of his free will known in advance by the higher powers? Indeed sir, we can tell how that person will exercise his free will. It depends upon the individual whether free will is predestined. Remember the word *free will*. You have a choice: to do it or not to do it. You are where you are in life right now in life because of the series of sequences in exercising your free will. [Regarding the second part of the question]: We get together, my dear sir, and we gamble at what you are going to do and what you are not going to do. That is based on how you have exercised your free will in the past. You can change your mind, sir.

Some people believe that the overall evolution black race is somewhat less than that of other races because they have tended to repeatedly reincarnate into the same race. Is there any truth in that belief? Originally, all humans on Earth were black. I have said before that the reason you changed into different races was climate. There is some truth in that the black race tends somewhat to reincarnate into the same race.

It seems there is much more dishonesty among people on Earth nowadays than there was several decades ago. Is that so, or does it just appear that way? Is our society more decadent today than it was many years ago? It's the same thing. It is just advertised. It just appears that there is more dishonesty. Overall, society in America is not more decadent. The same, sir. There's more people, you know.

Do reptilian-human hybrids exist anywhere on Earth today? Indeed, sir. That is obvious. They are not mostly below the surface of the earth. They are on the surface.

Theoretically, could memories that emanate from a person's ancestors be stored within the cells of the person's body? In other words, could he have memories not just of his own lifetime but also have some of his ancestors' memories? No, sir. In other words, because of your cells, you don't have any memories of your ancestors with you.

When a person has what we refer to as a near death experience, does that person actually enter the spirit world? Are NDE's preplanned or are they spontaneous? Some do enter the spirit world and some do not. Each individual is individual. They [the experiences] are not preplanned. You cannot preplan.

When we dream at night, are we fully conscious in the spirit world or are we only hazily conscious? It depends upon the dream, sir. In some dreams you are only partly in the physical world but in other dreams your consciousness is fully in the spirit world.

Is it true that in the earth's sphere there are about ten times as many souls in the spirit world than there are in the physical world? Correct.

You have frequently said that humans are stupid. Can humans overcome stupidity through specific actions or will that only occur through a slow evolutionary process? You know that you are ignorant, meaning that you just don't know but stupid implies that you don't have the capacity to learn readily. There are some that are ignorant and you cannot make any sense to them. They are stubborn. They are in their own world and you cannot deal with any person or people that think they are always right. By these questions [that I am answering you], I am helping you to become more aware, in other words to become less ignorant. That is what my existence here [is for], to be with you, and help you, and serve you and answer your questions. I am helping you to raise your level of awareness or consciousness. Some of you. And some we cannot open the door. It is stuck with Crazy Glue.

Are some humans more knowledgeable than some spirits in understanding the world and others around them? Indeed. The same is true regarding foreseeing the future. Some humans can see the future better than some spirits. However, there are few that can.

If a person is in a coma state, is that person able to think, or is the conscious mind shut down? The mind is shut down. He is not thinking. He is sleeping He is resting peacefully.

It appears that there are more mentally ill people on Earth today that ever before. Is that true? That is true. We have mentally ill people in my world also. This is a trend in society.

Do many human hybrids on Earth appear physically the same as other humans to us but are mentally and psychologically different? Yes [they appear physically the same]. They are more psychologically and emotionally different than they are physically different. The hybrids who are being integrated into your society are noticed by the way they think and act, not by the way they look.

L. GOD, CREATION AND THE UNIVERSE

1. God

How would you define what we humans call God? Is God something you worship as we do in our realm? You humans do not know God. No one knows God. My vision of God is tremendous and not explainable and it lies within each of us. We do not have any worship, sir. We do not worship other than ourselves. Each individual is an extension of God. We use the word God so loosely. I do not know what is meant or what is referred to as God. For I am God within myself. Within me is a God. Within each one of you there is a God. We call that God intuition. Within every soul there is intuition and there is a God. Within ourselves we are strong. Do not allow someone else to appoint what should be done or what will be done or could be. God could be defined as a conglomerate of all that exists. God is everything. Everything is a word that cannot be explained or expressed.

Is there a specific entity that oversees the operation of our universe? There is no single entity watching over all of creation. We have no god. There are many entities. God is within each individual. Like on your earth, everyone has their own soul. Different gods; different beliefs; different standards. There is no one specific entity in charge. We have groups of intelligent [entities] that get together and aid us to aid you. The work is done by committee.

Does each star system have some form of a conscious entity that oversees the development of that star system? Is there an overseer of all of creation? Indeed, we have different rules and organizations on our different star systems. We are the overseer [of all creation]. We have someone to put our efforts on, so why not blame God. We will not blame ourselves and sometimes we blame God. All of us together make up God.

Since you have already seemed to indicate that there is no single entity that we might think of as God overseeing everything in our universe, is there a hierarchy or committee of what we might think of as gods that oversee our universe? I must admit a smile on my face and show you there is such and it is consistent as you suggested. There is not a single entity but committees.

2. Places in the universe

Do many other universes in addition to our universe exist? When a soul experiences parallel lives, are those lives sometimes in different universes? Indeed. When a soul sometimes experiences parallel lives those lives can be in different universes.

Is there a center of the universe as some scientists feel? Indeed, sir. It is from that location that the life force emanates.

Are there other planets outside of our solar system which could support Earth humans in the physical as we now are? Indeed, very much so.

Do such places exist in the physical world where you can go through some kind of portal and emerge in faraway places in the universe? (MW) Indeed. Not only through one's mind but in the future. You can go into the future and into the past. They are what you may call black spaces. It is available to you. There is a network of underwater portals used by extraterrestrials. We look above but we do not look below. We must look below. Some are in our lakes and oceans and they are near here.

According to our scientists a black hole that is in our galaxy has a white hole at the other end of it, thus causing a tunnel that aliens could travel through. Were the scientists right? Indeed, that is correct.

In comparison with physical life in other star systems, what aspect of life would you say is the most difficult on Earth? The earth, my dear sir, is very difficult. Here on Earth we have promises. We have laws. We have concerns. There is much to learn. There are more rules and regulations on Earth than there are on other planets. The people, or entities, on other planets are nicer to each other than Earth people are to each other. We don't use the word "don't ". We do not use the word "do not". What makes the earth the most difficult planet to live on is not nature. [It is] people.

Was the planet Earth intentionally created to be the most difficult place for physical life or did it become that way because of the misguided but well meaning intentions of the angel Lucifer or some other entity?

Lucifer has definite intentions and they are not misguided. Lucifer's intentions in regard to the involvement with Earth are usually good but perhaps not to you, sir. It was because of Lucifer's actions that the earth became a most difficult place for physical life. The people made it [difficult], sir. The people disagree no matter what you do, no matter what you say. They don't know what they mean.

Is Zachariah Sitchin with you in your plane? Was he correct when he interpreted an ancient Sumerian tablet that said that there was once a planet between Jupiter and Mars that they called Tiamat? He is here now. He is telling her [Sondra Zecher] he loves her and wanted so much to meet her and he is holding her and he is charming. He loves the work that she is doing to assist and aid people and let average people know what it is to feel good about themselves. He is correct [regarding the planet between Jupiter and Mars]. That is why your horoscopes are changing. The planet that broke up created both the asteroid belt and the planet Earth. Indeed it was hit by Niburu and splintered off, having children. I am not quite sure but I will tell you that it is partially true that the earth was once part of that planet.

Are there pyramids on the moon and on Mars? Yes. There are pyramids on other planets in addition to Earth and Mars. Why should they be special? There are absolutely pyramids beneath the water in the earth. The earth has fallen. That is why there are pyramids [beneath] the level of the water.

Is there such a thing as complete silence or no kind of activity what-soever anywhere in the universe? Not that I am aware of, sir.

Are there entire cities beneath the ice in Antarctica today that are inhabited by extraterrestrials? Indeed, and air and water are necessary for the entities beneath the surface of Antarctica. It is necessary for flowers and anything that needs air. There is also vegetable and animal life beneath the surface. I have said that at one time there was an Earth shift and what was Atlantis became Antarctica. That is why it is a highly evolved civilization.

Was our moon created and placed into our solar system by extraterrestrials? Indeed. Your moon was strategically placed by beings more advanced than humans so that life on Earth could take place.

Was the planet Pluto originally a moon of Saturn that was hit by the planet Niburu? If you wish to believe it, sir, it is true. Pluto was originally revolving around the planet Saturn. Then the planet Niburu influenced it and threw it out of the orbit of Saturn.

Are there additional undiscovered planets in our solar system? Indeed. Some of those are as large as the earth. There are seven or nine undiscovered planets as large as the earth. They are as far out as the planet Niburu.

Just as there are many different physical worlds, are there also many different spirit worlds? Each planet that has humanoid life has a spirit world.

Is there more than one star in our solar system? Indeed sir. There are many stars. The earth revolves around more than just what you think of as your sun.

Is Earth one of the most recent planets to be inhabited by human-like entities? There are more than Earth. There is another planet that is exactly like Earth. I have told you that human life on Earth is the least advanced of all planets. The beings on the other planet that is just like Earth are at the same level as humans. You will have contact with those beings if you live long enough. That planet is in your solar system. It will be difficult to communicate with them. I'm not talking about Ceres but something further.

Do spirit worlds exist on planets or other celestial bodies where no physical humanoid life exists? Indeed. There can be spirits on the moon but no humanoid life on the moon. There is energy everywhere. Spirits are energy. When I say there is energy everywhere, I am saying that there are spirits everywhere even though physical beings are not everywhere.

Was the Earth inhabited by spirits before it was inhabited by humans? Yes.

3. Evolution of cosmic entities

Some people believe that highly advanced entities that were once on this plateau can eventually evolve to the state that they can become a planet or a star. Is that true? (GK) Indeed, sir. That is at a higher level. Souls can evolve into the sun or things like that. These are highly advanced souls. There are many stars. You can always be a star. So we can say that all the billions of stars out there are souls. It's hard to believe. That's why we wish upon a star; do we not? Planets and stars have a level of consciousness that is above the level of that of humans. I will not start up with a star. To become a star you must be knowledgeable. Humans have the potential of someday becoming a star. Indeed if you are good in school, you will become a star. I will not tangle with a star because they are more knowledgeable.

Since you have said that planets and stars are souls, do those souls sometimes withdraw from the planets and stars just as our souls withdraw from our physical bodies? What happens to the planet or star after the soul withdraws? Indeed, sir. After the soul withdraws, it goes on to another. It goes on and on. It's like playing hopscotch. The planet or stars continue to exist without a soul. They are mightier than we are. Your sun has a soul, many bright lights, many peaks of energy. When they refer to your sun as the logos of your solar system that implies that the sun has a soul.

Are all stars, planets and other celestial beings manifestations of souls? In a way, sir, yes. Your souls are manifested as physical humans but eventually as you continue to evolve in the physical, your soul can manifest itself as a planet. Not all planets are manifestations of souls. Some are and some aren't.

In addition to planets and stars, are all celestial beings, such as comets and meteors, also the manifestations of souls? Many souls are resting on different stars. Indeed. The same is true of comets and meteors. They are different energies.

Are there multiple spirit worlds just as there are multiple physical worlds or is there just one world of spirits? (E) Indeed, there are also multiple spirit worlds. Spirits such as I can instantaneously travel from one spirit world to another. My origin is not on this earth. Thank goodness for that. That is why it takes me a lot of energy to travel to you from one spirit world to another.

Are there celestial bodies in the spirit world as well as in the physical? That is, do the celestial bodies have a spirit component just as humans have both physical and spirit components? Indeed, sir.

Did life on Earth begin because organic material was brought here from elsewhere? Extraterrestrials were able to bring organic materials to start off physical life. They had manipulated and they are still doing so. They are here where we need the most help. Earth human beings are the least advanced in the universe but I see them evolving to the status of extraterrestrials. They have a long ways to go, a very long ways.

Is our solar system one of the youngest in the universe? Indeed, sir. New solar systems are continuously being created.

Did all life in the universe begin at one specific location and then spread throughout the universe? It was like an ant. It keeps spreading and spreading. The process of spreading out is continuing even today.

4. Other Kingdoms

Do nature spirits or elementals watch over nature and the vegetable kingdoms as do angels over the animal and human kingdoms? Does any force watch over the mineral kingdom? I do not like the elementals, leprechauns, gnomes and things like that. They cause turbulence in any kingdom. They can get in your way and help you to fall or trip. They certainly do watch over the vegetable kingdom. There is a force watching over the mineral kingdom. It's something comparable to angels watching over the human kingdom.

Is the purpose of elementals to watch over nature? In their evolution, do they always remain as such or do they move up to a higher level? What do they become? I have said that I particularly don't like elementals. They can move up to a higher level when they come back. It may take time to become humans but they can do that. It does take time.

You have said that leprechauns and fairies are very childish and immature and that they do not evolve into angels. Do they evolve into a higher level being or do they remain childish and immature? My dear sir, there is nothing wrong with remaining childish and immature. There are always souls that remain childish and immature. That can be as far as they evolve. That's all that counts. Their happiness. There is nothing wrong, sir, with being that way. There is nothing wrong with being stupid.

Are new souls still continuing to come into existence? Indeed, sir. The soul exists throughout the entity's evolution from the mineral kingdom through the vegetable and animal kingdoms and finally to the human kingdom. The soul is right from the beginning.

We know that those in the animal kingdom and the human kingdom have souls. Do those in the mineral and vegetable kingdoms have souls? When does the soul come into existence? Indeed not, sir. The soul begins in the transition from the vegetable kingdom to the animal kingdom, when it's procreating. [Note: This appears to contradict the previous question.]

You have said that the soul is there in the beginning and that minerals have souls. You have also said that souls begin with the transition from the vegetable kingdom to the animal kingdom. Does this mean that elements or fragments of a soul are in the mineral kingdom and the vegetable kingdom and then those elements coalesce upon the entry into the animal kingdom? Indeed.

Do vegetables have awareness? They have consciousness of some kind for a moment. They communicate with other vegetables. It is possible that they communicate with people for a very short period while they are alive. The purpose of vegetables is to provide nutrition for insects, animals and humans.

Is there ever a blending of the vegetable world and the animal world? That is, are there creatures that are part vegetable and part animal? Is this true on other planets as well? That is what they tell me. That is true everywhere you go.

You have said in the past to us that animals can evolve into humans and that birds can evolve into angels. What do fish evolve into? They are just as a vegetable, sir. A fish does not have a brain, depending upon the fish, if you are talking about a goldfish or an octopus. What category do you put fish in? They do evolve further, just as a rock does. A rock progresses.

We know that there is no distinction between male and female in the spirit world. When we speak of both gods and goddesses, in that realm does gender distinction exist? No. Society is progressing so that there is increasingly less distinction between male and female. The future shows that there will be less distinction. Notice the clothing. Notice the hairdos. Notice the people. Notice how everything is going away from gender to gender. This is a natural or normal type of progression or evolution.

5. Miscellaneous

Is there considerable accuracy in the letters of those individuals in your realm who channeled the Urantia Book? (K) There is some accuracy in some of the Urantia statements.

Are the fundamental principles presented in Theosophy correct for the most part? (K) Indeed sir. Indeed sir. You could learn and grow if you looked into Blavatsky's work, the Secret Doctrine and things like that. It is of use to find out where others have failed so you can prevail. You will do so.

You have said that the soul is there in the beginning and that minerals have souls. You have also said that souls begin with the transition from the vegetable kingdom to the animal kingdom. Does this mean that elements or fragments of a soul are in the mineral kingdom and the vegetable kingdom and then those elements coalesce with upon the entry into the animal kingdom? Indeed, sir.

If not simultaneously, which came first, the creation of the spirit world or the creation of the physical world? The spirit world.

You have indicated that there are about ten times the number of entities in the earth's spirit world as there are in its physical world. Of those in the spirit world, is there a large number who no longer have the need to reincarnate? I myself do not need to reincarnate. There is a large number of entities in my world who do not need to come back into the physical.

Could the information in the book called the Kolbrin Bible be worthy of our consideration? It is worthy of your consideration to be knowledgeable. Indeed, sir.

Must a soul follow the same line of evolution in all star systems when in the physical; that is, a progression from the mineral, to the vegetable, to the animal before evolving as a human-type being? Yes.

Did some form of individual entities exist before the creation of our universe? Indeed, sir. Believe your museums, sir.

If a large meteorite should totally destroy the earth, what would happen to the spirits of all those in the earth's spirit world? You would have to find somewhere else to go. In other words the earth's spirit world would no longer exist and those spirits would have to go to the spirit world of a different planet.

From your own experience, would you say that physical life on this planet is more difficult that physical life in other star systems? My experience? They are all shaking their heads. Physical life on this plateau? They do not want to come back. So I would assume that from this experience, no one wants to come back.

Is there such a thing as what scientists call the God particle? Indeed, sir. It is held by people that are together as they are here before me. I am saying that the God particle is like a conglomeration of souls or something like that.

Does the soul manifest itself only in the physical realm and in the astral realm or are there also other realms where the soul resides? There are other realms. I have visited those realms if you wish to refer to them as higher realms.

M. EXTRATERRESTRIAL INVOLVEMENT WITH EARTH

1. Extraterrestrials and the U.S. government

Is there secret cooperation between our government and aliens? (T) Indeed. Indeed. Indeed. Your government is not without an odor.

Does the United States have military installations that house extraterrestrial beings? Oh, yes, yes, indeed. They are around you everywhere and they change their form and position so often.

Is there a hidden city beneath the earth near Dulce, New Mexico in which thousands of extraterrestrials live under the cooperation and observation of the United States government (U)(Laughing) Indeed, sir. There has been a pact between you and the aliens. I will answer in your language "sort of". These extraterrestrials experiment on humans there. They share their technology with you. They keep up to their part of the agreement, sort of.

Are there more than one hundred secret underground military installations in the United States? In addition to the installation in Dulce New Mexico, do any of them house extraterrestrials? (U) Indeed sir, a hundred is not a good number. In addition to the one in Dulce, New Mexico, some of those house extraterrestrial beings.

Is the government installation in Roswell, New Mexico still the home of aliens? (Laughing) Yes. I must see my family there.

Is NASA withholding some very significant information from us regarding the universe and extraterrestrial life? (U) Indeed they are holding information as you well know.

Is the HAARP facility in Alaska to control weather a potentially dangerous experiment to the earth and mankind? (U) 'Tis funny, you know. Ridiculous. You cannot control anything that's going to happen. The danger will be when the people doing the experiment drown. There is no extraterrestrial involvement at this time There will be a time that others will need help but at this time, no. No help. Your government is using the HAARP facility in Alaska for nefarious purposes, such as mind control. There is secrecy about the HAARP facility that the government is not publicizing.

What is the reason for the intense secrecy surrounding Area 51 in the air force base in Nevada? (U) 'Tis always that way, sir. Is it not? Security is needed. Your government chooses that. They wish that it is a secret. They are hiding information about aliens, UFOs, equipment and things like that. They're hiding it without too much success, you know.

Have some of our technologies been achieved through analyzing equipment found on crashed UFO's? (UV) More recently, sir? They have been there for years. What is so different? There is nothing different you know. The United States government is involved in programs of reverse engineering of alien spacecraft or other alien technology. They are examining things they found and then cover it.

Are there members of our government who are aliens disguised as Earth human beings? Do they mean to do us good or harm or both? Indeed. Both. Without knowledge [that they are aliens].

Are extraterrestrials monitoring our nuclear facilities because they are concerned about the direction our civilization is taking? (R) Indeed, sir. They are very concerned about these directions. They are very curious, sir. They wish to be in control. They are not fearful of what you might do. They wish to control. They are seeking control. There may as well be a potential that there will be a nuclear war but it will not come to that end. You will wipe out Syria [Isis?] and you will come to the aid of Israel. Israel has forces as such that no man has created. The Jews have secrets. Indeed, Israel is being guided by a powerful extraterrestrial force. They want so much to be existing.

Was the information in the U.S. government *Project Blue Book* about human encounters with extraterrestrials mostly accurate or mostly fiction? Accurate, sir. It was declassified to make it seem as though it was not true, even though it was true. It is not the only question that has been declassified. They do not wish you to be anxious or cause raucous or cause another war. Sometimes when the government declassifies information it is to make you believe it was false.

2. Extraterrestrials and the evolution of mankind

Is it true that Adam and Eve were super humans who came here from somewhere else to infuse their DNA with that of the humans on Earth at that time? Indeed. It was a long time ago, even before my time. Yes, they were here before any of us were here. Along with help from people from outer space.

Did the Anunnaki play a significant role in the development of mankind? If so, what did they do? Everyone who comes into this plateau serves a purpose whether you wish to call it significant or useful or nonsense is up to you. They come from another star system. There are star systems other than the earth. They raised human consciousness. Now the humans have a greater sense of responsibility which not every race has.

Did the Anunnaki create or assist in the creation or modifications of human beings for the purpose of being workers for mining the gold which they needed? (K) Indeed. sir. The Anunnaki did take part in the creation of human beings, and they enjoyed it too. They had a mixture [of animals]. May I add that you can attribute your beings, the way you look now to the Anunnaki if you wish?

Did the royal lines of kings and queens originate with extraterrestrial involvement? Why do we refer to them as "blue bloods"? Some are from alien beings, some are a mixture. Their blood is blue indeed. When it hits oxygen it turns red and sometimes yellow which is ill. Indeed. It started from nonsense to begin with. They had the same blood as everyone else. There is nothing special about the royal bloodline. We make people into royals by idolizing them and putting them on pedestals.

Have epidemics or plagues that have affected humans been caused by microbes on meteorites and asteroids that have hit the earth? Were some deliberately sent by extraterrestrial entities? (S) Indeed, sir. My answer to you is yes. Some of those hitting the were intentionally sent by extraterrestrial technology to help reduce the population.

Are there diseases afflicting humans in today's world that were intentionally caused by extraterrestrials? They meant no harm but they were caused by extraterrestrials. Those diseases are neurological in nature. It was not intentional. It was experimental.

Have extraterrestrial beings created genetically modified both humans and animals on Earth? Yes, sir. They tell me to say yes. I don't know what I am saying yes to but they tell me yes.

Were our distant ancestors given increased intelligence or intellectual ability by modification of their DNA by extraterrestrial beings? (K) Indeed, sir. This is still going on today. Why not?

Did aliens introduce their DNA to the then developing human race in order to jumpstart humans to make them evolve more rapidly? (K) It's a mixture. It's an interpretation. A mixture.

Were the Atlanteans evolved humans or a hybrid race of humans and extraterrestrials? (P) The Atlanteans were a combination, sir, as we are.

From what star system was there the most extraterrestrial intervention in the development of the human race? (K) There are many star systems that we all come from on Earth. There are many inhabitants in your system. Your Earthly beings are so simple as you well know. There wasn't one single system that had more influence.

Have the Pleiadians had considerable involvement on our planet? Indeed, sir, perhaps more so than those of any other star systems but that is my opinion, sir.

Was the origin of the system of priests in various religions actually humans who were able to communicate with extraterrestrials and act as intermediaries between them and Earth people? Was Aaron, the brother of Moses, one such person? (Q) Indeed, sir. Aaron was one such person; not well liked but Moses was well liked. I was on Earth at the time of Moses.

Can we usually assume that if one of a person's parents was a human and the other an extraterrestrial that his physical appearance would appear somewhat unusual to other humans? (K) There is interbreeding between extraterrestrials and humans. If an extraterrestrial should interbreed with a human, that child will not look completely different from a human but there will be a time that robots will take place. This is already in existence at this time. They are robots and they are people from outer space. There will be robots invented to be sexual partners for humans. That will be in your lifetime. They are right now.

You have said that extraterrestrials have influenced the development of mankind. Have they also had an influence on the creation or the development of insects and animals on Earth? (T) Indeed.

In our times, are babies with reptilian features sometimes born of human mothers who have had sexual contact with extraterrestrials? That is true. There are still babies being born. They are being raised by Earth mothers [rather than by the extraterrestrials].

Were the various types of humanoids such as the Neanderthal man, the Cro-Magnons etc. created by the Anunnaki as prototypes that lead to the development of the modern Homosapiens? (KP) Indeed, sir. They were models of humans created as an aid and consistency to continue. The Anunnaki are very much involved in the creation of the next humanoid species after the Homosapiens that some people refer to as the Homonoeticus.

Were early forms of writing such as the Egyptian hieroglyphs, runes, and the Sumerian alphabet given to humans by extraterrestrials? (P) They were invented by humans at that time. I am saying that after the extraterrestrials left, then the humans in order to record the events, came up with different ways of putting them into writing.

Throughout the history of the earth, including the present time, have there been both good and evil extraterrestrials attempting to direct the evolution of mankind on Earth? Indeed, sir, as you well know. Right now you have good intended and bad intended extraterrestrials involved with you as always.

3. Extraterrestrials and the development of the planet Earth

Was the Great Flood engineered by the Anunnaki to rid the earth of the Nephilim giants? (Q) The Great Flood was caused by alien intelligence to purge the earth. It was not to rid it of any specific species. It was a great cleansing. It was engineered by the Anunnaki.

Was the Gulf Stream engineered by the Atlanteans or other intelligent entities? (PW) Not manmade. I would like to say other intelligent entities, not a natural phenomenon, not the Atlanteans. By many people, extraterrestrials. The purpose was to keep the lands to the north warmer.

Ages ago did extraterrestrials who visited the earth encourage human and animal sacrifices? Why? No. They encouraged the sacrificing of animals. They believed the animals were beneath them and they were not all animals. They were creatures.

4. Physical evidence of ancient extraterrestrials

From what beings were the ancient elongated skulls found in Egypt and in the Americas? (P) Aliens, sir. And some were human. A mixture. The humans didn't try to imitate the aliens by forcing the skulls to become longer. They did it by having relationships, sir. They had fun with each other.

What is the origin of the drawings of the caves of Lascaux in France? (P) The drawings are their ways of communication, what we would say to you is their writings. They are able to communicate. They were both Earth people and extraterrestrials. They are existing on this planet. They have not left. They have been here many a century.

Can you tell us something about the construction of the Coral Castle in Homestead, Florida? (VW) Aliens were involved to help him [Edward Leedskalnin] to do so. He was too little to do this himself. His ability to communicate was remarkable.

Who were the architects and builders of the pyramids in the Yucatan and Guatemala? (PW) People that are striving from your past are reaching out and wish to serve in your future. They were actually built by those of another star system, the Pleiades. They also built the pyramids in Egypt and that is how they got to the top. The Pleiades are one of the most advanced groups. Our secret people were building your pyramids that they could reach from the top down. Humans provided a lot of the labor but extraterrestrials provided the technology.

Do the Dogu (Dogoo) statues found in Japan represent aliens in space suits? (W) Indeed, sir.

Regarding the Nazca Plateau in Peru, what was the purpose of the numerous very long lines, drawings of animals, geometrical shapes and mathematical diagrams that can only be seen from the air? (W) For those that are up high in the sky they can read it easier when above the land it is written on. I am talking about extraterrestrial UFO's. They were constructed by extraterrestrials for the purpose of providing instructions or information to the people of Earth. The same could be said about the various crop circles that have been appearing throughout the world. They are messages or instructions to Earth people from extraterrestrials. They are in your face. They are right there. They are trying to assist you and aid you. They are trying to be heard.

Have extraterrestrials imbued certain objects with special powers, perhaps such as the crystal sculls or other physical objects? (W) Yes, they have been cleansed and have special powers. Again I think about that. They have been cleansed. They are very clever. They are very intelligent. If they gather together that will be a tremendous powerful force, a controlling force. When those glass skulls are brought together power will occur, power to the extraterrestrial groups that made them. Extremely powerful. There are other objects located on Earth that are endowed with powers, such as you humans have power that was endowed by extraterrestrials. Humans will be using the crystal skulls relatively soon to communicate with extraterrestrials.

What caused the formation of the Devil's Tower in Wyoming? (W) Extraterrestrials were involved. We have been there and we created it. Extraterrestrials are still involved in the Devil's Tower. We are everywhere, sir. We have been here for centuries.

Does the dress of Betty Hill, who claims she and her husband were abducted by aliens in 1961, actually contain DNA evidence from an extraterrestrial? Indeed, sir.

Are the ancient astronauts that are depicted in stone carvings throughout the world both extraterrestrials and human time travelers from our future? They are both. Some of those rock carvings are actually humans in the future.

5. Extraterrestrials in the Bible

Are many events portrayed in the Old Testament of the Bible actually a recounting of encounters with entities from other worlds? (I) Some are precisely that situation. Some are true but not all.

Are the accounts of angels in various cultures, including the Bible, often references to extraterrestrial beings? (I) On some occasions. Not all occasions.

Were some of the people in the Bible actually extraterrestrial beings disguised as humans with the intent of the betterment of humankind? (I) If you want an answer, some of it would be yes.

I will read seven events portrayed in the Bible. After each one would you tell us if there was any involvement of aliens or their technology? (I)

1. Moses receiving the ten commandments — Indeed
2. The Israelites crossing the Red Sea — Natural
3. The manna provided to the Jews in the wilderness — Natural
4. Enoch's ascension into the heavens — Ridiculous! Indeed not!
5. Ezekiel's account of a wheel within a wheel — Indeed
6. Jonah in the belly of a big fish — Ridiculous, fairy tales
7. The walls of Jericho that crumbled — It was sounds
The power of sound will crumble anything.

Did the Nephilim, often considered as the race of giants that existed in Biblical times really exist? Was Goliath one of them? Were they extraterrestrial in origin? (IQ) Indeed. Indeed. They were not the offspring of fallen angels. They were not fallen angels. They were extraterrestrial in nature. Goliath in the Bible was one of them.

Can you tell us anything about the involvement of space people in Biblical times? The same space people are involved here now as were in Biblical times. They are not all welcomed and some are evil.

Did many of the world's great religions today come about as the result of encounters with extraterrestrials? (I) Indeed. Many of the confusions. It could be said that Jehovah was an extraterrestrial.

6. Extraterrestrials currently on our planet

Are extraterrestrials as active now on our planet as they were a thousand or so years ago? Indeed, my dear lady. Very much so. Very, very much so. They are not easily accepted depending on time. Messages are left and found. Not only have we been watched over for many thousands of years but we have been joined by them. It is important to note that many are noble but some are not so noble.

Are there other forms of intelligence in the universe that know about us? Indeed there are other forms of intelligence that are more intelligent than you. They are here to assist you and sometimes they are not assisting you.

You have said that there are aliens on the planet among us. What is their agenda? They mean to be helpful and kind. Their agenda is to be wise and kind and helpful. And they will continue to do so. They will help and guide us and aid us.

Are there what is often referred to as "little people" from other systems living in isolated places on Earth? Yes, sir. There are little people and there are tall giant people too.

Are there many different alien races currently residing on our planet? There are many different alien races present here right now. They sit among you here in this room right now.

What are what we call "Black Eyed Children"? They are knowledgeable children. They seek deep within. They are children that come back again. There is something evil about them. They cause damage and distress. It comes from within. They are selected children that come back again with anger. They are extraterrestrials.

Are what we refer to as shape shifters actually alien beings disguised as humans? What are some of the characteristics that might help us identify them? Are they all dangerous to humanity? Indeed, sir. There are not certain features that you can look for. There is nothing that you can see. They are made to be identified yet you cannot identify them. They are not dangerous to humanity. They are there to help you and comfort you. You have shape shifters in your government. 'Tis only a rumor that Obama is a shape shifter but with every rumor there is some truth. Is that not true?

Are extraterrestrials on Earth only from other star systems in our galaxy or are they from other star systems in other galaxies as well? They are on Earth and they are as well from other galaxies. They are among you. Perhaps they are you.

Is there a connection between the Grand Canyon and star beings as thought by native American Indians in that area? (W) Indeed sir. Star beings are from the Grand Canyon. They are imbedded in the Grand Canyon and remain so for protection.

Are there undersea UFO bases on the earth? Indeed yes! There are activities under the sea. If you wish to give them a name, I would call them extraterrestrials that know how to swim. Air is not needed.

You always say that the aliens are here with us now and you have said that they are here to help us. Why don't the show themselves or expose themselves to us? They do, sir, but they are not acknowledged. She [Sondra] can tell you where they have helped her and they have disappeared into the earth or into their dwellings.

Can extraterrestrials show themselves in the physical to people on Earth as something different from what they actually are, much the same as angels do? Yes, sir. They can make themselves look like a human if they so choose. They can make themselves look like an animal. Some are.

Although you have said that there are many aliens among us who look exactly like humans, are there also extraterrestrial beings on Earth who look different from humans? Are there any communities on Earth composed solely of them? Indeed, sir. It is not what I would suggest you call communities. It is fragments: lightning, the clouds, the rain. There are many differences that are shown here.

When you said that Hitler was playing a predestined role and was guided by extraterrestrials, was it the goal of that group of extraterrestrials to take over the world? (Q) No my dear sir. They were following his orders, not their own orders. This is the same group of extraterrestrials that is assisting ISIS today. We must get rid of them. You are on the same path with ISIS as you were with Hitler. They are a fungus.

Long ago did some ancient extraterrestrials seek to have humans worship them as gods? Is the same true today? If you wish to term them as gods. What is "gods"? Extraterrestrials on Earth today are just like most humans. Some are of a positive nature and some are of a negative nature.

Are there extraterrestrials who try to influence humans by tricking them into believing they are something they are not? Indeed, sir. Some call them trixter gods. They are evil.

7. Current extraterrestrial activities on Earth

Do the Anunnaki continue to play a role protective of mankind on Earth? (K) Indeed, sir. They are in control.

At the present time, is there any one star system that has more influence on the activities on Earth than other star systems? They are all together. They are all working together. They are working as a unified group. They are not in conflict with each other. Not at this time.

You mentioned that there are extraterrestrials helping on both sides with ISIS. Are there multiple alien races fighting each other on Earth?

Indeed, sir. You have both good and bad. You can get hurt sometimes because of that. There is no way to tell the difference. [This appears to contradict the previous answer.]

Are some of the extraterrestrials that are influencing us people from our future controlling our present time? Indeed, sir, yes.

Does Israel receive help with their technology, such as the Iron Dome, from extraterrestrial intelligence? Yes. Israel knows much more than you know. They are more capable. You know those Jews keep secrets. I have said that Jehovah is an extraterrestrial guiding the Jews. Jehovah is still involved with guiding the Jews.

Is the formation of the numerous crop circles throughout the world caused by extraterrestrials who are attempting to communicate with the people on Earth? Is mathematics used as the basic form of communication? (U) Indeed, sir. Sometimes it is easier to use mathematics.

Do extraterrestrials communicate with us through dreams? At times when you remember your dreams but how many of us remember our dreams?

What was the cause of the numerous mutilizations of animals across America in recent years in which certain organs had been surgically removed? (T) It happened for experimental reasons, sir, by extraterrestrials indeed, and the organs were removed for research.

Are people currently being abducted by extraterrestrials for sexual experimentation and breeding? Indeed. They come here on UFO's and actually have sexual contact. They are having fun, you know. 'Tis fun. They won't harm anyone, just blood sharing blood as you well know?

In our times, have extraterrestrials abducted humans and implanted devises beneath their skin? Indeed, sir, that is for sending information back to them. That is also for manipulating and controlling them. There are people in this room who have been abducted without their knowledge. There has also been a pregnancy by an extraterrestrial by someone in this room but not your wife. Someone has been impregnated by an extraterrestrial in the past, not recently. The child is an adult now.

Are or were extraterrestrials interested in getting gold from our planet? They still are, sir, more groups than just the Anunnaki. Gold, sir, has tremendous healing. Gold heals.

Are there extraterrestrials whispering to different tribes causing the wars? Some do cause wars and some try to cause peace. So we have man who causes wars and man who causes peace. We are waiting for the extraterrestrials to appear and we don't know whether they will be good or bad. So let's pray for good.

Does the St. Louis Arch have any effect on the weather in that region? (W) Indeed. Extraterrestrials were instrumental in providing information for its design. They want to know if they were good designers. Part of the purpose was to affect the weather.

Is the research and information presented by Barbara Lamb credible regarding extraterrestrials and their interaction with humans? Indeed, sir, very credible.

Do opposing forces among the extraterrestrials pose a serious potential threat to mankind? No.

There seems to be different species or visitors from other planets and they seem to be at war with each other. Are those battles carried on among us that we can't see? Not as you claim battles but disagreements.

Is there such a thing as an intergalactic federation composed of various extraterrestrial groups? (EN) Yes, there are many. Human hybrids are placed on Earth to help humans to connect with extraterrestrials to the point that Earth may become part of the federation. Indeed just as the young lady that I have just spoken to, there are a number of you in this room who are hybrids. I do not wish to offend you but you all look so strange. Where I am from, my physical appearance is not the same as the appearance of the Earth people. We do not have male or female. There is no such thing as division into sexes. We have more fun than you have. We are able to please ourselves. We don't rely on others to please us. I would say that we are what you might call hermaphrodite. We're just like a bug that reproduces. They're [those with the guide]showing me a white bug that reproduces themselves. Some of it would be like a starfish where you cut of part of and a new entity [appears] but there are other ways of reproduction. I prefer my own physical appearance over yours.

8. The Greys and other extraterrestrial entities

What is the intent of the alien beings that we call the Greys? (O) They wish to dominate, sir. They wish to dominate and they may. They are a mixture of Earthlings in a star system at this time and there is another system that has been recently discovered by your people on Earth. Another system with more people as you wish to call people or those or things or it.

What or who was the god Quetzalcoatl that the Aztec Indians worshipped? (P) It is their god, you know, what they call god. It is their worship, sir. There was such a person. He is of extraterrestrial nature. He is with me now. He says hello. He can communicate with me. He is not on Earth. He thanks you for the recognition.

Were the ancient Sumerian gods actually extraterrestrial beings? Some were. There were many of them that were extraterrestrial.

Since you have already said that Jehovah was extraterrestrial being, does he still guide the Jews in modern times? Is Jehovah in your realm? (I) Some of the Jews. He is here now. I am speaking [telling] some of your questions for him to aid me in guiding you. In answering your questions now, I have assistance from Jehovah. I am not alone, sir.

9. Extraterrestrials in recorded history and mythology

Was the Incan empire created or significantly influenced by extraterrestrials? (P) Extraterrestrials are indeed among them. They will interfere as they do with you Earth people.

Were the early Egyptian pharaohs either extraterrestrials or descendants of extraterrestrials? Sometimes, sir, they were both or either.

Was the role of the ancient priests of antiquity to serve as messengers between extraterrestrials and the people of Earth? (Q) Yes. In a way that is very nicely put.

Did George Washington have encounters with non-human intelligences during the Revolutionary War? (Q) Indeed. He thought people were being misled. He appeared to think that people were going not well mentally. Extraterrestrials helped him with the war.

Was Queen Nefertiti in ancient Egypt an extraterrestrial or was she an Earth human? (P) She showed herself as an Earth human but she was not an Earth human. The same is true of the Egyptian King Akhenaton. They are buried near King Tut's tomb but not in the same place.

In ancient times were there wars on the earth or in the skies above the earth between opposing groups of extraterrestrials (P) Indeed, sir. They were often portrayed in various mythologies. That is how we get the answers resolved.

Is it true that much of the ancient mythologies regarding the various gods and goddesses are actually references to aliens who visited the earth? 'Tis true in some ways, you know. Some facts come through. Some are true but facts are facts. In a way, sir, there is no doubt. Gods like Zeus or Jupiter actually were extraterrestrials.

If there was such an event, what was the war that we call the Clash of the Titans between Zeus and his siblings? Indeed there was not such a war. There are always wars, people killing each other. The Clash of the Titans did exist but was not important. It was a battle of tongues, all extraterrestrials.

Is there factual historical significance to the American Indian mythologies which often portray beings that are part ants and part humans? (T) Indeed, sir. Such beings did exist. They still exist. They exist on Earth.

10. Extraterrestrial travel

Do such places exist in the physical world where you can go through some kind of portal and emerge in faraway places in the universe? (LW) Indeed. Not only through one's mind but in the future. You can go into the future and into the past. They are what you may call black spaces. It is available to you. There is a network of underwater portals used by extraterrestrials. We look above but we do not look below. We must look below. Some are in our lakes and oceans and they are near here.

Will humans be able to travel to the home planet or the universe of the extraterrestrials who helped build the pyramids? How will they travel to the planet of the aliens who came and helped build the pyramids? (R) Indeed. sir. Indeed. It is coming shortly. They will travel the same way they arrived. I am not able to give that information [how humans will travel] but with your mind you can do so much. So many of you have bright minds and we don't use our minds. We have so much to offer and so much to give. So we come therefore [to give] more help. Open up your minds and you will get there.

Did the Anunnaki use any type of spaceship to travel from their home planet to Earth? Indeed, sir. They did not use any type of vortex or wormhole to travel here. They are here.

Are some entities that we call extraterrestrials actually time travelers from our own future? Indeed. The Greys are such.

Are there UFO's large enough to transport hundreds of people? (O) Not at this time. UFO's from other star systems cannot transport hundreds of people at this time.

Why are there more UFO sightings in America than in other parts of the world? They are all over, sir. They are everywhere. It is not that you are more observant but you are more forceful. You are more talkative. You have more freedom. There are just as many UFO's in Africa, Australia and other places.

11. Miscellaneous

Will the time come in the not too distant future when we humans will have visual physical contact with extraterrestrials who are very recognizably different from us physically? (R) Would you prefer a yes or no or more detail? For your benefit, yes. Next neighbor to you is questionable if you wish. That will be in the lifetime of people already here. There are people in your world who have already seen these extraterrestrials.

Do you have contact with human beings in other star systems? (E) Indeed I do! They are all the same or similar, just different systems.

Is Erich Von Daniken on the right track in his book *Chariots of the Gods*? (K) There is some truth in what he has written.

Would mathematics provide a universal means of communication between those on Earth and physical entities in every civilization in other worlds? Mathematics is an answer to all your questions. Some of it you have yet to learn.

Did the activities of L. Ron Hubbard, the founder of Scientology, and Jack Parsons have any involvement with increased UFO activities? No.

Is there a high degree of accuracy in the television program called *Ancient Aliens* on the History Channel? Is our government attempting to condition the American people to be less fearful of extraterrestrials by in some way promoting this program? Indeed, sir, [there a high degree of accuracy]. Your government is not promoting the program, sir. The government is withholding. They are trying to condition the American people to accept extraterrestrials. They are walking among you sir. They are right next to you. You are holding their hand. You are them. They do look like the typical human beings, sir. Some, such as the Greys, don't look like human beings. The next will be the robots. There are many people without a brain.

Are there secret files in the Vatican that support the existence of UFO's and extraterrestrials? (I) Indeed, sir. Indeed. Files and rows of books. They are in control. They are keeping it secret so they can keep control.

We understand that when you speak to us, we are communicating with an extraterrestrial through a channeler but will the time come within the near future that there will be overt face-to-face physical communication with extraterrestrials whose appearance is noticeably different from ours? Indeed, sir. You have it right now, sir, but you would be fearful because it is not a human. There are extraterrestrials who look like humans and there are extraterrestrials who look very different from humans.

Will any of us here ever see a humanoid being in the physical from a different planet who appears totally unhuman. (R) Indeed. People in this room will meet face-to-face with people that look like me, but not me, and actually see them. A lot of those beings are housed in Area 51 in Nevada beneath the ground now and in other places in the United States. They look totally different from humans and live mostly underground. They can change. Your government is aware of that. And the government has shown it. They have presented it.

Is the reason that we sometimes cannot see extraterrestrials because they are of a higher dimension? Do they not have disease because of their being in a higher dimension and the reason that we have disease is because we are in a lower division? I would say yes to your questions.

Have highly advanced extraterrestrial civilizations been able to imbue robots with sentience or some level of consciousness? (V)Indeed. Absolutely.

Using the DNA in bone fragments of dead persons, have extraterrestrials been able to clone the bodies of those persons? They tell me to say yes and then they tell me to say no. So I am confused in answering your question.

N. OTHER PLANETS AND THEIR INHABITANTS

1. Other planets in the universe

Some people believe that there is another planet in our solar system, often referred to as Niburu, that revolves around our sun in a huge elliptical orbit. Does such a planet exist? Is what we refer to as the planet Niburu actually a dwarf brown star with planets circling it, as some scientists claim? Indeed. Scientists are men who do not know all that is given. There are more than that. Many more stars and planets. There are many planets revolving around our sun. The Anunnaki are still on this planet.

Do some other planets have both days and nights and others have no distinction between day and night? Indeed, sir.

Do many other planets, like Earth, have several land masses surrounded by water? Indeed. All [inhabited] planets have water. There are planets that have only surface water and no dry land. Surface water sometimes freezes and turns to ice on other planets. The water on all other planets is not the same as on Earth; that is, chemically not H2O. There are other kinds of water on other planets.

Are there inhabited planets which have no moons? Indeed not. Most inhabited planets have one or more moons.

Do all of the elements on Earth exist throughout the universe? Does Earth contain more gold than most other planets? Since you have said that gold is an element that is treasured throughout the universe, can extraterrestrials change other elements into gold? There are more elements that are not on Earth that are on other planets. Earth does not contain more gold than other planets. Extraterrestrials wish they had the ability to change other elements into gold but they are still trying. Just like salt at one time, more worthy than gold.

Do planets in other star systems which support human life have both climate and weather as does our earth? Indeed, sir.

What color or colors are the skies on other planets? There are no skies on other planets. They do not have skies. There is always atmosphere.

Are there planets which once supported physical life but no longer do so? Indeed. A planet which does not have physical life on it can have spirit life on it. Most all of them do even though they may not have physical life.

Are there many physical worlds that are more advanced than Earth? Indeed, sir. Other worlds are more advanced than Earth. They've been here before, sir. Go back in the centuries and the earth is the last to be involved.

Are there any planets or moons in other star systems that could support human life exactly as the earth does (light, air, temperature, nutrition, etc.)? My answer is simply yes. You will be amazed to find out how Mars has many features that are on your earth. There are human-like entities on Mars right now in the physical.

Are there other planets or moons in our solar system that were once inhabited by physical beings? If you wish to call them physical, yes. You did not call them human. Physical, yes. They did not look like you.

Was the asteroid belt between Mars and Jupiter once a planet? It is a planet, my dear sir, but not in the traditional sense that you call planets. It is broken up into many pieces. It was a once single piece. It was broken up by the atmosphere of the planet. There is a civilization on planets other than Earth. There is a civilization on the dwarf planet called Ceres. And you will not like them. The appearance of their planet will not entice you. The planet that was once between Jupiter and Mars was destroyed because of being close to Earth. Warring extraterrestrials. Some Earth people are the descendants of the winners. It is a choice. Extraterrestrials do not war against each other in your times like you have war. They are not one of extinguishing each another. They are at war with words not with extinguishing like you have. We do not diminish each other.

Is there such a thing as an intergalactic federation composed of various extra terrestrial groups? (EM) Yes, there are many. Human hybrids are placed on Earth to help humans to connect with extraterrestrials to the point that Earth may become part of the federation. Indeed just as the young lady that I have just spoken to, there are a number of you in this room who are hybrids. I do not wish to offend you but you all look so strange. Where I am from, my physical appearance is not the same as the appearance of Earth people. We do not have male or female. There is no such thing as division into sexes. We have more fun than you have. We are able to please ourselves. We don't rely on others to please us. I would say that we are what you might call hermaphrodite. We're just like a bug that reproduces. They're [those with the guide] showing me a white bug that reproduces itself. Some of it would be like a starfish where you cut of part of and a new entity [appears] but there are other ways of reproduction. I prefer my own physical appearance over yours.

2 Nature, climate, and land features

Are the land features of some other planets similar to those on Earth; that is, are there mountains, valleys, deserts, jungles, rivers, oceans etc.? Indeed, sir, of many colors. Many issues. There are other planets that are inhabited by human-type beings where the land features are noticeably different from those on Earth.

Is there a wide range of atmospheric temperatures on most of the other planets as there is on Earth? Indeed, a wide range. Some planets have a very limited range of temperatures.

Is the air on some other planets similar to that on Earth? There are planets which have a very different kind of air from that on Earth.

Do other planets have periodic cataclysms such as earthquakes, floods, tornados, hurricanes etc. as on Earth? Indeed, sir, just as I said before about those serpent mounds. It is somewhat the same as Earth as far as weather conditions.

Do all planets have mineral, vegetable and animal kingdoms? [At this point there was a loud clap of thunder.] That is your answer. You can assume that that means yes. There are planets that do not have human-like beings.

Are there many varieties of insects, birds, land animals and sea creatures on other planets? Indeed, sir. Some of those are the same as those on Earth. Actually, every planet has life, different forms of life, insect life and animal life. Every [inhabited] planet has something similar to human life.

On other planets is the vegetation mostly green in color as it is on Earth? Leaves on trees on Earth are usually green. The same is not true on other planets. Trees can be different colors.

Do other planets have fruits and vegetables very similar to those on Earth? Not similar sir. They can vary. There are many different kinds of fruits and vegetables on different planets. Some of your fruits and vegetables have been brought to Earth by extraterrestrials by mistake.

Does fire exist on all other inhabited planets? Indeed, sir. Visible fire exists that the inhabitants can make use of. That is a strong thing. That is your weapon on Earth, fire. Your only [natural] weapon on Earth is fire. Guns are manmade. Since fire exists on all [inhabited] planets, you can assume that hydrogen and oxygen exist on all planets. And water. I have said that on some planets it is a different kind of water than you have, a different formula.

You have said that Earth is the least advanced planet in regard to the evolution of its inhabitants. How does the earth compare with other planets in regard to land features, nature. vegetation and animals? Indeed, the vegetation on Earth is comparable to that on other planets. It is on its way to be discovered that there are other planets that have just as much vitality. If you want to compare animal life to Earth, it is difficult to say because there are different animals.

Does it rain and snow on other inhabited planets? Indeed, sir.

Is oxygen poisonous to the humanoid beings on some planets? Yes. Too much of it can be.

3. Physical appearance of inhabitants

Are there entities on other planets who are very similar to Earth people in appearance? Are there still others who do not have a humanoid form? They are not human beings. They are on another planets and they do not look like you. There is no other place in the universe that looks like you. They are similar to you. Indeed on different plateaus. We have many other plateaus, not only on Earth. There are others who are very different but have a humanoid form; a head, torso, arms, legs etc. Whether they have a humanoid form depends on what planet they are, what planet that will elevate their souls. Some planets have [entities with] a form like yours, although they may be different. They are all different. There are some that are not human-like that are living among you now. They do not look like people. You can recognize those conscious entities. It is not the cockroaches. It is animals, some animals like cats and dogs, closer to humans that understand the human language.

Are there humanoid beings on other planets whose physical bodies are not as dense as those of Earth people? Indeed, sir. They are more like the Lemurians in your history. Some have larger heads and more brains. There are planets whose humanoid beings are of greater density than those of Earth.

You mentioned that some extraterrestrials were covered with feathers rather than with skin. Was Quetzalcoatl one such individual? [He was covered with feathers] and skin. There are other kinds of external coverings rather than feathers and skin. For example some extraterrestrials have scales like reptiles.

Are there alien races which are not as human-like in appearance but rather more like insects, such as ants and praying mantises? Indeed, sir.

Are there extraterrestrials of skin colors different from those of humans? Indeed, sir. All extraterrestrials have skin, if you wish to call it that. There are some that would have feathers.

In addition to having arms, legs, a head and a torso, are there extraterrestrial humanoids who have other visible human like features such as skin, fingers, fingernails, toes and hair? Not all extraterrestrials have fingers. Some are covered in feathers or scales or things like that. They do not all have hair.

Do the physical characteristics of the inhabitants of other planets provide any indication of their age, as they do for Earth people? Ridiculous, sir. You can look at those from other planets and those who have been in the physical longer don't look any different from those who have recently incarnated. You are what you want to be.

Are there physical differences among the people of other planets in regard to their height, weight, skin color, and facial features as there are among Earth people? There is as much variety on the people of other planets as there is among Earth people as far as facial features, height, weight etc.

On other planets, as with humans, can a person's facial expressions be an indication of their emotions? Indeed, sir. Other humanoid beings that don't look like humans have facial expressions that tell something about their emotions. A prune will always look like a prune. A prune will not look like an apple. [Note: Answers to other questions state that at least some other extraterrestrials do not have emotions.]

Does each star system or planet have a unique form of humanoid being that does not exist elsewhere in the universe or are some forms of humanoid beings on several different planets? On different planets. Each planet has its unique form. There are planets in the universe which have the same humanoid being. In other words, you can confer with different planets.

4. Gender and reproduction features of inhabitants

Although there are many individual exceptions, is the need or desire to reproduce implanted into the minds of individuals in all star systems? Indeed, sir, and to reproduce is very important. It keeps the whole ball rolling.

On other planets, are there genders like male and female? And bisexual. I have told you that on some planets there are three genders but in the realm of the spirits there is no such thing as gender. Since spirits have had physical incarnations as both male and female, they can portray themselves as either male or female to humans. I portray myself as a male [to you] but in some other situations to some other peoples, I portray myself as a female. As you well know, my talk on gender is not always accurate. You have noticed that sometimes a woman can be speaking to me and I will say "sir" because I really don't see the gender distinction as you do.

Are humans or humanoids in other star systems divided into two sexes as they are in our world? Are both sexes necessary for reproduction? There are many more than just two. At times it takes two beings to reproduce. At times a single being can reproduce itself. At times more than two beings get together to reproduce.

Are there physical extraterrestrial entities who visit the earth who are neither male nor female? Correct. Likewise there are some who are either male or female. I have said that in the spirit world there is no distinction between male or female. I am neither male nor female. The division into sexes is only in the physical world.

Does the majority of other planets that have human-like beings have both male and female genders, as do Earth people? Does homosexuality exist on those planets? Are there planets which have more than two genders? Indeed. Homosexuality exists on those planets. There are also planets that do not have the division into sexes, only one sex. Most of those planets are bisexual and all of you human cultures are bisexual. There are planets that have more than two genders. A third gender. Male, female and something else. They do not need all three genders for reproduction purposes. All you need is one.

Considering that there are various means of the reproductive process in other star systems, is the reproductive process designed to begin with a pleasurable experience as it is with Earth humans? Yes. Sometimes it takes just one person, sometimes two and sometimes three in some systems to reproduce but it is always a pleasurable experience. Ask any animal.

Are there some planets where the reproductive process is similar to that of Earth people? Male and female. Similar. On the other hand there are some planets where the reproductive process is totally different from on Earth. Shaking hands is sometimes a reproduction. I have mentioned that some are hermaphroditic and some are like starfish where you cut off a piece that grows into another being. [There is] cloning and other means of reproducing.

5. Internal physical aspects of the inhabitants

Are the internal organs of the people on some planets basically similar to those of Earth humans and, on other planets, very different? Do all extraterrestrials have blood of some type? Indeed, sir, and on other planets a little different. They all don't have what you call blood or something similar to blood. They don't need blood to function.

On other planets do all human-like inhabitants have the same five senses as do Earth humans? Indeed sir. They sometimes have additional senses that Earth people do not have. They have senses that are not physical; and that is intuition. They have senses that are more acute than those of Earth people. They hear sounds that are beyond the frequency range of humans. The same is true of sight and colors. There are colors that they can see that you can't see.

On other planets are there physical beings above the level of animals who can breathe under water and fly as well as walk? Indeed, sir. They have forms different from that of Earth humans.

6. Non-physical aspects of inhabitants

Is the overall level of consciousness of Earthlings higher or lower than that of physical beings on other planets? I would say mostly lower on Earth. Conversely, physical beings on other planets are at a higher level of consciousness.

Do humans or humanoids in other star systems have the attitudes and desires as part of their being? Indeed, sir. Indeed they do.

Do inhabitants of other planets have similar emotions as Earth people? No, they do not have emotions. That is manmade. The Greys do not have emotions. They have facts. They work on facts. That is not emotional. They do not cry like the humans cry or [have] the fear that the humans fear. They have a sense of humor. All life is a sense of humor, sir. I show you that I have a sense of humor and I am from a different world. People on other planets have a sense of humor. There is variation among the intellectual abilities of the inhabitants of all other planets.

Regarding the extraterrestrials that we call Greys, do they have the depth of emotions that humans have or are they more emotionless? Do they reproduce mainly by cloning? What I would term as emotionless, sir. Emotions only are in humans. They do not reproduce exactly the same way as humans but they enjoy it. They have done a lot of cloning over the years and sometimes that does damage to their DNA.

How do humans or humanoids on planets in other star systems compare with Earthlings in their propensity for creating warfare? Warfare is one of the human race that wishes to win when you don't agree. They do not kill each other like you do if you don't agree. I would say they are more advanced [in their evolution] because they do not dissolve the person who does not agree with them. In other systems they are more technologically advanced.

From your own experiences, is life on Earth more warlike than that in other places? Indeed sir. I could say that life is more peaceful in other systems than it is on Earth. That is one of the reasons I don't like life on Earth. Too many rules here sir and your religion is a rule. Other star systems do not have religions. Religion is manmade.

Do those who inhabit other planets appreciate the beauty of plant life and create beautiful gardens such as some of us do on Earth? Indeed.

Are people on other planets more sensitive to animals than are Earth people? Do they keep animals as pets in their homes like we do? They often keep animals in their homes but not as pets. People on other planets are sensitive to those around them. They get close to certain animals as you do to dogs and cats.

Are there any other star systems in which physical entities can create physical objects with just their minds, similar to the manner in which spirits create in the astral world? Indeed, sir. It is going on at this moment. Physical beings can absolutely create physical things with just their minds. We can make things happen and it wasn't until I left your dear Earth that I could make things happen. And that is why I do not want to come back. In those systems where the physical entities can create physical things with just their minds, they are not on more highly evolved planets than Earth. It is just an ability that they have developed that you have not. You haven't desired to develop that but if you tried, you could create with just your minds to a great extent.

Do the mineral, vegetable and animal kingdoms exist on all inhabited planets? Indeed, sir. Humanoid beings evolve through the mineral, vegetable and animal kingdoms as they do on Earth, somewhat. In other words, some don't start off in the mineral kingdom and some bypass the vegetable kingdom. All humans go through the animal stage before evolving into a human. The animal kingdom is very aggressive and that will be human after the animal.

Is the lifespan of individuals on other planets comparable to that of Earth humans? Much longer. More than five generations of a family can exist together if they want to.

Misery seems to be a prevalent part of human life. Is there misery among extraterrestrials? There is always unhappiness when we don't get what we [want to] receive. All extraterrestrials do not have the depth of emotions that humans have. Some extraterrestrials have no emotions. I have said that the Greys are extraterrestrials with no emotions and that at least some of the Greys are human time travelers from the future.

7. The Anunnaki

All of the Anunnaki questions also appear in other chapters.

Who are the Anunnaki? They are people on a different planet. It is what you call the tenth planet in your solar system. It is part of your solar system. They can be visualized. The Anunnaki also inhabited Mars in the distant past.

Was the human body designed by the Anunnaki to look like them? In a simple way, yes my dear sir. They modified the bodies of the then existing Earth beings by infusing their DNA into them. That is how they made them to look more like them. When your Bible said that God created man in his own image, that was actually in reference to the Anunnaki creating humans in their image.

Did the Anunnaki create or assist in the creation or modifications of human beings for the purpose of being workers for mining the gold which they needed? Indeed. The Anunnaki did take part in the creation of human beings, and they enjoyed it too. They had a mixture [of animals]. May I add that you can attribute your beings, the way you look now, to the Anunnaki if you wish?

Were the various types of humanoids such as the Neanderthal man, the Cro-Magnons etc. created by the Anunnaki as prototypes that led to the development of the modern Homosapiens? (KP) Indeed, sir. They were models of humans created as an aid and consistency to continue. The Anunnaki are very much involved in the creation of the next humanoid species after the Homosapiens that some people refer to as the Homonoeticus.

Were humanoid beings introduced to our planet by extraterrestrials or was there a form of a humanoid being that was indigenous to our planet before the intervention of extraterrestrials. There are annoyances. Yes. There were some humanoid beings on your planet before the Anunnaki came and changed them.

Has the human mind as well as the human body been expanded with the infusion of DNA of the Anunnaki? In a way, yes. More the body than the mind.

Was the Great Flood engineered by the Anunnaki to rid the earth of the Nephilim giants? The Great Flood was caused by alien intelligence to purge the earth. It was not to rid it of any specific species. It was a great cleansing. It was engineered by the Anunnaki.

Do the Anunnaki continue to play a role protective of mankind on Earth? Indeed, sir. They are in control.

Did the Anunnaki use any type of spaceship to travel from their home planet to Earth? Indeed, sir. They did not use any type of vortex or wormhole to travel here. They are here.

8. Extraterrestrial species

Are the Arcturians the most advanced civilization in our galaxy? I cannot answer that question because there are many advanced [beings] that come to your earth.

What is the intent of the alien beings that we call the Greys? (M) They wish to dominate, sir. They wish to dominate and they may. They are a mixture of Earthlings in a star system at this time and there is another system that has been recently discovered by your people on Earth. Another system with more people as you wish to call people or those things or it.

Are there at the present time any human-like physical entities on any other planet or moon in our solar system? Yes, sir, walking among you on your planet. On other planets, they are above ground and underground. It depends on what area you are. The civilization on Ceres is half and half, the same as Earth. There are physical entities on Mars below the ground. They are above the ground also, sir. They are like lightning. You see them and yet you don't. Like a flash of lightning. You see them for the moment and then you don't but they are human-like entities.

Has there been warfare between the inhabitants of different planets? Does that continue in our times? Indeed, sir, and that continues in your time. They are not fighting, sir. They have differences of opinions. We are not like you humans are. We don't kill each other. We do not have physical warfare. We have mental warfare.

Are there planets whose inhabitants do not live on the surface but only beneath the surface? Indeed, sir. There are actually human-like beings living beneath the surface of the Earth but they do not look like humans. There are some that have a human-like form but with the head of a bird or a reptile if you wish to refer that way.

How does the density of population on other planets compare with the density of that on Earth? It is not greater. It is not lesser. It is the same.

Has society existed on other planets for what we might say hundreds of thousands of years more than Earth society? Indeed, sir.

Are other planets considered to be more pleasant places to incarnate than is the earth? Is our Earth considered among the least pleasant planets on which to incarnate? If you ask me, sir, personally I do not wish to come back to Earth. For me the earth is not the most comfortable place. There is always war, fighting and destruction. I have had experiences in other places in order to make the comparison. When you live as long as I have, and I have, you can compare. It can be said that the earth is considered among the least pleasant planets on which to incarnate. The earth is made up of people who only want to profit, as far as what you would call money. Money seems to play an important role on Earth.

Do humanoid beings in other star systems also have spirit guides as we have on Earth? Indeed, sir. We are not alone. We are not alone as you well know. I myself assist other physical beings in other star systems than Earth when it is needed. When I am called for, sir, I am there to serve as your [Charles'] mother is and she has learned to deal.

Are there physical monuments or structures on other planets or moons in our solar system that are not natural creations but rather created by other physical humanoid beings? (M) Indeed, sir. My answer to you would be simple even though your question is not simple but when you go to the star systems, you will see these wonderful awarenesses. There are structures on Mars that were created by human-type beings.

Are there objects created by intelligent beings within the rings around planets? Indeed, sir.

The ancient Sanskrit writings state that there are some 400,000 human-like species of extraterrestrials? Is that correct? Indeed, sir. There are more than that.

Are Earth humans the only species in the universe whose physical bodies were created or modified by extraterrestrials? No. Indeed, no. There are humanoid beings and animals on other planets whose physical bodies were modified. There are animals that are more human that are so much not to be taken [for granted?], like your dogs who know the weather. They know the future.

O. LIFE ON OTHER PLANETS

1. Institutions and society

Does marriage exist on other planets? Is it a natural social institution or the result of religious doctrine invented by man? It is manmade. It does not exist on other planets. Do your dogs get married? Do your cats get married? There are some swans that keep one mate but is that marriage? There are some monogamous animals. You can be monogamous without being married. In other star systems, monogamous relationships are not necessary.

Does the concept of family exist on other planets? The concept of family, my dear sir, is attachment. It doesn't mean that you have to be born into, because we are born into the same race. We are all the same. Parents take part in the raising of their young. It is turning toward a communal thing that you are going into. It is like in Israel. This planet is gradually becoming so that the family unit will not be as important in the raising of the young as a communal. On other planets it is not more communal. Monogamy is absolutely not practiced in all other star systems. We are having fun. We do not have rules and restrictions as you do. Marriage is something that is an Earth feature rather than in other star systems. Your cats and dogs do not get married either.

Do extraterrestrials on various planets usually live with their families as do Earth people? We do not have families. On other planets the family concept does not exist. Parents don't oversee the upbringing of their children. There is a different way of raising children. It is more of a community way. [Note that the preceding answer says that parents take part in the raising of their young but this answer says that they don't oversee their upbringing.]

Do religions exist in any star systems in addition to ours? (I) Religion, sir, is manmade. You make up rules. You make up your art. Your theater is manmade. Your music is manmade. Religion does not exist elsewhere, only on Earth. Art, theater, music etc. is individual. It is what is perceived by the individual. That occurs in other star systems.

Do individuals on other planets have professions or special areas of work? Indeed, sir. They have activities ahead for them and they are here. Some of them wish to bring rewards to the people here. They are waiting anxiously and happy to be called upon and wish to assist and aid those in pain.

Are those on other planets more attentive to the needs and care of their planet than are Earth people? Earth people are at this moment more concerned. Earth people should be more concerned about climate warming if they wish to. Earth people cause much disdain [?] in their emotional life. Regarding climate change, a lot of what is occurring is natural.

On other planets do individuals wear clothing or some kind of covering of the body? Their skin is enough to cover their bodies if they have that. That is not necessary. Some have feathers. They don't have something comparable to your clothing but it is always nice to adorn with clothing.

On other planets, how are bodies of the dead disposed of: buried in the ground, cremated, cast in the sea, or in what other manner? Evaporate. Do we not all turn to dust? We just dissolve. We don't have to be buried, sir. They just disintegrate. They make themselves disappear. There is no need. They make their bodies disintegrate just like the wind. Do you see the wind? In your language some individuals live a couple of hundred years and some less.

As on Earth, are people on other planets interested in recording or preserving their history? Not necessarily a habit. They do not have things comparable to your museums. They have no interest in such rubbish.

Are there planets which have some form of government, such as we have on Earth, with leaders, laws, or politics etc.? If you want to call it that, there are questionable people always who take charge.

Do those on other planets treat each other more kindly and cooperate more with each other than do Earth people? Well, they listen more. They are not ones that think while you are talking. There are [Earth] people who, as you are speaking to them, are thinking their own mind and usually their own problems.

2. Dwellings and buildings

Is the residential architecture on other planets somewhat similar to ours? What materials are used in their construction? Somewhat. Sometimes. It varies a great deal among the different planets. Stone is very common and some are like stone. Wood decays. It is mostly stone, like caves.

Do those who inhabit planets in other star systems live both in what we might call metropolitan areas and in rural areas much the same as those on Earth? There are different areas where people choose to be at rest and that depends. There are people that like to be in rural areas and they lead lives that way much the same as you do.

On other planets are dwellings used as they are on Earth; that is, for individuals or families for both protection and privacy? Indeed, sir. Those shelters are usually manmade rather than natural. They are usually beneath the surface of the planet, sometimes several stories deep.

Do the interiors of the dwellings on other planets have divisions used for specific purposes comparable to our rooms such as kitchens, bedrooms, recreation areas etc.? Not necessarily. That is not true.

Do some planets have buildings above ground that are many stories in height? Indeed. Some of those buildings are higher than those on Earth. And beneath also, sir. I have told you that on many other planets the civilizations are beneath the ground. Indeed, much more than one is aware of at this moment. There is civilization beneath the ground on your Earth, mainly of extraterrestrial nature.

Do those on other planets have both public and private plumbing systems for obtaining water and disposal of sewerage? Nothing compared to yours. Yours is more elaborate if you wish to say it that way. Water is not necessary for physical life on all the other planets.

Do residences on other planets have furnishings similar to ours; such as tables, chairs, beds and things like that? They do not need that, sir, unless they wish that. Some have them, some don't. They don't need any furnishings at all. It is all in one's mind. Some humanoid beings on other planets can just live in nature without any thing of comfort. Nature is the most comfort.

3. Communication and education

Do those on other planets communicate to each other through spoken language? Are there multiple spoken languages on other planets as there are on Earth? You need not speak in words. You can mind read. They do not have spoken language unless you mean hand language. The Earth is the only planet where you have to communicate with voice.

Do most extraterrestrial groups readily communicate with other extraterrestrials from other planets? Indeed, sir. They use mostly spoken language like you do. In other words, they don't communicate as those in the spirit world. They don't read thoughts but they will be able to read thoughts as most of you think you do. You will eventually evolve as humans where you can read thoughts. [This answers appears to contradict the previous answer.]

Do those on other planets have schools or learning centers where they can obtain knowledge? Are there places of learning for the adult population similar to our universities or libraries? Indeed, sir, but not as you have them.

On other planets are the young provided with what might be considered a formal school type of education as they are on Earth? No. They are educated in some other manner, if you wish to call it educated. They grow up without it. You can grow up without a wisdom tooth.

Do those on other planets communicate with the angels, spirits and entities on other worlds? If they are friendly. They do communicate with angels the same as you do.

4. Nutrition and health

Is the consumption of vegetables a source of nourishment for human or human-like beings on all inhabited planets in the universe? Indeed. Vegetables are necessary for all human life.

Do bodily diseases occur among the population of those on other planets? Only on Earth, sir. Disease does not exist except on Earth. Disease is manmade, sir. Individuals on other planets can be injured and need help to repair strength. They need strength. The help comes from external but not necessarily just from within. They do not have places where these people can go to have their bodies repaired. We do not have physicians. We do not have medications. We have our own resources which is our own mental ability. There is no equivalent of medical doctors. We need mental people.

Is agriculture practiced on most other worlds to provide nutrition for their inhabitants? That is another way of expressing oneself, sir. Inhabitants on other planets have farms that they create in order to feed the inhabitants and they take things from nature without planning.

Is the food of those on other planets harvested directly as it comes from nature or is there also a form of farming? Food is not food as you think of as food. I have said that nutrition on other planets is comparable to you putting gas in a car. Different kinds of gasoline are needed. Nutrition comes somewhat from the vegetable kingdom, somewhat from the sea kingdom, not all from the animal kingdom. Animals that live in the sea and vegetables that live in the sea and vegetables that live in the earth like worms. I don't want to make a complete vegetarian out of you. I can tell you stories that you wouldn't believe. People eat people. They used to and some still do. On other planets some of the humanoid beings eat animal flesh also.

Are those on other planets more conscientious of their nutrition than are Earth people? They do not eat the way Earth people eat. Earth people eat for taste. It is like filling up your car for gas. It needs gas, your car. Is that not true? So you purchase the gas your car needs. You don't fill it with sugar. The sense of taste is not as important for extraterrestrials as it is for Earth people.

Do those on other planets consume mind altering substances comparable to our alcohol and drugs? Isn't that ridiculous? They don't. They just have their own mind to deal with. That is enough.

Do the bodies of those on other planets need rest and sleep? Everyone needs rest, but sleep, no. And do not worry about sleep. Not everyone in the universe sleeps. You can rejuvenate yourself just by resting. Dreaming when you are asleep belongs more to humans. Sometimes humans dream when they are awake. By dream they hope and they wish. The same is true of extraterrestrials when they are awake. They are no different than the wonderful humans except that they don't sleep and they don't go to the bathroom as you call it.

5. Transportation and technology

Are there UFO's large enough to transport hundreds of people? (M) Not at this time. UFO's from other star systems cannot transport hundreds of people at this time.

Is the wheel used for forms of transportation in other star systems? (V) Indeed, sir. There are star systems in which the wheel is not used at all [for transportation]. They do learn to fly. They can fly and rise up and be in the sky and fly above. In Atlantis they did both. They flew and travelled on land. They have ground vehicles with and without wheels on other planets. The wheel is an invention on all planets.

Are there any civilizations on other planets where the inhabitants do not need mechanical means to travel from one place to another but instead are able to use their minds to teleport themselves wherever they wish to go in the physical? (K) Yes, my dear sir. You can do that now. Earth people can learn teleportation.

Do those on other planets use electricity? On other planets electricity is not a form of energy that is needed. Scalar energy is a major form of energy that is used throughout the universe.

Do those on other planets measure such things as distance, weight, volume, energy etc.? In a different way from on Earth.

On other planets is there artificial lighting, heating and cooling, systems for the disposal of rubbish? You can have anything you wish. Nothing has to be artificial. Technologies such as air conditioning are not necessary.

Do those on other planets have means for reproducing sounds, sights and visual activities; that is sound recordings, still photography, and motion pictures.? Indeed, sir. All the trivialities you are talking about. They have that technology.

Do those on other planets measure time as we do, something comparable to our hours, days, weeks, months and years? They have no knowledge as to what you are talking to. Time is not important and therefore they don't have any instruments such as clocks or calendars. [Today is New Year's Day on Earth but] there is no such thing as New Year's Day on other planets. Holidays are manmade, my dear lady. Holidays are not what you think they are. They are not holy days. This is a manmade situation as your religion is manmade.

When humanoid beings on other planets want to travel from one place to another, do they use land vehicles on roadways comparable to our streets and highways? We do not need that, sir. That is instruments that are not necessary. If they want to travel from one place to another in the physical they can fly instead if you want to use that term. We do not have airplanes, sir. Teleportation is probably the most common means of transportation. People on Earth are now teleporting by their daydreams, their visual dreams. The mind can do it but the body won't.

Do those on other planets have vehicles like our ships that travel on the surface of the earth as well as vehicles that travel beneath the surface? Yes they do, sir.

6. Work, business and leisure

Do those on other planets enjoy playing mental games with each other? Indeed.

Do those individuals on other planets enjoy the visual arts such as painting and sculpture etc.? There are many forms of art. There is music. That is also considered an art. It does exist on other planets if you wish to call it that. The arts do not exist in the spirit world. They exist in one's mind if one has a mind. Not everyone has. It is not the same on other planets. They look at us as ridiculous. Playing with dolls. Those on other planets are far more advanced than Earth people. People on Earth are one of the least developed cultures on the various planets. In fact, most Earth people are not so bright. They do not listen to their first thought, which is wisdom.

On other planets, are there places to which people go to play or to observe sports and various athletic or exercise activities? Sports, sir, are like religion. It is manmade. There are always games. Games are manmade. On other planets they do not have physical activities. They don't have bodies like you have or like I used to have. They don't need physical activities because of their bodies.

Does private ownership exist on other planets or does everyone share ownership? They do not have the conditions you have on Earth but they are able to share ownership. They are more like the American Indians were. There is no private ownership of land. And they are able to share.

On other planets, are there specific places that house the various kinds of materials or goods that individuals may need where they can obtain them? We make our own, sir. We can initiate and make our own. Everybody makes themselves whatever they need. Humans on Earth are the least advanced of any other planet. That would mean then that those entities on other planets can do much more than Earth people can do. They are more capable. They do not have any limitations as we put upon ourselves on this planet. I have been myself to this planet many times and I would say when I was on your planet, "I cannot do this?" Is that not true? Life on this planet is more difficult than any other place.

Do individuals on other planets travel for both work and pleasure? It is indeed a privilege to travel either way, sir. It is pretty much the same as for Earth humans. You travel for work and you travel for pleasure and you travel for nonsense. It is the same on other planets.

Do entertainment and activities for pleasure like those on Earth exist on other planets? If this is what they seek. What is entertainment? It is comparable to humans.

Do those individuals on other planets have commerce as well as communication with those on various other planets? Indeed, sir.

7. Miscellaneous

Is gold an element that is treasured throughout the physical universe? (V) Gold, silver and platinum are treasured in other star systems.

Are rare gems such as diamonds, emeralds and rubies valued in other star systems? Are less rare gemstones such as amethyst, quartz, and jade of value also? Not the way it is humanized. They do not put a dollar sign on them. Sometimes they make use of the less rare gemstones. They are healthy and they will bring on energy from different sources. They bring on energy. The way you use amethyst, for example, is for beauty and culture. You use it to bring about love but not everyone in the universe is aware. A diamond brings on love; the bigger the diamond, the more love. [This last sentence is an example of the guide's sense of humor which he used frequently in the answers to personal questions asked by the group's participants.]

All of life on Earth comes basically from the same DNA. Is that same DNA throughout the universe? Do all the other planets operate with the same DNA manifest in different forms? Different forms. Different blood. I do not have an answer [regarding if the DNA is the same].

Are there multiple births on other planets, like twins or triplets? Indeed, madam, of course there are.

P. THE WORLD BEFORE BIBLICAL TIMES

1. The planet

Did the Nile River flow into the Atlantic Ocean at the time of Atlantis? (W) Yes.

Was there a time when India and the area around it were not connected to the rest of Asia? (W) Indeed.

Were ocean levels much lower before the Great Flood than they are now, thus causing many coastal areas to be inundated? Indeed sir. The total land mass of the earth was greater then than it is now.

Was the Gulf Stream engineered by the Atlanteans or other intelligent entities? (MW) Not manmade. I would like to say other intelligent entities. Not a natural phenomenon. Not the Atlanteans. By many people, extraterrestrials. The purpose was to keep the lands to the north warmer.

Thousands of years ago was the Libyan Desert Glass created by a nuclear explosion? (W) Indeed sir, indeed. It was not caused by people. It was caused by gasses. It was natural.

Did a large asteroid that hit the earth millions of years ago cause the extinction of many of the huge animals that threatened the existence of humanity? Was this event engineered by extraterrestrials? Indeed, sir. It was not engineered by extraterrestrials. It was a natural phenomenon.

Since many ancient cities have been discovered beneath the water in the Mediterranean Sea, can we assume the sea was dry land before the Great Flood? Indeed, sir. Perhaps we can assume that it was the Great Flood that covered those cities. It was responsible, at least in part, for the creation of the Mediterranean Sea.

In the ancient past was what is now the New York City area located many miles from the ocean? Yes. Like everything else a long time ago it was much further inland and then the ocean rose. The ocean rose and then shrank and then shrank again. Alaska will be shrinking. This is a process that goes on repeatedly over and over again throughout history.

2. Extraterrestrials and vestiges of ancient civilizations

Who masterminded the construction of Stonehenge? (E) Many of us masterminded the construction. We had what you call architects. The extraterrestrials, the name you have selected to call us, are here now too. We are the bright ones, you know. You can call me an extraterrestrial also but I have had many lifetimes on Earth. I'm not coming back. No way! I do not like to live on Earth. Too many rules. I have been here many, many times.

Can the prehistoric cave paintings throughout the world be considered something like a key to our understanding of the history and future of mankind? There is hidden meaning in those drawings. The interpretation of those drawings tells of your history and your future.

What is the origin of drawings of the Lascaux caves in France? (M) The drawings are their ways of communication, what we would say to you is their writings. They are able to communicate. They were both Earth people and extraterrestrials. They are existing on this planet. They have not left. They have been here many a century ago.

From what beings were the ancient elongated skulls found in Egypt and in the Americas? (M) Aliens, sir, and some were human, a mixture. The humans didn't try to imitate the aliens by forcing the skulls to become longer. They did it by having relationships, sir. They had fun with each other.

Can you tell us about the origin and original usage of the huge statues on Easter Island? (W) Manmade, sir. They were products of people they worshipped. Extraterrestrials had an improvement in them. They improved it. They had more strength. The Lemurians played a role in the creation of the many large statues on Easter Island. The statues represented extraterrestrials and people that are [of] stature.

Is there any what we might call "mystical" connection to the scarab beetles portrayed in ancient Egyptian beliefs or drawings? (T) Indeed, yes. They are a happening of the past. They were extraterrestrials, what I would refer to as reincarnation. The ancient Egyptians drew them and revered these beetles.

What was the purpose of the construction of the great pyramid at Giza? (W) The great pyramid was built for electricity. It was a power plant to provide energy. Many Egyptians built it. The labor was made by humans and extraterrestrials too, as they are now with you. The extraterrestrials designed the pyramid and the humans built it using extraterrestrial technology.

Was the Cheops pyramid in Egypt built by the power of thought? It was built by manpower.

Who were the architects and builders of the pyramids in the Yucatan and Guatemala? (W) People that are striving from your past are reaching out and wish to serve in your future. They were actually built by those of another star system, the Pleiades. They also built the pyramids in Egypt and that is how they got to the top. The Pleiades are one of the most advanced groups. Our secret people were building your pyramids that they could reach from the top down. Humans provided a lot of the labor but extraterrestrials provided the technology.

Is there validity or accuracy in the books called *The Pyramid Power* and *The Pyramid Prophecies* written by Max Toth? Max is here with me and he sends you his love. He is enjoying the pleasure of being departed and he has experienced [?] his books. Max has left New York and he is very comfortable now and glad to be here now and happy that you remembered him. You can rely on the information he gives to you.

What is the story of Lake Titicaca in Peru and its underwater city with sunken ruins? (W) It has been in Peru many, many times [eons] ago. It was covered with earth and then with water. It was there before the Great Flood. Indeed an earthquake occurred and then water. The earth opened up here and allowed the water to overflow. I was not there. That is what I have been told. There are many cities that existed before the Great Flood. There are still remnants now.

How can we explain the existence of the same type of hieroglyphs and cuneiform writings that are found in both ancient Sumer and near Lake Titicaca in *Peru*? (W) The same way as in some caves or such other areas that were left. They were writings and messages left for the future. Some were left by extraterrestrials.

Since ancient stone carvings seem to possibly indicate so, did ancient rulers of various lands throughout the world have reptilian bloodlines? Indeed, sir.

3. Atlantis and Lemuria

Some scientists believe that the earth's crust has moved and that there was an island in the middle of the Atlantic Ocean that went south. Is that true? (W) Indeed, but we have no trace of it. You have no trace of it but it did exist. It is the origin of the Great Flood.

Was Antarctica once an inhabited continent? Did a shift of the crust of the earth cause it to be at its current location at the South Pole? Did it have anything to do with the Atlanteans? (W) Indeed it was once. The earth has shifted, rotated. Regarding the Atlanteans, I will simply say "yes".

Are there ruins of an ancient civilization beneath the ice in Antarctica? Indeed there is although I have not lived through that. I have not been a witness to that but it is also told from previous lives that this existed. It was before the Great Flood. It had to do with Atlantis. Atlantis was a beautiful city although I myself had not had the pleasure. I have been told by many other entities that it was a beautiful town, country or civilization and very much advanced as you are today.

When it was at its largest size, with what country or land mass today was Atlantis approximately the same size in total land mass area? They're showing me a map that goes into India and China combined.

Were the underwater rock formations north of Bimini in the Bahamas remnants of Atlantis? Indeed, sir.

Was one of the several breakups of the continent of Atlantis caused by their technology? It was a natural disaster. It was nature's harm or nature's good, not their technology, sir, but someone else's. It was a question of being earthbound. It came from within the earth. It was like what you would call an earthquake.

What destroyed the continent of Lemuria? Earthquakes. They also helped destroy Atlantis.

Were the Atlanteans evolved humans or a hybrid race of humans and extraterrestrials? The Atlanteans were a combination, sir, as we are.

Were the Atlanteans meat eaters? Indeed, sir. I have said before that many of the oriental people alive today are reincarnations of the Atlanteans.

Were the Atlanteans physically different from us to the point that we could easily see that they were not like modern humans? (K) No, sir. The Atlanteans are beautiful human beings. They are beautiful and well cared for. They did not resemble one of the current races more than the others. They covered many races, not only one race. The American Indians were the closest to what the Atlanteans looked like. The brown skin, a mixture, sir. They are beautiful souls.

Have there been previous human civilizations on this earth before Atlantis that were more technologically advanced than our current civilization? (V) Indeed. Intelligently advanced.

Can you mention some of the technologies that the Atlanteans had that we do not have? (V) They were very imaginative but you are doing quite well since the time of your typewriter. They were more interested in building and the mechanics of their building. You will find pyramids in Wyoming under water.

Would you describe the transportation used by the Atlanteans? (V) They had air travel but they did not need ground vehicles for transportation. Flying machines were much easier. They were powered by crystals. Cars were not important.

Are some of the crystals that the Atlanteans used to transmit energy still in operation under the sea today? Is that the cause of the disappearance of so many ships and airplanes in the area known as the Bermuda Triangle? (VW) Yes. They are the cause of the disappearance of planes and ships. They are not causing disturbance. They have power. It is caused by your friends that are not visible to you. Some are not friends that are visible and some [are not friends and] are not visible to you.

Did humans of long ago have medical knowledge that exceeds that which we have today? Very much so. The medical knowledge of the Atlanteans exceeded what you know.

Was the architecture of the homes in Atlantis similar to that of ancient Greece or Rome? What can you tell us about the homes of the Atlanteans? Indeed sir. They had no doors. They had big wide spaces and there was no structure. It was beautiful. It was freedom. And their tiles were artistically carved. Indeed it was a pleasant place to live.

Was the role of the ancient Druids in England to preserve the ancient Atlantean knowledge? Indeed sir, yes. They still exist and they uphold their quest for knowledge. Is that not true?

Did the two books that Plato wrote about Atlantis contain information that was, to a great extent, accurate? Indeed, sir. He wants you to know he's a good friend [of mine].

What were the major ways in which the physical characteristics of the Lemurians were different from Homosapiens? (K) Indeed, sir. They were hermaphrodites, quite different from physical human beings. Before that they reproduced like starfish, cut off a part of themselves.

Were the Hawaiian Islands once part of Lemuria? Indeed, sir.

Although it is generally assumed that Lemuria preceded Atlantis, did Atlantis and Lemuria ever coexist for a while? Different elements, sir, different time. different elements.

Are the American Indians the physical ancestors of the Lemurians? Some are. Some resemble what the Lemurians looked like.

Were the writings of James Churchward regarding the continent of Mu for the most part accurate? For the most part it is claimed that it is accurate, which is not completely true.

Are we going to have more information about the influence of the people of the land of Mu? Indeed there is information each day that is arriving and more appealing and understanding to you at this time. It will be given publicly but very little appreciation will be given.

Did the destruction of the island of Santorini in the Mediterranean Sea by a volcano have any connection with Atlantis that Plato described? Indeed so. Plato enjoyed life. He loved his territory. He loved the columns, the business in his life. He just loved life. He loved life and he loved Socrates. He wrote about the island of Santorini as being part of Atlantis; yet I have also said that Atlantis was a large land mass, a continent in the Atlantic Ocean that, when there was an earth shift, it slipped to what is now Antarctica. Antarctica was once Atlantis. Plato was not incorrect when he said that the island of Santorini was part of Atlantis. It was part of the land slide.

4. Early humans

The first 14 questions in this section have appeared in previous chapters.

Were the various types of humanoids such as the Neanderthal man, the Cro-Magnons etc. created by the Anunnaki as prototypes that led to the development of the modern Homosapiens? (KM) Indeed, sir. They were models of humans created as an aid and consistency to continue. The Anunnaki are very much involved in the creation of the next species after the Homosapiens that some people refer to as the Homonoeticus.

Did the human race, both the Neanderthals and the Homosapiens, first appear on Earth in Africa? (K) Yes. In Africa.

What is the origin of the different races on Earth? (K) There was only one human race before the Great Flood. We were all here together and we all separated different ways. When we separated we became different races. Until then we were all one. It goes back many, many years even before I was born. Atmosphere changed the color of the skin. The current races are one race that went to different atmospheres or, as you well know, climate. They are becoming more similar. They are blending and blending.

In our ancient past, were there once several different varieties of human or humanoid beings on Earth at the same time, including Neanderthals and Homosapiens etc.? (K) Indeed sir, and there was a mixture and that is why you are so odd. Many of you are like part Neanderthal.

Was there a time when reptilian physical characteristics were prevalent in a large portion of Earth people? Are there still such people on Earth living underground? (K) Indeed, sir, and they are still under the earth too.

Did the early physical humans communicate by telepathy or did spoken language gradually evolve and become their means of communication? (K) Telepathy, probably so. Telepathy is much easier when we would read other people's minds and actions.

Was there a time in the distant past when physical humans were not divided into sexes? (K) Indeed. They were not divided into sexes. They reproduced both ways. They were hermaphroditic.

What was the cause for the apparent leap in human consciousness from the Neanderthal Man to the Homosapiens? (K) An awakening, my dear sir, an awakening. Extraterrestrials were absolutely involved and they are always there. It was an infusion of their DNA into the Neanderthal man.

Did either the Neanderthals or the Homosapiens ever co-exist with the Atlanteans (K) [The Atlanteans were] before, sir.

Did the Neanderthal humans and Homosapiens ever co-exist peacefully? Was there warfare between them? Were they of equal intelligence? (K) Not peacefully sir. Not warfare as you stated. Different opinions. They were of equal intelligence.

Did the Ice Age affect the development and physical appearance of the Neanderthals? (K) Yes. The skin color changed. That was primarily the many colors you have endured. The climate had an effect on the development of the races today. The races were created by climatic conditions.

Did volcanic ash of approximately 39,000 years ago have an effect on the demise of the Neanderthals? (K) Indeed, sir. If you were being burnt by the ashes wouldn't you say that you would be disappearing?

Was the Great Flood engineered by the Anunnaki to rid the earth of the Nephilim giants? (Q) The Great Flood was caused by alien intelligence to purge the earth. It was not to rid it of any specific species. It was a great cleansing. It was engineered by the Anunnaki.

Were the ancient Egyptians able to perform brain surgery? (V) Indeed, sir. That was taught by extraterrestrials in a way yes and in a way no. They had some assistance from the aliens but they were able to progress on their own.

Are there still any full-breed Neanderthals on the earth today? No, but then I want to answer him yes. They're pulling me and tugging me, tell him yes. So my answer again I wish is yes. There are hidden enclaves in the caves in southern Spain.

Is there a significant degree of accuracy in the writings of Damon T. Berry in his work called *The Knowledge of the Forever Time?* Interesting. There is accuracy in that, and interesting. It would be worthwhile to read it. It is only his words but there is a lot of truth with his words.

Since there are many prehistoric drawings of humans with birdlike heads throughout the world, can we assume that such beings did exist on Earth at one time? If you wish. They were drawings of Earth inhabitants.

Were there physical humans on Earth before the Lemurians? Indeed, sir. Some of their bodies were as dense as your bodies are now. Some were lighter.

Was it solely for extraterrestrial observation and their travel that the ancient humans placed so much focus on astronomy by building a great number of observatories throughout the world? Indeed.

Was there atomic warfare on Earth in ancient times? In ancient times before the Great Flood, indeed, sir.

5. Animals

Was there a time in the ancient past when animals, including humans, could mate with animals of different species, thus producing strange looking offspring? (L) Not true.

What was the cause of the disappearance of dinosaurs many years ago? (T) Earthquakes. Explosions. Earthquakes devoured the earth at that time.

Was the earthquake that caused the disappearance of dinosaurs from Earth engineered by extraterrestrials or was it a natural occurrence?(T) Both. It was intentional in part to get rid of the dinosaurs. Dinosaurs have shrunk to many little lizards. Have you noticed the lizards? Lizards and many of the reptiles were dinosaurs at one time.

Did the grotesque beings part subhuman and part animal with weird appendages that Edgar Cayce described actually exist? Indeed, sir, and they still exist.

6. Languages

Was there originally just one language rather than the proliferation of languages that exist in the world today? (K) Yes. And then we separated and went different ways. Language was given by those that were able to communicate by sounds and grunts and sounds of pleasure. We speak many languages on Earth. Your grunts are closest to the original language.

More and more linguists are finding out that our languages are not that separate at all and that they are all flowing from an original language. Can we say that Hebrew and Sumerian are very near to that original language and is there one that is before? Correct. There was one before definitely one before. Indeed before the Flood.

Since you have said that there was only one language before the Great Flood, what caused the proliferation of languages? People going to different climates and they will speak differently but there is only one language that will occur and that is no language at all. Telepathy. So, my dear sir, you don't have to learn another language. Just think it.

7. Technology

Did humans of long ago use the power of sound, taught to them by extraterrestrials, to accomplish such feats as moving extremely heavy objects? (VW) Indeed. You don't need an education to find that interesting. Sound was used in the construction of some of the unusual ancient monuments we find throughout the world. Sound was used in the construction of the great pyramids. Sound was also used when the Israelites went around the walls of Jericho and made the walls crumble. The frequency of the sound. And do you not have a place of interest [i.e. the Coral Castle in Homestead, Florida] in the area where you live? He [Edward Leedskalnin] used sound to raise those heavy stones. That is the same way you have seen opera singers break [drinking] glasses. Sound was used to move stones at Stonehenge.

Does antigravity technology exist? (V) Antigravity does exist. Indeed it does. It was used in the construction of ancient structures if you wish to call it that way.

Did laser technology exist in the ancient world? (V) Indeed.

In ancient times were there occasions in which great numbers of people were killed by radiation from atomic explosions caused by intelligent entities, perhaps such as in Mohenjo-Daro Pakistan? (V) Indeed, and your ancient times might even be referred to as now.

Was there electric lighting in the ancient tombs in Egypt? Indeed, sir. They made use of other electrical devices, something that begins with [the letter] R with protection of wiring in the tombs. The tombs were wired.

In ancient times was there a global wireless energy network throughout the world (V) Indeed. It was used by extraterrestrials and it was used by previous civilizations of Earth peoples. All star systems need similar kinds of energies. The energy system that was on Earth was used in other parts of the universe. Other star systems picked up on the energy that was on the Earth. Electricity. It was created on Earth but used in other star systems.

Did highly sophisticated robots exist on Earth in our ancient past? (V) Indeed, sir, and they will exist again and they do exist.

Was the Great Pyramid at Giza used as a hydrogen power plant to produce electrical or scalar energy? (V) Yes, a hydrogen power plant.

Can electricity be broadcast wirelessly as Tesla thought? (V) Indeed, sir, Tesla was right. The many ancient obelisks throughout the world were used for broadcasting electricity wirelessly.

Were early forms of writing such as the Egyptian hieroglyphs, runes, and the Sumerian alphabet given to humans by extraterrestrials? (M) They were invented by humans at that time. I am saying that after the extraterrestrials left, the humans, in order to record the events, came up with different ways of putting them into writing.

Prior to the Great Flood was the civilization on Earth as technologically advanced as our current civilization? You think your civilization is advanced, sir? It was more advanced.

8. Personalities

Was Queen Nefertiti in ancient Egypt an extraterrestrial or was she an Earth human? (M) She showed herself as an Earth human but she was not an Earth human. The same is true of the Egyptian Pharaoh Akhenaton. They are buried near King Tut's tomb but not in the same place.

Why did the ancient Egyptians try to erase evidence to references that Queen Nefertiti and King Akhenaton ever existed? They felt that they had too much power and they wanted the dead to be deceased. They were full-fledged extraterrestrials, not hybrids.

What or who was the god Quetzalcoatl that the Aztec Indians worshipped? (M) It is their god, you know, what they call god. It is their worship, sir. There was such a person. He is of extraterrestrial nature. He is with me now. He says hello. He can communicate with me. He is not on Earth. He thanks you for the recognition.

Who was Amelius as mentioned in Edgar Cayce's readings? He was a high spirit such as I. Like Adam had a wife called Eve, he had a wife called Lilith. Amelius was a spirit. He manifested himself in the spiritual. They were of extraterrestrial origin.

Do the spirits of the Nephilim giants of long ago still walk among us? Yes, this is true. You cannot recognize those who walk among you. It is through different feelings, gut feelings.

Is has been said that Osiris, the Egyptian god of the underworld, was actually a robot. Is that correct? Manmade.

9. Miscellaneous

Where was the original home of the ancestors of the American Indians? All over what you call the United States. The original home was in the heat area [desert] in Asia. They migrated to America.

Did Cyclops ever exist? We all make up stories. There are people who see more with one eye. It is nonsense.

Was the Java Man found in Indonesia in the late 1890's the remains of an early species of humans or was it the remains of a giant ape? (Laughing) It is a giant with hair.

Is there reality in the belief of the ancient Egyptians that there are five parts of the human soul.; ren, ba and ka etc.? Indeed. Yes, sir. There are five parts to the human soul including the soul.

Is the human population of the earth greater today than it ever was in ancient history? My dear sir, there are many more people on your earth today than it was in the past, even in the time of Atlantis and Lemuria.

Throughout history there were plagues and epidemics that affected humans. These plagues were often preceded by a shower of red rain. Were those showers related to the plagues and epidemics or were they, what you might say, coincidental? They were related, sir. Those plagues and epidemics were caused by both what you might say a natural occurrence and by extraterrestrials.

Was the ancient Sumerian civilization the first after the Great Flood to be advanced by extraterrestrials? It was helped by extraterrestrials. There were other civilizations at that same time that were helped by extraterrestrials.

Long ago did some ancient extraterrestrials seek to have humans worship them as gods? Is the same true today? If you wish to term them as gods. What is "gods"? Extraterrestrials on earth today are just like most humans. Some are of a positive nature and some are of a negative nature.

Q. THE WORLD FROM BIBLICAL TIMES TO THE PRESENT

1. The book of Genesis

All of the questions in this section appeared in Chapter I: Religion.

Who were Adam and Eve? What was the Garden of Eden? (I) Your mother and father. A name you derived for a peaceful habitat for people. A "Pleasantville" in your dimension. Adam and Eve come from people who make up names.

Where on the present day Earth was the Biblical Garden of Eden? (I) Wherever we place it. It will survive. Everybody wishes it was a specific place on the planet. There were several places, different Gardens of Eden in China, in Japan, in Italy. Everyone has their own Garden of Eden.

Did the Nephilim, often considered as the race of giants that existed in Biblical times really exist? Was Goliath one of them? (IM) Indeed. Indeed. They were not the offspring of fallen angels. They were not fallen angels. They were extraterrestrial in nature. Goliath in the Bible was one of them.

Was the original purpose of male circumcision to identify those men who were descendants of Adam or the superhuman race created at least in part by aliens? (I) Indeed the answer to your question was it was to be part of a tribe. Purely identification reasons. They were not knowledgeable at that time about health reasons. This was purely identification reasons.

Were the ten plagues of Egypt in the Bible actually the result of a sequence of events of natural causes? (I) Indeed, sir.

What is the historical significance of the Stone of Scone that is placed under the throne of the British monarchy? (I) Nonsense. It is not the pillow that Jacob slept on in the Bible. Jacob took his pillow with him and it has since disintegrated. The stone is of meaningless significance.

Is some of the ancient history portrayed in the Bible, including that of the Great Flood, a recounting of earlier Sumerian legends? (I) All is recounting of interesting stories. Some happened and some did not happen. Some of what is in the Bible is taken from earlier civilizations and embellished.

2. Noah and the Great Flood

Were the land masses of this world before the Great Flood considerably different from the way they are today? (W) Indeed, sir, considerably different.

What was the cause of the Great Flood that is mentioned in the Bible and in the lore of other ancient civilizations throughout the world? (I) The accumulation of weather that had formed was not an accident you know. It was precisely planned. It was planned by aliens and to be helpful.

Was the Great Flood engineered by the Anunnaki to rid the earth of the Nephilim giants? (M) The Flood was caused by alien intelligence to purge the earth. It was not to rid of any specific species. It was a great cleansing. It was engineered by the Anunnaki.

At the time of the Flood were there cultures throughout the world that survived by going underground? Indeed sir. There were cultures that were underground. It was safer, you know, to be underground than above ground, as it will be in the future. Underground will be more positive for you.

Did the Biblical characters from Adam to Noah actually live very long lifetimes? (I) May I ask you what do you consider a lengthy lifetime? More than one hundred twenty years is not considered a lengthy lifetime.

Was the Black Sea created by the Great Flood? No, ridiculous, sir. The Great Flood did create new bodies of water such as lakes.

3. From Biblical times to the 18th century

Was the Incan empire created or significantly influenced by extraterrestrials?(M) Extraterrestrials are indeed among them. They will interfere as they do with you Earth people.

Why was Machu Picchu in Peru abandoned after a hundred or so years? It was not very comfortable to live there. It was very high up in altitude. The climate and its past history had a tendency to have some reflection on those that are fearful of living there. Most of the people didn't survive because of the climate.

It is estimated that approximately ninety-five percent of the Mayan civilization disappeared more than 1000 years ago, long before the arrival of the Europeans. What was the cause of the disappearance of so many people? Earthquakes, my dear sir, earthquakes. There were earthquakes in Central America where the Mayans were.

Did the Mayan Indians have settlements in the state of Georgia? Are they related to the Creek Indians. They had settlements everywhere, not just in Mexico. Many places. I don't know if they are related to the Creek Indians in Georgia.

Who is responsible for the creation of the maps copied by Piri Reis about five centuries ago? There was assistance from extraterrestrials because when we stand on a higher hill, we see more of the mountain.

Was the origin of the system of priests in various religions actually humans who were able to communicate with extraterrestrials and act as intermediaries between them and Earth people? Was Aaron, the brother of Moses, one such person? (M) Indeed, sir. Aaron was one such person; not well liked but Moses was well liked. I was on Earth at the time of Moses.

Did the magician Merlin as portrayed in the Arthurian legends of England actually exist? (Laughing) In many ways, no, he did not exist. It is made up again, stories concocted by human souls. The human soul is so good at making up a story, like Noah's ark.

Was the letter about Jesus supposedly written by Pontius Pilate to the Emperor Tiberius a forgery written several centuries later? Yes.

Was it a UFO that Christopher Columbus saw rising from the sea or was it a natural phenomenon? It was a natural phenomena, not a UFO.

Was the Black Plague actually caused naturally by rats or was it created by extraterrestrials for rats to reduce the earth's population? It was to reduce the earth's population. It was intentionally designed by extraterrestrials to reduce the earth's population. Poison gas was used. Everything was used. Right now we are working on that, decreasing the world's population by both physical disease and warfare.

Is Leonardo DaVinci's painting of the Mona Lisa a self portrait? Who was the Mona Lisa that Leonardo DaVinci painted? In a way, yes. Well, it's part of him he's expressing in a feminine way. It is not a painting of a natural person. It was more a self-portrait he created. It was his smile.

Was Freemasonry encoded in the design of Shakespeare's Globe Theater? Does the number 72 play a significant role in its design? Yes. [The number 72 is] 9 and if you put it upside down it is evil. The design of the theater incorporates secret hermetic knowledge.

Is there a connection between the Catholic Inquisition many centuries ago in which great numbers of infidels were killed and the current radical Moslem movement in which the infidels are killed? (I) They are disassociated occurrences. It is not the same group reincarnating. They are similar but not the same but I have said that the current group of Moslem terrorists is the reincarnation of the Nazis. That is a fact.

Centuries ago, did the Indians throw a great amount gold into the lakes in South America so the Spaniards could not take possession of it? Indeed. There is still a lot of gold at the bottom of many of the lakes in South America.

Who built the huge underground city which could house 20,000 people in Derinkuyu in Turkey? Why? That was built by your slavery. That was built underground like the pyramids were built by humans that acted as slaves. That was not built by extraterrestrials. It was built to be a safe place. Humans built the city without any connection or advice from extraterrestrials.

Is there historical basis for the existence of the city that we refer to as El Dorado? Is Lake Guatavita in Colombia part of that basis? Indeed. Lake Guatavita in Colombia has nothing to do with El Dorado.

<u>What caused the disappearance of the lost colony of Roanoke, Virginia in 1587?</u> It was what you would call an earthquake. The earth swallowed them. It wasn't unfriendly Indians. It was an earthquake like the grounds here that swallow up people.

<u>Was Joan of Arc influenced by extraterrestrials in order to avoid the negative consequences if the English won the battle against the French?</u> Extraterrestrials were actually assisting Joan of Arc.

4. The 18th and 19th centuries

<u>Did George Washington have encounters with non-human intelligences during the Revolutionary War? (M)</u> Indeed. He thought people were going misled. He appeared to think that people were going not well mentally. Extraterrestrials helped him with the war.

<u>Was the purpose of the street designs in Washington D.C. so that they could be seen from the sky?</u> It can be seen from any angle, not necessarily from above but from below also. Below is very important, sir, not just on the earth but beneath the earth. There is activity going on beneath the earth and in the oceans, not just on the surface of the earth. It was a plan, my dear sir. It was a plan based on ancient wisdom. There are many intelligent beings on your planet.

<u>Were some of the major founding fathers of this country influenced by higher level conscious entities?</u> Yes.

<u>Was there extraterrestrial or angel involvement in aiding the Americans in the fight against the British in the War of 1812 in regard to the manipulation of weather conditions? (D)</u> Ridiculous, but angels and extraterrestrials were always there to help the Americans.

<u>Did the Freemasons have a significant impact on the founding of our country? What was the source of the Freemasons' information? (U)</u> Indeed, sir. The source was extraterrestrial.

<u>Were Napoleon Bonaparte and Adolf Hitler the first two of the three</u>

antichrists that Nostradamus predicted? Has the third one been born yet? (I) Yes. The third one has been born.

5. World War II and the Nazis

During World War II did both the Axis and the Allied powers use psychics and channelers to assist them in their war efforts? Was there assistance or influence from extraterrestrials? Indeed, sir. The Germans used everything imaginable. There was influence from extraterrestrials. That is why they lost. They were deliberately misled.

Did the United States government know in advance that Japan would attack Pearl Harbor and declare war on this country? They had the inkling. They did not know the day.

Did the Nazis receive technology information from the extraterrestrials through reverse engineering of their crashed UFO's? (V) Indeed, sir, and so is ISIS. Extraterrestrials are helping ISIS. There are also some who want to defeat ISIS. ISIS will be defeated. It will take some time for ISIS to be defeated. ISIS is gaining weight. ISIS will strike again with the magnitude of the Wall Street Towers. They will go back to New York and they are eyeing at this moment Washington. They are trying to hit the root of your government like they did in Brussels. They are in South Florida now where you are. They are around but they figure that all old people are in Florida. They are going for young people and young children.

There is speculation that Hitler escaped from Germany and died somewhere else? Where did Hitler die? He died in Germany. He did not die a natural death. He was shot. He was killed. He did not escape and go on.

Did the Nordic race of extraterrestrials aid the Germans in World War II. Is that correct? (D) Indeed. They are disliked by other extraterrestrials.

Did the Nazi's make contact with extraterrestrials living beneath the surface of Antarctica? Oh, yes. They got some of their ideas for waging war there.

Did the German stealth aircraft exist during World War II? Indeed, sir, it did actually exist and it was not successful.

6. The 20th century

Was a foreign country involved in the assassination of President Kennedy? Can you tell us anything more about the assassination that is not generally known by the public? (U) No, ridiculous! It was another government official who was behind the assassination. [The name of a U.S. president was given but we choose not to state it here.]

It has been reported that our government found dead bodies of extraterrestrials in a UFO that landed in Roswell, New Mexico in 1947. Did they find such bodies? Indeed, they found such bodies and they still are finding more from that crash. They didn't find any live extraterrestrials. Perhaps they were human time travelers from your future, the extraterrestrials that you call the Greys. The Greys are humans of the future.

Was Lee Harvey Oswald recruited either directly or indirectly by a government official in the assassination of John Kennedy? Was Jack Ruby? He was so but not successfully. He was not involved in recruiting Jack Ruby. Ruby was honest and faithful and loyal and stupid.

What can you tell us about why and where Amelia Earhart's plane crashed? Amelia Earhart's plane crash made some delicious food for those in the jungle in that era. It did not crash in the ocean. It crashed on land. It crashed because the oil in the machinery did not work well. It got dry.

Was the death of Princess Diana accidental or was she murdered? She was accidently murdered. She was killed in the car. It was the fault of the driver. He was speeding. He was under the influence of legal medication and not enough sleep.

Was the death of the actress Natalie Wood many years ago accidental or was she murdered? Indeed, it was accidental, sir. She slipped and fell and drowned, not able to swim.

In 1949 did our Secretary of Defense Admiral Forrestal commit suicide or was he murdered by the U.S. government because he had secret knowledge regarding Antarctica? (U) Indeed, sir. He was disposed of because of his secret knowledge and he was not the only one. There were others too. Your government is wonderful.

What happened to the five airplanes that disappeared in the Bermuda Triangle in 1945? Did they go off course and crash in the Georgia swamp as some people theorize? They went into the black hole, the mystery of life. They ended up somewhere else in the universe because there is a stargate in the Bermuda Triangle.

Many years ago, in the 1940's, did Admiral Byrd discover advanced underground civilizations at the earth's poles? (U) Indeed, sir, with people living underground at both poles. There was a cover-up by our government regarding Admiral Byrd's expedition to Antarctica after World War II.

What was the cause of the automobile accident in which princess Grace Kelly of Monaco was killed? Her daughter was driving and she was young and they were arguing. She was arguing with her mother and she was a young driver of perhaps the age of fourteen. It was an accident and it was hush-hushed that the daughter was driving. There was a rumor that [the cause of the accident was that] Grace Kelly had a stroke but the stroke was after the accident.

Who killed Jean Benet Ramsey? The murderer of the child is a lowly person who creeped [crept] into the hall of the basement of that child and crawled into bed with her. Greasy old man who was imprisoned. Overlooked, over minded, like many of the individuals that are on Earth. He is another earthworm hiding in the basement of their home. Crawling through the basement window of their home and remained there. She appeared to be as a young adult.

Did President Eisenhower and some of his advisors have face to face discussions with an extraterrestrial named Valiant Thor who said he was from Venus and who looked like a human, in Washington D.C. V.I.P. during the late 50's? Indeed. The man who looked like a human was actually manifesting himself as a human but was from Venus. They are among us always. I have said that extraterrestrials have far more abilities than you have since you are one of the least developed planets in the universe.

7. The 21st century

Is there a government cover-up regarding the destruction of the World Trade Center Towers? (U) Indeed yes, everything. They do not want to cause fear.

What can human beings do to stop or slow down the acceleration of the earth becoming warmer to the point where polar ice will melt, thus causing the inundation of many coastal areas, and the extinction of some animal life forms? (W) It is the rotation of the earth. Nothing can be done. This is going to happen in many years to come. You won't be here. There's nothing we can do about global warming. That is the existence of your past and your future.

When the airplanes hit Building One and Building Two in the World Trade Center, why did Building Seven collapse in the same manner? Poor structure, sir, not explosives. Mismanagement of electrical wiring.

Are extraterrestrials monitoring our nuclear facilities because they are concerned about the direction our civilization is taking? (M) Indeed, sir. They are very concerned about these directions. They are very curious, sir. They wish to be in control. They are not fearful of what you might do. They wish to control. They are seeking control. There may as well be a potential that there will be a nuclear war but it will not come to that end. You will wipe out Syria [Isis?] and you will come to the aid of Israel. Israel has forces as such that no man has created. The Jews have secrets. Indeed, Israel is being guided by a powerful extraterrestrial force. They want so much to be existing.

Is the present group of Islamic terrorists who, as you have said are reincarnations of the Nazis, also the reincarnations of many groups throughout the history of our world? Indeed sir. They come back again and back again and reincarnate. They travel as a group through their incarnations. The same group we call the Islamic Terrorists has appeared as a group at various times throughout history.

Is our government becoming increasingly corrupt or has it always been as corrupt as it now is? You answered your own question. It has always been corrupt and it always will be corrupt.

Was the spread of Lyme's disease the result of experiments done with ticks by our government on Plum Island, N.Y.? (TU) Indeed, much was spread in this special place on Long Island. Experiments taking place on Plum Island are dangerous for people. Other diseases have been created by your government, experimenting, sir. That is the reason why there has been so much cancer on Long Island. And that was explained to your wife. At that time she was aware on the North Shore.

Will the book we are writing, in which you give answers to the questions we ask, be a worthwhile project that will be of interest to many people? Anyone who is closely tied in with religion will not accept this book. Not in control. It is control we are fighting. This book will be helpful to other people. Very much so, and even those who slam it down and say "bull shit". It will keep the mind thinking. If you ever get it finished, it will be popular. I am always right.

Was it solely because of his health or age as he stated, that Pope Benedict resigned? (I) Anything that would cause health [problems] would be the reason he was resigning. It was only for health reasons and for gallbladder. It was because of differences of opinion. That can cause a gallbladder [problem].That is why he resigned but he is there and will be of assistance. He is a dear, darling person, kind and genuine.

When you said that Hitler was playing a predestined role and was guided by extraterrestrials, was it the goal of that group of extraterrestrials to take over the world? (M) No my dear sir. They were following his orders, not their own orders. This is the same group of extraterrestrials that is assisting ISIS today. We must get rid of them. You are on the same path with ISIS as you were with Hitler. They are a fungus.

Is the media in the United States as controlled, dishonest or biased as some people portray it to be? The media in this country does not know how to tell the truth. There is right in what is said. There is an awful misconception in your country. They keep secrets. Everything is a secret.

Do the ten guides or commandments known as the Guide Stones in Georgia contain coded messages for the impending apocalypse? The thinking of the creator was influenced by unseen sources. I want to go back to Stonehenge and Coral Castle in your neighborhood. They are elsewhere too. They are coded messages. The code will be broken.

Did Saddam Hussein discover a stargate? Indeed, sir. He was planning on using the stargate for nefarious purposes. He was interested in control, a very controlling person. That is why the Unites States invaded Iraq. They were aware that he had discovered a stargate. Your government is aware of stargates. They went after Hussein so he couldn't make use of that stargate.

The U.S. technology now has an unmanned space shuttle that was in orbit for two years. Is that shuttle capable of disabling enemy satellites?(V) Absolutely. What is already in space can disable satellites. Disabling satellites has already been done. Ask Israel that made the satellite. They know what to do with their satellite. This [the unmanned satellite] has to do with North Korea's satellites misfiring. You are protecting yourselves through that satellite.

R. THE WORLD OF THE FUTURE

1. Planet Changes

Will a major Earth shift occur within the next century? (W) Indeed, sir. 'Tis happening. The areas least affected will be all the places not near water. Water is delicate[?] to the interior. As Edgar Cayce said, I still see the Virginia Beach area as safe.

Do you foresee a major Earth shift in the next thousand years, such as when Atlantis virtually disappeared? (W) Indeed yes. Not in your lifetime.

It is said that the most powerful volcanoes on Earth today are in the United States. Will those volcanoes ever cause a major effect on the development of humanity? No.

How many more years do you think we have in south Florida before the rise of the ocean makes it not a good idea to buy land here? (W) Well, it's a good idea to buy land because you will be here. It is true about the water rising. I do not have dates about the water rising. It will not be in your lifetime but it looks like the rising of the water is eminent in Florida. Water from the rising seas will intrude into your community in the next century.

Will we see the rise of Atlantis during next few years? No.

In the future when our Earth experiences severe cataclysms and changes, will a sizeable portion of the people be rescued and placed aboard UFO's? Indeed, sir. You can assume that it will be many centuries from now but that is not true. It will be sooner than that. It will not be in the lifetime of anyone in this room now.

Steven Hawking has said that we have only about another hundred years on this planet and we need to find somewhere else to go. Do you concur with that? Yes. You will go on to different planets. A few of you will remain.

Will the answer to global warming be solved within the foreseeable future in a different direction from where they are going now? Indeed, there will be a different direction. There will always be arguments when people don't agree. Global warming is a natural thing that is going to occur no matter what but you can slow it down. Reducing what you call the carbon footprint can retard or slow down.

2. Warfare

Will China dominate the world within the next century? Indeed, sir. The people of China are smart and intelligent. They continue to build and will someday inherit the earth. They are currently working with extraterrestrials regarding their plan to overtake America. There will be economic warfare with the United States. The Chinese will win. They will dominate the world within the next century. I cannot answer if it will be in your lifetimes. Other countries in the world will be involved in this, including ISIS which will fail. Russia and China [will be on the same side]. The European countries are confused. The African countries will join in on America's side. I do not have an answer for South America. The conflict between the United States and China will not lead to a third world war but Isis will lead to a third world war.

Are there any present day nations other than China that will ever present a dangerous major threat to our country? Do we have more to fear from radical religious groups than we do from nations? Indeed it is true that you will be going to war with China but that will not be a physical war, more economic control. At this moment there are other countries that you are in disagreement with but there will not be any action such as you perceive as war. There will indeed be nuclear war between other countries. There will be mismanagement of opinions. Iran is insignificantly not knowledgeable [regarding the detonation of an atomic bomb]. Regarding atomic weapons, the country that you have most to fear from is yourselves. North Korea is very limited.

Will there be any more wars as great as World War II? There will be many wars between man and woman on this earth. People fight all the time. There are mean people among us. Future wars may not involve uniforms. World War II taught people lessons. The wars to come will be different.

When will there be peace in Israel? When you ask for peace, there is peace in Israel but there is also war and that is religion. So as long as we have our religions we will continue to have war.

Will there ever be a World War III? Yes, but not immediately, not now. World War III will not be a world war. It will not be as other wars that you have presented. It will not be a world war as you perceive a world war. It is ridiculous, my dear lady, to have a world war. It will not be a war as other wars. You have a world war right now on your streets. The enemy does not wear a uniform. You have a war among yourselves right now. It could be your neighbor. There is a world war right now. You are fighting that war now. It is not a war like a war in the past. In the past the wars wore uniforms. The uniforms are not worn today. There is a war now, even your racial war which is nonsense, absolutely nonsense. People fighting each other for no reason, that is why we call it ignorance.

Do you foresee any atomic warfare in our lifetime? It has already begun and has been with you. There are countries or groups of people who are definitely making plans to use atomic bombs. You have most to fear from North Korea. It will be North Korea. Iran will attempt to use atomic warfare but they are very slow and very ignorant people, you know. They are not a people of stature. Russia will not consider using atomic warfare. China would use atomic warfare. They will inherit the Earth. They are the brightest culture of all. She [Sondra Zecher] loves the oriental Chinese people. They are so humble and kind and so misguided. The United States will use the atomic bomb again. That will be in the lifetime of some here today. That depends on how long they are going to stay. It is not in the near future but much further off.

Will there be a bomb dropped on the United States within the next five years and on what city? It will not be in any city that you are aware of. They do not wish to alarm you about a bomb dropping. They are saying no, not in your educated mind. You are at war at this moment but you won't have to worry about nuclear war. You won't be here anyway.

Will the radical Muslim movement become less of a serious threat to us in this generation? (I) It is making a good point of its generation and more radicals will prove with time. It will still be here in twenty years and it will progress to be more of a threat. This will not come to an end soon. It was always there. It is a very serious situation with Syria. Eventually there will be an end to the threat. Fifty years from now there will be more peace on Earth after more destruction.

Do you foresee a big terrorist attack in the United States anytime soon? Indeed. It will be in New York. It's been planning to where most people gravitate, Times Square, and also Los Angeles where they gravitate. Chicago comes in too. There's a bombing devise that they will use. They are fierce and not knowledgeable but know how to work their killing process.

There is an alarming number of mass shooting these days, some of which are terrorists and some domestics. Is that going to stop soon? It will only get more. It will only be bigger, sir.

Is there any other country outside of America that will be safer during the time when terrorism strikes? Go to a safer country than America? At this moment there is no such thing as safe. It is not safe when you get up in the morning. It is not safe when you go to sleep in the evening. There is not such a thing as any complete safety. What is predicted is predicted.

Will there ever be a devastating war in our country, caused by the invasion of other countries, in which more than a million people die? Indeed, sir. It is arising. It is arising now. Now is the time to stop this evil force. ISIS is a crisis.

With all the confrontations we are having with North Korea, Russia and China, is there going to be some kind of military action? Indeed, eventually, sir. It will take time for this to be in progress. It is a meeting of the mind.

Will North Korea ever detonate a nuclear bomb? Will North Korea and South Korea ever be reunited? They will never bomb another country. It will backfire on them. I see that occurring within the lifetime of those here. North Korea will become friends with your country. The leader in North Korea has a mishap in his brain. He is a young man who is really in love with himself. He will last as a leader and he will not be that successful. I see North Korea and South Korea being united within the next twenty years and they will become one country.

Will Iran team up with North Korea for a nuclear ballistic-type missile? Will they ever hit United States or another country with any kind of missile? No, my dear sir, 'tis not the object. They will try to hit another country with a missile but it will not and has not been successful. They are aiming towards Japan but actually the U.S. is their obstacle [objective]. They want to hit from behind and sneak up on the United States which they will not be successful. They will go for Seoul South Korea but it will not be of any success. So you need not worry for your own being, sir.

3. America and international relations

Will the Amero be an accepted currency in the United States within the next two generations? (V) It is already, my dear sir, acceptable. Is it not true? The dollar, the piece of paper will disappear. 'Tis true you know. They have already proceeded and will continue to do so at a rapid pace.

Which of the present major world countries will have the most stable currency for the remainder of this century? There's nothing like the U.S. buck. Is that not true?

Will speakers of Spanish someday comprise more than one-third of the population of the United States? Will our country ever have an official language? Indeed, especially in your region [i.e. South Florida]. Your country will have an official language and that will be no language. In other words, you will be able to read thoughts. That will not really be a long time off.

Will the European Union exist at least for several more generations? Will the Euro remain a stable currency? Yes it will continue but will be broken up in different ways. The Euro will not decline in value. It will increase.

Will America remain a dominant force in the world for a long period of time in the future, at least until the end of this century? Until China takes over. China and Russia will be a strong force. Not in your lifetime.

In regard to the international political situation, what is the United States place: leading, following or trailing? America will be very strong and very opinionated and will succeed. America will be successful. It will be difficult but it's what's in the end that counts.

Why is China building islands in the water? To extinguish America. They are getting ready like Japan did on the American troops. The Chinese are getting ready to do same. Similar conduct, this is true. You will increase your knowledge of water. The sea and under the sea we will have troops which we already have. It is not above the land. It is below the land that we must be mindful of.

The higher denominations of money were eliminated in the banks of India. Will that happen here? Indeed, has it not already? You went down from the thousand dollar bill and the five hundred dollar bill to the hundred dollar bill.

4. Society and religion

Will there ever come a time when there will be peace throughout the world and wars will be a thing of the past? Man was put upon Earth to outdo each other. When I was on Earth I was fighting to survive but I was better than you, stronger than you, more intelligent than you. I look back and think about what you call "what a dummy". There will always be confrontations, always confrontations from the beginning of mankind.

Will there be a time in the future where civilization will return to something similar to the so-called Dark Ages before wars end? Is that not available at this time? Are there not animals on your earth at this time, people that act as animals? 'Tis bad enough now. I cannot tell if the condition will get worse. In other words, we do not wish to tell you.

Will women become the dominant gender at some point in the future? (K) Your wife will. Women will take more leadership roles in different areas of the world. Do not fear if it will be in the relative near or distant future.

Will the time come when there will be large numbers of designer babies created; that is, selected DNA from more than two parents or even a community of parents? Isn't that available at this moment, sir? I see them. That will increase in numbers. That happens on other planets also.

Will we as a society ever get past the point where the one with the most money rules and makes the rules and oppresses those that have less money? No, sir. It has always existed. Money is a god.

Someone once said that human nature is the reason that socialism as a form of government will never endure. Do you agree? In your realm it will exist.

Years from now, will we still have Christians, Jews and Moslems or will we be all one? (I) In many times there will be one bank, there will be one car, there will be one time. Is that understood? So your religious beliefs will continue to be one. One religion after many, many, many failures and many deaths. Fighting over religion is ridiculous. It does not matter what you believe. It's all one.

Do you see an end to religious beliefs? (I) It will no longer exist centuries from now. It will slowly dissolve and it is coming about showing you now very slightly how it is dissolving. The big churches that you perceive will become less and less.

Will a major crisis or scandal occur in the Catholic church within the next decade? (I) It is now sir. That scandal will be the cause of the demise of the papacy. It is on its way out, sir. This is your final Pope. Pope Francis will be the last Pope.

5. Science and technology

Will the genetic manipulation of human DNA to create a more advanced human being by our scientists become a reality in the near future? (K) It is already sir. It is in progress definitely and they are experimenting and this also will come to light in a very short time. The danger in what they will create is another person. It is not being developed for negativity. It is being developed to be used in a harmless way but everything harmless turns out with some negativity.

Will humans be able to travel to the home planet or the universe of the extraterrestrials who helped build the pyramids? How will they travel to the planet of the aliens who came and helped build the pyramids? (M) Indeed. sir. Indeed. It is coming shortly. They will travel the same way they arrived. I am not able to give that information [how humans will travel] but with your mind you can do so much. So many of you have bright minds and you don't use our minds. You have so much to offer and so much to give. We come therefore [to give] more help. Open up your minds and you will get there.

Will physical humans ever be able to time travel? Indeed, sir. Time is manmade.

Will scientists rediscover the means of counteracting gravity? Will that technology ever be put to use? (V) Indeed, sir. That technology has already been put to use but it is not publicized. That technology was from extraterrestrials. We got some of it from crashed spaceships.

Will the Doomsday Vault in Norway which stores the seeds of various varieties of vegetation ever be used in the event of an Earth catastrophe? It will be successful for humans to have this. It is not needed.

Will we ever discover and take advantage of more abundant sources of energy than we now have? Indeed. There are many energies coming your way. Your lifestyle will be very different. You will not see this in your lifetime but you will come back and see.

Will automobiles without wheels someday run on our streets and highways? (V) Indeed. It will be in this century. Is that not true? Your planes will have another engine. It is necessary for your airplanes and helicopters to have another engine for safety reasons. They have ground vehicles with and without wheels on other planets. The wheel is an invention on all planets.

Within the lifetime of those alive today, will the government require microchips to be implanted in the skin of all newborn babies? Indeed, sir. While some of you are still alive, that will be a requirement of the government. Like animals, you will be micro chipped. That will be for control and identification. The birth certificate is no longer needed. There will be microchips. This is an action indeed influenced a little bit by the

Illuminati, one world control. All will be chipped. You don't have to worry about that.

Will the time ever come when human-like robots will be self-reproducing? (V) Robots won't be able to reproduce.

6. Miscellaneous

Are there major forces at work in many countries to create a one world government? Will there ever be a one world government? (U) [There will be a one world government] in time but not in your time. In another era there will be [a one world government]. Yes, it takes much time, centuries from now.

Will the time come in the not too distant future when we humans will have visual physical contact with extraterrestrials who are very recognizably different from us physically? (M) For your benefit, yes. Next neighbor to you is questionable if you wish. That will be in the lifetime of people already here. There are people in your world who have already seen these extraterrestrials.

We make a big deal about Atlantis but if we think about what has happened after World War II, the first thing that happened was the Atlantic Alliance. That created in a certain way an Atlantic civilization between all Atlantic Europe and all Atlantic America. So do we really need an island between both as a civilization between both coasts of the Atlantic? No, it will not be necessary. It will not be split as it is now. Atlantic and Pacific will all be reunited.

Edgar Cayce has stated that there is a chamber under one of the paws of the sphinx called the Hall of Records that contains a full account of the pre-history of mankind. Does such a chamber exist? Yes. The contents of that chamber will be exposed to mankind. I see that occurring within the lifetime of some of those alive today.

Will there be disclosures from the extraterrestrials before the year 2020 in the U.S.A.? There will be somewhat. The government claims it. It will not release the disclosure. The government is in control.

It seems these days that truth is almost irrelevant. No one seems to care anymore. Is truth going to be valued again. Are we going to seek it out? Truth is the only important word. The truth is the only word that is important. The truth is your answer to everything. And many of us do not follow the truth. Is that not true? It will regain the respect that it deserves. That will come in the future.

S. HEALTH, HEALING AND PROTECTION

1. Healing devises and external aids

Will any object whatsoever that a person believes to have healing qualities be effective in healing if the person believes that it will heal? If you believe so, no matter how nonsensical it may be, it is true if you choose to believe. Why not?

Is scalar energy an effective healing modality? (V) It has to be looked into. No question that it should not be avoided. To some degree it will help others.

Is the Aura Ring effective for healing? Is it scalar energy? (V) To some degree.

Can the wearing of a battery powered wrist watch be of healing benefit in some cases? Is the same true of magnets? Indeed, yes. It will bring anything to the victim. Sometimes 'tis true. It depends on the magnet.

Will the E-power healing machine be an effective healing modality even if you don't believe in it? When you believe in it, sir, it will be effective at times. If you don't believe in it, it won't be effective.

Is there truth to the theory that, because of modern technology, humans are being excessively bombarded with positive ions and this is having a negative effect on our health? Are devices that are imbued with negative ions of benefit to our health? (V) No, this is not true. Such devices are not of importance.

Is the wearing of gold of benefit to the health of the human physical body? Indeed.

Is much of what is said about various kinds of crystals being able to aid humans or to bring healing correct? When one's soul wishes it to be of assistance, when one believes that this will be, it will be. When you hold a religious article, or what you call religious, it will be. It is very easy to be.

When one wishes, what is true will be true. When you believe in good, it will be good. When you believe in bad, it will be bad, or not good.

Is the use of castor oil packs for health reasons as described by Edgar Cayce effective? They will be effective if you believe in them. They will not if you don't believe in them. If you don't take it, it won't be effective.

Is it therapeutic for people to be in the ocean water? Indeed, sir. It is relaxing and you will find you Earth beings will be more aware of the ocean. There is more to come of the ocean. The ocean will be something that humans will be relating to; no longer a mystery as it has been in the past.

Can using a laser beam on water or food before it is consumed be more beneficial to a person's health than if the laser beam had not been used? Yes. The same is true of using a laser beam on the meridian lines of the body to promote healing. You can say that the instrument that Jeff Starkman presented to you is of value to you.

Will any of the following healing devices be effective even if the person using them is doubtful about their usefulness?

The Grounding Pad	It depends if one believes.
The Body Shaper	It will help your heart condition.
The E-Power machine	If one believes then it will succeed.
The Aura Ring	If one believes.

Does Irving Pheterson's invention, the Body Charger, provide the healing benefits that he claims? It is worth using if the mind wishes to use. It will work for other things, not for what you wish.

In the 1930's Wilhelm Reich invented the Orgone Box. Did that device have any healing effects on the person inside of it? To the person that sat inside of it, it could actually have some effect if they believed it. Whatever you believe, sir, will be.

We have heard that if a man wears a fourteen carat gold ring on the ring finger of the left hand he will be more susceptible to lung problems. Is there any truth in that? It's ridiculous.

2. Foods

Are genetically engineered vegetables such as corn harmful to our health? At times yes indeed. It will improve in the future. They will use less germicide.

Is eating meat a reflection of lower level consciousness? (K) You can raise your level of consciousness by avoiding red meat. Definitely. Eating red meat is not beneficial to your health.

Will the time come when the great majority of humans will no longer eat the flesh of animals? (R) Indeed, sir. It is becoming slowly. Slowly in your future.

Why is it generally believed that eating fish is more acceptable than eating the meat of land animals? I don't know who made it acceptable. Fish is better for you than meat. It is more healthy for you.

Is seaweed a food that would be beneficial to add to our daily diet? Indeed, sir, as long as it is not moving.

Is eating organically grown fruits and vegetables significantly better for our health than eating most of the fruits and vegetables that are sold in supermarkets? For years and centuries before, we Earth ones were eating fruits and vegetables and survived. So now we give it a new name [i.e. organically grown]. Is that not true? Now you use a lot of chemicals and fertilizers to make them grow better. You would do better to eat fruits and vegetables that haven't been treated by chemicals.

For those of us who continue to eat meat, is it better for our health to eat the meat of animals that have been fed organically grown food? Is the meat from buffalo less harmful to our bodies than the meat from cattle? Yes, it would be better to eat organically grown food. If you insist on continuing to eat red meat, the meat from buffalo is less harmful to your bodies than the meat from cattle.

When you said that eating red meat was not good for our health, were you referring to the meat of all four-legged animals, not just cattle?

Are fish and fowl preferable? All. It is not good to eat meat. I have said that it reduces your level of spirituality by eating meat. Fish and fowl are preferable to eating the meat of four-legged animals.

Is there a danger in drinking filtered water because that will leach out essential minerals and trace elements from your body? Indeed, sir. Drinking filtered water is not really a good thing. It is silly. It is ridiculous.

Is it possible for humans to exist solely on a type of green algae for nutrition? Indeed, sir, but not solely. There are grasses that will help you.

Many people believe that drinking bottled spring water is better for your health than drinking the water that is piped into our homes. Is that correct? No, my dear sir, water is water. You don't have to buy any water.

3. Herbs, drugs and supplements

What herb would you recommend for the improvement of our memory? Vitamin B12 is one that would be good. Medications are not my advice to you. Be careful of medications. Vitamins are medications.

Are health supplements such as turmeric, green tea and aloe healthful to the body? Indeed, sir, so is water, just plain water. It is very needed for the body to be good.

Do herbs found on Earth and other natural remedies exist for curing all human diseases? Indeed, sir. Definitely, yes, sir.

Is ionized air of benefit to our health? Is the same true of ionized water? It depends on who is asking for it. For some people, yes. For other people, no.

You have said that it is not good to stand in front of a microwave oven while in use but is eating food or drinking a liquid that has been heated in a microwave oven detrimental to our health? Indeed. You should avoid heating things in a microwave oven if possible. Don't stand in front while you press the buttons so you don't get the electricity. Standing three feet away is not far enough away. Three feet away is dangerous, sir.

Is drinking a glass of water with a spoonful or two of apple cider vinegar everyday good for your health? Actually, sir, I would not advise you [Charles Zecher] to do that. It is of no [value].

Is there any truth to what we have seen on television about hemp oil or marijuana helping with cancer? Absolutely. Absolutely. A great deal of truth. It is real true but the government does control and that is why you selected your government control.

Is there such a thing as very limited use of marijuana for people who have illnesses where you wouldn't be smoking enough to do any damage to your lungs? One doesn't have to smoke. It is only a plant and all medication comes from plants. There are different parts of it [marijuana] that are good for some illnesses.

Can the use of marijuana take a person to a higher level of thinking? Can a controlled or limited use of marijuana be noticeably detrimental to a person's health? Indeed. It can take one to a higher level and to a lower level. Even a controlled or limited use of marijuana can be detrimental to a person's health as smoking [cigarettes] is. If you smoke marijuana it will have the same effect on your lungs and arteries as cigarettes but then there are stages that marijuana is helpful.

Can the use of mind-altering drugs enhance a person's creativity or mental abilities by connecting the person with a higher level form of intelligence? For a moment. It is for the moment. The use of mind altering drugs can make a person temporarily creative.

Are there certain types of coffee that we should avoid or are there some that are okay? Yes, coffee that was not triggered with some liquid. The coffee that stimulates the growth is very healthy for you because it stimulates the veins. Starbucks coffee contains nicotine. That is why people need their fix in the morning. Be careful not to overdose. I would have a little drink now and then. The nicotine is fine to open up different arteries and is necessary to open up the arteries. Sometimes it is made positive. It is a drug that is positive. Forget about decaffeinated coffee. No decaf.

Does the ingestion of DMT (Dimethyltryptamine) cause meaningless hallucinations or does it help in making connections with higher intelligence beings? Both. There are certain groups that use it in Africa. Some of you think marijuana does the same. Sometimes it can take you to meaningful connections with higher intelligence and sometimes it is meaningless hallucinations.

If a person uses a lot of artificial sugar in his diet, is there an increased likelihood that the person will develop cancer? Is artificial sugar worse than natural sugar for our health if it is used in moderation? Sugar substitutes such as Sweet & Lo are not harmful to our health if you don't overdo it. Nothing is harmful if not in abundance. Yes and no [regarding cancer]. It depends on the health of the person. In some conditions artificial sugar is not helpful. If a person has bad teeth, it is not going to make the teeth any better. If a person has bad teeth, it is preferable to use artificial sugar.

4. Protection

Can a person endow any object to serve as an effective good luck charm or an object of protection if they believe in it? If you think that something is a lucky charm for you, it can become so. It can actually be effective if you feel that way. I think you are limiting your potential if you do not believe in good luck charms. The only good luck charm, sir, is you. You make your way.

Can physical objects such as a statue of St. Jude placed on the dashboard of your car or a mezuzah placed at the doorway of your home or amulets be imbued with special powers, such as for protection or healing? (D) It only comforts those who believe. It is a comfort to believe in nonsense.

Does placing a glass of water on your nightstand help keep negative energy away? Indeed it does if you do not use if for nurturing yourself. It will keep evil spirits away as they are fearful of water.

Is there such a thing as holy water or is all water the same? Can water dissolve negativity that is potentially harmful to humans? Water is water. It is no more effective if it has been blessed by priest than out of the faucet. Water is water from the ocean, from the sea. [Regarding dissolving negativity] it depends upon your thoughts. Where are your thoughts? It can keep fire away. It can extinguish fire. It can extinguish hotheadedness, heat. It can cool off and experience no longer having heat.

Does making the sign of the cross with your hand in front of your chest, as the Catholics do, actually bring assistance or protection to the individual doing so? If they feel that, sir, it gives them peace of mind but that is ridiculous.

5. Visualization and channeling energy

When we visualize surrounding someone with white light can that be of actual benefit to that person? Indeed 'tis true. White light can be beneficial to most.

Can a person send healing energy to another person merely by his thoughts? Correct.

Is it possible for us to take on someone else's disease or problem when we are channeling healing energy to them? If you are weak and cannot resist the flow of negative energy. Do not worry about your wife. She is strong.

6. Diseases: diagnoses, causes and cures

Is there a known cure for cancer? (U) Correct. Your government is creating a cover-up. Your physicians. We do have a cure. There are many cures for cancer. They are here among you. There are many kinds of cancer and there is a cure.

Have epidemics or plagues that have affected humans been caused by microbes on meteorites and asteroids that have hit the earth? Were some deliberately sent by extraterrestrial entities? (M) Indeed, sir. My answer to you is yes. Some of those hitting the were intentionally sent by extraterrestrial technology to help reduce the population.

Are there diseases afflicting humans in today's world that were intentionally caused by extraterrestrials? (M) They meant no harm but they were caused by extraterrestrials. Those diseases are neurological in nature. It was not intentional. It was experimental.

Are physical ailments frequently the result of emotional disorders? Many of them are, sir, such as a headache.

Do people sometimes make the choice at the soul level to have a particular disease or physical problem so that they can advance more rapidly in their spiritual evolution? (G) My answer to you would be yes. People before they incarnate can choose to have an infirmity so they can advance more rapidly.

Is the cause of the 2014 Ebola virus outbreak a natural occurrence, manmade, or of some other origin? Ridiculous fear. No more fear than a cold in your atmosphere. There is no fear. It is a natural occurrence, not something that was intentionally started.

Can the sound of a person's voice when he speaks indicate specific health problems he might have? Indeed, sir. Indeed. That technology is available to you now if you wish for physicians to take knowledge.

There has been research where they are curing cancer with viruses like measles and cold viruses. Are these therapies going to become cures? In a way. They are experimenting, sir, but the most important experiment is that you will be cured.

Can a long painful death, such as from cancer, help resolve what we might call karmic debts? (G) If you wish.

Can we stop ourselves from having fatal illnesses by understanding that something is wrong in our life and by changing it? Indeed. We can do it but mainly, in answer to your question, attitudes are very important. We can say that the material written by Louise Hay can pertain to your question.

Can the Zika mosquito be used in some manner for the improvement of a person's health, such as stopping the growth of cancer? Indeed, sir, it will be found to be able to halt any more growth of tumors. The injections will be made and they will be made to be a positive use. It's not all negative, you know. I see that they can make use of it after science and the doctors find out.

Has the Zika virus been caused by the use of chemicals on agriculture? No. The mosquitoes have often good to offer. It will be put down as something we will be grateful for when used properly. The children infected with the Zika virus will have some[thing] injected into their system to offer for a chemical for different viruses affecting other people.

Can we assume that what appears as defects, such as blindness or deformed body, is intentionally done by those conscious entities responsible for the construction, growth and maintenance of our physical bodies rather than such conditions occurring just by random chance? No such thing, sir, as random chance. It is a learning ability. If a person is born with some kind of defect whatever, that was intentionally done in the creation of that person's physical form.

7. Miscellaneous

What is the cause or the reason for the different blood types of physical humans? The cause of different blood types is the cause of different people. What caused you to be a male or your wife to be a female? She chose to be a female and she chose her blood type. Some blood types are negative and some positive. Just a spin of the wheel. It does not matter.

Does an individual's blood type indicate which kinds of food are best suited to that individual? Is the information in the *Book Eat Right 4 your Type* basically correct? Indeed, sir. It can help. The information in the book is administered to you by a dentist who gave you the information that he found out. There is some correct information to a degree in the book *Eat Right For Your Type*. The information he found out is good as far as your human type is concerned. The food mentioned for your blood type would help you to a degree. All that is written is not 100% correct. There is some basic core of correct.

Do organ transplants and blood transfusions affect the recipient in more ways other than just on the physical body? Yes, there are times. Yes, on the emotional and mental [levels] at times. Sometimes yes, and sometimes no. When the recipients are sensitive, they can pick up the memories of the donor.

Are stem cell implants a healing modality that is worthy of continued injections and further research? Indeed, sir. Indeed. Very worthy when given the correct stem cells. They are experimenting with animal stem cells for humans. Rather than rabbits, pigs would be better. They are more like humans than other animals.

Will sleeping with your body aligned with the polarity of the earth, that is your head facing north, be of health benefit to the body? If that is what your mind thinks. I cannot help your thinking.

Could the intentional provocation of an out-of-body experience be detrimental to an individual's physical health? It could be detrimental to individuals if they do not protect themselves.

Since you have said that the length of a person's life is predetermined but not cast in stone, can being of service to others help prolong a person's lifetime? Indeed, sir very much indeed. So all of you get out there and help other people. You will live longer if you help others. You will be happier.

Can an emotional shock create a fatal energy? Indeed, sir, indeed.

When an amputee feels pain where there was once a leg, why does that person feel pain if the leg is no longer there? The leg is always there, sir. It never goes away. Pain is located in the etheric body, not just in the physical body.

Is there sometimes a danger if a person is cremated too soon after dying because there is a possibility that the etheric body may not have fully separated from the physical body, thus causing the entity to feel pain? (A) It is absolutely true. It is painful, sir. You must wait two days before being cremated.

Can living near high tension electrical lines or a radio transmitting tower affect a person's health or affect the person's psychic or medium abilities? What about microwave ovens? To a degree. It can also claim more energy from person's psychic or medium abilities. They can deteriorate from such ability as well as experience more. It will be determined that standing in front of a microwave will affect a person's health. 'Tis true to a point that you should not use the microwave oven so much.

You have mentioned how the electromagnetic energy from overhead lines can interfere with us. What about the cell phones that so many of us carry? Is that interfering with our sensitivity? Is it not good for us to have as much electromagnetic radiation a la radio waves going through or bodies all the time with all the cell phones. Is that unhealthy for us? Indeed sir. Cell phones can affect your health.

Is either of the following two statements more effective than the other. The first is "I don't want to get sick." The second is "I want to stay well." You know, sir, staying well is much stronger. In other words, I am saying that when you pray or when you think or visualize something, you think in the positive, not the negative. Then it is heard. The negative is not heard. The negative brings a judgment cost among you people. The positive brings the happiness.

Is it true, as Edgar Cayce said, that there are health benefits to lying on the beach at Virginia Beach, Virginia because of the gold that is buried deep below the sand? There certainly is gold beneath the sand. The gold really doesn't do anything for the person's health.

Why has her (Sondra Zecher) illness (multiple sclerosis) happened to her? That is for others to see so she can help others. The illness that she has is to help others.

It appears that there is an increase in the incidence of neurological diseases. If that so, what is the cause of the increase? It is more recognizable. It is not an increase but you are just becoming more aware of it.

When a person is born deaf, or blind or in some way deformed, is the reason for that condition something the person has chosen at the soul level? (G) Not necessarily. It could be the result of karma or something that was chosen for their own advancement. It is very similar with animals.

It seems that a lot of people are now living to be in their nineties or over a hundred. What has caused that? A change in diet and a change in living. A change in mind control. People will be at a hundred and fifty. That will be the new young look. A hundred and fifty will be the new age for those that are a hundred.

Will humans be able to survive if a pig's heart is transplanted into them? Indeed, sir. It has been achieved so far. Many pigs are very much like animals that are on Earth. You don't necessarily need a human heart donor. It is possible to transplant a pig's heart into a human.

T. ANIMALS, INSECTS AND NON-HUMAN CREATURES

1. Evolution of animals

You have said that extraterrestrials have influenced the development of mankind. Have they also had an influence on the creation or the development of insects and animals on Earth? (M) Indeed.

Can all species of animals incarnate directly into the human kingdom or is there a chain of evolution among the animals? There are some animals that will become humans on their passing, such animals as cats, dogs; closer to humans. All animals will evolve to the human state. It will be eventually time. Animals who are pets and close to humans are more likely to reincarnate as a human.

Are some species of animals higher than other species on the evolutionary path to becoming humans? Believe it or not, sir, there are some animals that are better than some humans. Is that not true?

Do animals have soul groups, much the same as humans do? At times they [do] indeed so. Animals feel as we do.

Does karma play a role in the world of animals? (H) At times, yes. Poor souls.

Some people believe that whales and dolphins have a higher level connection with humans that others animals do not have? Do you agree with that? Not more than most. At times, whales and dolphins have a higher level of consciousness. They can reincarnate as humans.

Must animals incarnate in a variety of species before evolving into a human? Some do but some can be just one species and then evolve.

Can birds and flying insects evolve into angels? (J) 'Tis so. 'Tis so.

You have said that insects in their evolutionary journey can eventually evolve into angels. Can they evolve into elementals? Indeed, sir, insects also sometimes evolve into animals or birds. As far as I know, they cannot evolve into elementals.

Can any animals, including insects, fish and birds exist that are not part of a soul? No. Each animal has a soul. Even insects. Even an ant. They do not have awareness and sense when they are going to be stepped on. All forms of physical manifestations are part of a soul, any kind of soul.

Do animals sometimes choose to remain earthbound for a while rather than proceeding directly to the spirit world? Is this sometimes the case of pets who predecease their owners? They are very intuitive. They are much more intuitive than humans are. It depends [whether they go directly to the spirit world]. My answer cannot be yes or no.

2. Animals and reincarnation

All questions in this section, except for the last 3, have appeared in previous chapters.

Since you have previously said that humans often first incarnate as animals before incarnating as a human, is it possible for the reverse to occur? Can a human reincarnate as an animal? (G) Can a person become a dog? No, it is impossible.

Are domestic animals who have bonded with their human masters more likely to reincarnate as a human than are wild animals? (G) The answer to your question is yes. Are they not more like humans? You have a cat that is like a human. You have a dog that is like a human. They understand the human race.

Which species of animals are more likely than others to incarnate as a human rather than as an animal in their next incarnation? (G) Certain kinds of animals are not more likely to reincarnate as humans than other kinds. Domestic animals are more likely to reincarnate as humans.

You mentioned that animals also reincarnate the same as us and live in parallel lives. What do you mean by "parallel lives"? (G) They live in many lives like you do. People live many lives simultaneously.

Must all humans incarnate as an animal before becoming human? G) Not all, sir. Not all. Some never outgrow being an animal. They can be human but act like an animal. Many of you are pigs, snakes or elephants.

Do animals reincarnate as members of their former species until they finally incarnate as a human, or do they reincarnate in different species? (G) They reincarnate differently. A cat won't always reincarnate as a cat but a human will always reincarnate as a human. It is not completely true that there is no going backwards. Humans can act like animals.

If an animal died in a fire, is it likely that the entity might have fear of fire in when it incarnates as a human? (G) Indeed, sir. That is very possible and likely such as one drowning. It can transfer from the animal to the human if it was a fear.

When animals are about to cross over to the spirit world, are they aware of that? Indeed, sir. They are aware of it. They know when it is going to rain before it rains. They are much more sensitive than we are as humans. When I was a human, I was not as sensitive as my animals were. Animals are very psychic and know ahead of time when things are going to happen. And some come back as humans.

Are domestic animals sometimes predetermined to be with their owners? At times no, and sometimes yes. Some owners, you know, are like parents. They are not easy. Sometimes they do not wish to be like your children. Some children we bring up are not [easy]. They are enemies. Sometimes we bring up enemies and we call them children.

Can some animals have multiple simultaneous incarnations as humans do? Indeed, sir. Yes. True. Animals also reincarnate same as us and live in parallel lives.

3. Animals of the past

Was there a time in the ancient past when animals, including humans, could mate with animals of different species, thus producing strange looking offspring, as stated by Edgar Cayce? (P) Not true.

Are there remains of Noah's Ark that still exist? (EI) There are no physical remains that archeologists will ever find because it never existed. What we call Noah's ark was an extraterrestrial vehicle. I would prefer to call it a spaceship. It was not a real Noah's Ark. They were able to save not animals but the sperm [perhaps DNA] of the animals. That's how they got the thousands of animals into the ark.

What was the cause of the disappearance of dinosaurs many years ago? (P) Earthquakes. Explosions. Earthquakes devoured the earth at that time.

Was the earthquake that caused the disappearance of dinosaurs from Earth engineered by extraterrestrials or was it a natural occurrence? Both. It was intentional in part to get rid of the dinosaurs. Dinosaurs have shrunk to many little lizards. Have you noticed the lizards? Lizards and many of the reptiles were dinosaurs at one time.

4. Human and spirit connection with animals

Are animal totems that are said to hover over each person's head a reality? What is the purpose of a totem? (D) Indeed. Part of a composition. A build-up of strength to help the individual gain strength.

Should mankind endeavor to protect endangered animal species whose endangerment is not caused by mankind? That is a human decision as you well know. Why not keep all the bugs alive? They will come and sting you. It really doesn't matter whether we try to keep them alive. What purpose, sir, does it do? What is the purpose to keep alive all the humans that have passed away?

Will the time come when the great majority of humans will no longer eat the flesh of animals? (RS) Indeed, sir. It is becoming slowly. Slowly in your future.

Are animals sensitive to the thoughts and emotions of people? Indeed animals are very [sensitive]. They really can smell you a mile away. Some stink and some do not.

Some people believe apes are errant genetic descendants of humans rather than the reverse. Is that true? (K) Sometimes it's true.

Do the animal experiments conducted on Plum Island in New York pose a potential threat to those who live in the vicinity? (QU) Indeed, sir. Most of your hospitals in New York are filled with cancer patients on your North Shore. The experiments are causing cancer.

What can I do to help my cat who is getting older as far as her health goes? Talk to your cat and tell the cat how much you love her and how much you care. Talk to your cat. She will hear you and she will understand you. They know far more than you do.

Do humans or spirits ever have memories or emotions that developed from the time when they were incarnated as animals before they became humans perhaps such as certain fears? Indeed, sir. It does exist. You can have certain fears from before you were human.

When an entity reincarnates from the animal kingdom to the human kingdom, does the species of the animal have any effect on either the personality or the physical characteristics of the human? It will have an effect on the personality and very little effect on the physical. The kind of animal that incarnates as a human will have an effect on the personality of that new human.

Do those in your world communicate with animals on both your plateau and ours? (B) Some do, sir. We can communicate with physical animals as well as with animals in our realm. Influence animals too.

Can animals in your realm show themselves to humans much the same as do the spirits in your realm? Indeed, sir. Your dog who is now in my realm could show herself to you as do the spirits in my realm. Your dog Lady has appeared quite a few times.

Since entities in your world can create what they want with their mind, is it possible to create one of the person's animal pets who was on this plateau when they were here? (B) Yes.

5. Non-human creatures

If there was any truth in it, what was the basis for the legends about vampires? Ha, ha, ha. To scare you. Are not vampires the walking dead?

Does the concept of mermaids have any basis in reality? Made up stories. There never were beings that had the upper part of a woman and the lower part of a fish.

Do the underwater beings that we refer to as Telchines actually exist? Indeed sir. You will all be going underwater.

Are some of the strange creatures that have been reported seen throughout the centuries the offspring of a human and an extraterrestrial? Nonsense.

In your previous visit with us, us you used the term "creatures" as something that is distinct from humans or animals. What are they? They are part human and part animal. They act in animalistic ways. They are what Cayce referred to as the "things". They came into existence as through part development, not through genetic manipulation. It was development. They are among you right now.

6. Miscellaneous

Do animals have intuition as well as instinct? Absolutely.

Can animals be possessed by evil spirits? (C) Indeed, and they can be earthbound and not cross over.

Do angels sometimes manifest themselves as our pets that remain with us until they die? Do they sometimes manifest themselves as extraterrestrials? (J) Indeed. Sir. They can manifest themselves as bolts of lightning, flies, butterflies.

Is there any what we might call "mystical" connection to the scarab beetles portrayed in ancient Egyptian beliefs or drawings? (P) Indeed, yes. They are a happening of the past. They were extraterrestrials. What I would refer to as reincarnation. The ancient Egyptians drew them and revered these beetles.

Is there any factual historical significance to the American Indian mythologies which often portray beings that are part ants and part humans? (M) Indeed, sir. Such beings did exist. They still exist. They exist on Earth.

What was the cause of the numerous mutilizations of animals across America in recent years in which certain organs had been surgically removed? (M) It happened for experimental reasons, sir, by extraterrestrials indeed, and the organs were removed for research.

In addition to working with humans and spirits, do angels also work with animals? Do they work with the vegetable kingdom? (J) At times, sir. They do not work with the vegetable kingdom. The nature spirits take care of the vegetable kingdom.

Can memories in animals be passed on through the genes from one generation to the next? Indeed, sir. The same is true of some humans but not all. Theoretically, you could have memories of your ancestors. That is what makes confusion.

Do animals have free will? They do have free will and when love is expressed by the human the animal will respond with love. [Speaking to the woman who asked the question:]You should not feel guilt about the animals that you just had put down. Your animals are happy to be free and relieved. So do not feel despair because you have done them a favor so they can go on.

Dragons play a prominent role in Chinese drawings. Yet you have said that dragons do not exist. Was what the Chinese depict in their ancient drawings as dragons actually spaceships? Indeed, sir, if you wish to call it that. There is another name, as you well know, other than spaceships. As far as animals, there was no animal involved as dragons but that is how the Chinese interpreted what they saw in the sky.

Are Earth humans the only humanoid species in the universe whose physical bodies were created or modified by extraterrestrials? No. Indeed, no. There are humanoid beings and animals on other planets whose physical bodies were modified. There are animals that are more human that are so much not to be taken [for granted?], like your dogs who know the weather. They know the future.

U. GOVERNMENT COVER-UPS, CONSPIRACIES AND SECRET SOCIETIES

1. Secret societies and covert influences

Is it true that there are secret societies composed of human beings that control much of the activities on the earth? There are indeed. There is much power with money, both benign and malevolent.

What is the intent of the Illuminati? Are members of the Illuminati aware at the conscious level that they are such? They are people that want to control and take over. They don't want to let go. They leave and come back again. We don't care for them particularly. They are back again. I don't know if they are conscious of being such. The Illuminati have control or a strong influence on the popular music industry. Absolutely.

Are many of the current popular music stars, including the popular singer Lady Gaga, instruments of the Illuminati? Is the same true of the media? Indeed, sir. The same is true of movie and TV stars. The media is very much controlled by the Illuminati. They all get together and make your simple laws. You have something to fear from the Illuminati. You should ignore them or oppose them. Be strong and know what is better for you, each one of you individually.

Are there major forces at work in many countries to create a one world government? Will there ever be a one world government? (R) [There will be a one world government] in time but not in your time. In another era there will be [a one world government]. Yes, it takes much time, centuries from now.

Is our country run by mostly elected officials or mostly by certain behind the scene powers? You have many behind the scene powers as you suggested. It really does not matter who is elected president.

Did the Freemasons have a significant impact on the founding of our country? What was the source of the Freemasons' information? (Q) Indeed, sir. The source was extraterrestrial.

Does there exist a secret private organization for space exploration that is not connected with the government of any country? Indeed, sir, it is all secret. Everything is secret. Your country is a secret. This organization will be successful. They will attempt to control.

2. Our government and aliens

All questions in this section, except the last 3, have appeared in previous chapters.

Is there secret cooperation between our government and aliens? (M) Indeed. Indeed. Indeed. Your government is not without an odor.

Is NASA withholding some very significant information from us regarding the universe and extraterrestrial life? (M) Indeed they are holding information as you well know.

Have some of our technologies been achieved through analyzing equipment found on crashed UFO's? (MV) More recently, sir? They have been there for years. What is so different? There is nothing different you know. The United States government is involved in programs of reverse engineering of alien spacecraft or other alien technology. They are examining things they found and then cover it.

What is the reason for the intense secrecy surrounding Area 51 in the air force base in Nevada? (M) 'Tis always that way, sir. Is it not? Security is needed. Your government chooses that. They wish that it is a secret. They are hiding information about aliens, UFOs, equipment and things like that. They're hiding it without too much success, you know.

Is the formation of the numerous crop circles throughout the world caused by extraterrestrials who are attempting to communicate with the people on Earth? Is mathematics used as the basic form of communication? (M) Indeed, sir. Sometimes it is easier to use mathematics.

Will any of us here ever see a humanoid being in the physical from a different planet who appears totally unhuman. (R) Indeed. People in this room will meet face-to-face with people that look like me, but not me, and actually see them. A lot of those beings are housed in Area 51 in Nevada beneath the ground now and in other places in the United States. They look totally different from humans and live mostly underground. They can change. Your government is aware of that. The government has shown it. They have presented it.

Does our government have direct communication with physical extraterrestrials from several different star systems? Indeed, sir. Are you not aware of it? Your government is with many different kinds of extraterrestrials. It will come to light in a very short time. They are being heard at this very moment. There are some currently on Earth. Some live underground mysteriously but not in the way that you present it.

Is there a time in the immediate future that Earth people will know there are aliens and the government will come forward and say that there are? It does exist now, my dear lady. It does exist and they are among us. All of us. I see full disclosure of the alien presence coming soon. Indeed, sir. They are there now. They have been there and they are there now.

Is our government currently spending more than one trillion dollars each year for secret facilities and searching for extraterrestrial life? They have been doing so for numerous years. Years before. I don't know the exact amount as you perceive it but it is not generally given to the public. It is not for public airing.

3. Government withholding information

Will the Amero be an accepted currency in the United States within the next two generations? (R) It is already, my dear sir. Acceptable. Is it not true? The dollar, the piece of paper will disappear. 'Tis true you know. They have already proceeded and will continue to do so at a rapid pace.

Is there a government cover-up regarding the destruction of the World Trade Center Towers? (Q) Indeed yes, everything. They do not want to cause fear. They had nothing to do with it.

Is there a known cure for cancer? (S) Correct. Your government is creating a cover-up. Your physicians. We do have a cure. There are many cures for cancer. They are here among you. There are many kinds of cancer and there is a cure.

Was there a conspiracy and a government cover-up regarding the death of Marilyn Monroe? Dorothy Kilgallen? Was the CIA involved? Indeed, sir. 'Tis going on again. The CIA was involved, if you want to call them that. Regarding Dorothy Kilgallen, not that much but because of her loud mouth. She died of an overdose as reported in the news. It was self-inflicted also. She was a drinker, you know. It was drinking and medications.

Is there a government cover-up regarding the *Blue Planet Project*? Indeed, there is a cover-up. The information in its publication is not too accurate, but somewhat accurate. There is some truth behind every lie.

In 1949 did our Secretary of Defense Admiral Forrestal commit suicide or was he murdered by the U.S. government because he had secret knowledge regarding Antarctica? (Q) Indeed, sir. He was disposed of because of his secret knowledge and he was not the only one. There were others too. Your government is wonderful.

Many years ago, in the 1940's, did Admiral Byrd discover advanced underground civilizations at the earth's poles? (Q) Indeed, sir, with people living underground at both poles. There was a cover-up by our government regarding Admiral Byrd's expedition to Antarctica after World War II.

Many years ago, a man named G. E. Kincade found artifacts in the caves in the walls of the Grand Canyon. Why did the Smithsonian Museum remove them and deny their existence? Fearful that if they do not understand and fearful that others will not understand. Those artifacts were of ancient human origin [not extraterrestrial]. They were leaving their customs behind, a writing of their history for later humans to discover and learn.

4. Secret government activities and places

Do the animal experiments conducted on Plum Island in New York pose a potential threat to those who live in the vicinity? (QT) Indeed, sir.

Most of your hospitals in New York are filled with cancer patients on your North Shore. The experiments are causing cancer.

Is there a secret government installation beneath the Denver airport? Indeed. I am not able to share [the information].

Is there a hidden city beneath the earth near Dulce, New Mexico in which thousands of extraterrestrials live under the cooperation and observation of the United States government? (M) (Laughing) Indeed, sir. There has been a pact between you and the aliens. I will answer in your language "sort of". These extraterrestrials experiment on humans there. They share their technology with you. They keep up to their part of the agreement, sort of.

Are there more than one hundred secret underground military installations in the United States. In addition to the installation in Dulce New Mexico, do any of them house extraterrestrials? (M) Indeed sir, a hundred is not a good number. In addition to the one in Dulce, New Mexico, some of those house extraterrestrial beings.

Does the United States government regulate the price of gold? Indeed. Indeed it does. Gold and silver and diamonds.

Would we be correct in fearing what the pharmaceutical companies are doing to mankind? Indeed, sir, indeed. They need the money and they are making the money. They want power and they have the power. They are misusing the power for humanity. Indeed, they are not fair to humanity to mislead them in the wrong direction and they know it. The pharmaceutical companies exert influence on politics. Indeed, more knowledge must be given. They are very controlling, your organizations.

Does Project Mercury of the National Security Administration actually record telephone conversations of a large majority of Americans? Yes. They are recording the conversations of some of the people in this room. Particularly there are special people in this room that are being recorded. They [those with the Guide] do not wish me to reveal [who are being recorded]. I would say that you should be more careful of what you say in your telephone conversations, and your thoughts also. A wired phone in your home is not safer than a cell phone.

Has our government been able to erase certain memories from people, especially memories of secret government projects on which they have been working? Indeed, sir. Your government has the power to tamper with your memories.

As in the movie *Manchurian Candidate* years ago, will we be mind controlled by the government? In a way, it never not existed. It was always available. It is part of your government.

Is our government experimenting with modifying the DNA of humans in a manner similar to what the Anunnaki has done? Indeed, sir. Your government is secretly experimenting with changing the DNA of humans.

Does the United States have military bases beneath the ice in Antarctica? The United States absolutely does have military bases beneath the ice.

5. Miscellaneous

Was a foreign country involved in the assassination of President Kennedy? Can you tell us anything more about the assassination that is not generally known by the public? (Q) No, ridiculous! It was another government official who was behind the assassination. [The name of a U.S. president was given but we choose not to state it here.]

Recently it was announced that astronomers are getting a signal from a planet that is nine light years away from ours. Is that from another planet? Indeed, sir. That is the voices that I have been addressing you to. Scientists are now backpedaling on that because there is a government conspiracy to shut that up. It is control.

In regards to our space program, why do we not go back to the moon? Bigger and trying effort to do so. The fear of the government. The government hates to take us in the direction. Something was discovered on the moon that has caused our country fear to go back. Your government conceals much of its awareness.

Do time travelers exist? Indeed, sir. There are many of them on Earth now. Some of the current members of your government are from your future. They are planted everywhere, sir. Some of your leaders are actually from your future.

Some people think that, in addition to providing health care, Obama care was designed by behind the scene powers as a means to control society. Is that correct? Indeed, sir. It ain't no lie. The Illuminati are controlling the scene there. The belief is that if the government can control your health, they can control many facets of your life eventually, like even where you live or what kind of work you do. You are being manipulated. It is to your advantage to resist that manipulation. Manipulation is not a positive thing for you but it will be controlled.

V. SCIENCE AND TECHNOLOGY

1. Ancient technology

All questions in this section except the last 2 have appeared in previous chapters.

Have there been previous human civilizations on this earth before Atlantis that were more technologically advanced than our current civilization? (P) Indeed. Intelligently advanced.

Did humans of long ago use the power of sound, taught to them by extraterrestrials, to accomplish such feats as moving extremely heavy objects? (PW) Indeed. You don't need an education to find that interesting. Sound was used in the construction of some of the unusual ancient monuments we find throughout the world. Sound was used in the construction of the great pyramids. Sound was also used when the Israelites went around the walls of Jericho and made the walls crumble. The frequency of the sound. And do you not have a place of interest [i.e. the Coral Castle in Homestead, Florida] in the area where you live? He used sound to raise those heavy stones. That is the same way you have seen opera singers break [drinking] glasses. Sound was used to move stones at Stonehenge.

Were some people knowledgeable about the creation of and the use of electricity in Biblical times? (I) Indeed, what you call electricity. Was there not lightening at that time? They were able to harness that. The pyramids were used to create electricity.

What was the role of or the importance of the Ark of the Covenant in the Bible? (I) It produced energy. It still exists today in your head. There is an Ark of the Covenant. Indeed, it will comfort you and you need to have that. It is hearsay that it is in Israel.

Was the technology encased within the Ark of the Covenant in the Bible instrumental in bringing down the walls of Jericho? (I) Indeed, sir. It was amplified sound waves of the blowing of the trumpets that caused the walls to fall. Loud noises can jar anything. The Biblical account of this event is accurate for the most part, and you know how interpretations get misconstrued.

In ancient times were there occasions in which great numbers of people were killed by radiation from atomic explosions caused by intelligent entities, perhaps such as in Mohenjo-Daro Pakistan? (P) Indeed, and your ancient times might even be referred to as now.

Did laser technology exist in the ancient world? (P) Indeed.

Can you mention some of the technologies that the Atlanteans had that we do not have? (P) They were very imaginative but you are doing quite well since the time of your typewriter. They were more interested in building and the mechanics of their building. You will find pyramids in Wyoming under water.

Would you describe the transportation used by the Atlanteans? (P) They had air travel but they did not need ground vehicles for transportation. Flying machines were much easier. They were powered by crystals. Cars were not important.

Does antigravity technology exist? (P) Antigravity does exist. Indeed it does. It was used in the construction of ancient structures if you wish to call it that way.

Were the ancient Egyptians able to perform brain surgery? (P) Indeed, sir. That was taught by extraterrestrials in a way yes and in a way no. They had some assistance from the aliens but they were able to progress on their own.

Did highly sophisticated robots exist on Earth in our ancient past? (P) Indeed, sir, they will exist again and they do exist.

Were some of the ancient structures on Earth built by melting rock and then reformed by putting it into molds? (W) Absolutely, sir.

Is what the ancients viewed as magic actually advanced technology? Indeed to a point. That is a wonderful way of expressing it.

2. Involvement of the spirits and extraterrestrials

The first 9 questions in this section have appeared in previous chapters.

Have some of our technologies been achieved through analyzing equipment found on crashed UFO's? (MU) More recently, sir? They have been there for years. What is so different? There is nothing different you know. The United States government is involved in programs of reverse engineering of alien spacecraft or other alien technology. They are examining things they found and then cover it.

Did the Nazis receive technology information from the extraterrestrials through reverse engineering of their crashed UFO's? (Q) Indeed, sir, and so is ISIS. Extraterrestrials are helping ISIS. There are also some who want to defeat ISIS. ISIS will be defeated. It will take some time for ISIS to be defeated. ISIS is gaining weight. ISIS will strike again with the magnitude of the Wall Street Towers. They will go back to New York and they are eyeing at this moment Washington. They are trying to hit the root of your government like they did in Brussels. They are in South Florida now where you are. They are around but they figure that all old people are in Florida. They are going for young people and young children.

Is it true that all modern communication technologies (computers, wi-fi etc.) are inspired to humans by spirits who previously experienced embodiment on more advanced worlds? (D) Yes. This is true. It was all here before you simple souls appeared. My good friend Plato had all of these advanced capabilities like your electricity.

Is the HAARP facility in Alaska to control weather a potentially dangerous experiment to the earth and mankind? (M) 'Tis funny, you know. Ridiculous. You cannot control anything that's going to happen. The danger will be when the people doing the experiment drown. There is no extraterrestrial involvement at this time. There will be a time that others will need help but at this time, no. No help. Your government using the HAARP facility in Alaska for nefarious purposes, such as mind control. There is secrecy about the HAARP facility that the government is not publicizing.

Can people in your world be knowledgeable about technologies they never knew during their lifetimes in the physical? (B) Indeed sir. Not all of us are advanced but we are aware. We have been knowledgeable about the future, have we not?

Did Steve Jobs, the founder of Apple Computer, receive information about his inventions from extraterrestrials? (D) Indeed, sir, and he took it with him. He couldn't explain it. It was given to him. He still has the information and that is why it is not publicized.

Has the earth been visited by machines that we humans believed were biological entities? (M) There have been robots on Earth that you thought were humans. They were from extraterrestrials. Aren't they now? They are not visible to your eyes but they are here.

Have highly advanced extraterrestrial civilizations been able to imbue robots with sentience or some level of consciousness? (M) Indeed. Absolutely.

Did Einstein use his psychic ability to develop the Theory of Relativity or was his work attributable to his high IQ? Both. He received assistance from extraterrestrials in developing that theory.

Is there or has there ever been a satellite traveling around the earth from pole to pole that was placed by extraterrestrials? Not like that, sir, but it was placed there by the earth, by humans. And they are still travelling, sir, from pole to pole.

Is the melting of the ice on the west coast of Antarctica and the growing of the ice on the east coast the result of energy being produced beneath the surface by humans or extraterrestrials? Indeed. The melting of the ice and the increasing of the ice is caused by intelligent beings.

Was liquid mercury used in the propulsion systems of UFO's to counteract the effects of gravity? Indeed, sir.

Is there currently technology retrieved from UFOs in the hands of nations which we consider our enemies, such as Iran, Russia, China, North

Korea? Indeed, sir. Some of that technology is dangerous and could lead to warfare. You are in war now. You have war on your hands now. For example, North Korea has gotten some of their technology from UFO's that have crashed.

Did the development of the transistor in the 1940's come from reverse engineering of objects found in crashed UFOs? Yes, sir.

From what source did Nicolai Testa receive advice regarding electricity? From many of our spirit friends, you know. He got his information from those in our world. Many of us have contributed. Lightning has been able to be shared with him. Lightning and the electricity in the Egyptian pyramids.

3. Energy

Does scalar energy have the potential to provide much of the world's energy needs and thus relieve us of our dependency on fossil fuels? Indeed. It will be much more possible in the future. The time is not given but it is in the process. Not in your lifetime. You needn't worry.

Is scalar energy an effective healing modality? (S) It has to be looked into. No question that it should not be avoided. To some degree it will help others.

Is the Aura Ring an effective for healing? Is it scalar energy? (S) To some degree.

Will we ever transmit electricity wirelessly through the air, on a large scale, as Tesla tried to do? Was that technology used in the time of the Atlanteans or before? Indeed, sir. There are people with their present attitude that are strong enough to do that. It is possible that electric lights can be turned on without wires. That technology was used in the time of the Atlanteans and even before that. Tesla was right. The many ancient obelisks throughout the world were used for broadcasting electricity wirelessly.

Was the Great Pyramid at Giza used as a hydrogen power plant to produce electrical or scalar energy? (P) Yes, a hydrogen power plant.

4. New and future technology

Does the technology exist for making cloaking devices to make objects appear invisible to the human eye? Indeed, sir.

Is it possible to develop prosthetic gills for humans so that oxygen could be extracted directly from water for when they are under water? What a wonderful idea. That technology already exists.

Does the technology exist that will transfer an individual's thoughts to another individual? Does what is known as "the God Helmet" do this? I wish to respond by saying yes. There are times that the God Helmet is possible to transfer one person's thoughts to another. It is very possible. You can put a thought into another individual. It doesn't say that you can put the will into another individual but you can put a thought. You cannot control another individual but you could put a thought.

Although alchemists have tried for ages without success to transmute common elements into gold, will the secret to doing so someday be discovered? It will be taken very seriously. The secret to gold will be the mixing of minerals. There will be many types of gold as there are now.

Will the technology become available in the next ten years to turn salt water into fresh water economically viable? In the next twenty-five years.

Can electro-magnetism be used to counteract the force of gravity? To a point sir. You will be able to witness that.

Can stargates be created through the use of technology? Does our government now have that technology? Will it ever have that technology? Indeed, sir, [stargates can be created through the use of technology]. Your government has that technology now. Your government is very well aware. They are not trying to create stargates now. They have created stargates.

Could the large Hadron Collider in Cern Switzerland present a potential serious danger to our planet? Could it open up a portal that will allow entities into this physical plane? (Laughing) No, [it will not present a danger.] Yes, they are bringing beings here. We have information and the technology has been reevaluated and they will not confuse[?] the detrimental part of it to the United States.

Will automobiles without wheels someday run on our streets and highways? (R) Indeed. It will be in this century. Is that not true? Your planes will have another engine. It is necessary for your airplanes and helicopters to have another engine for safety reasons. They have ground vehicles with and without wheels on other planets. The wheel is an invention on all planets.

Will the flying car invented by Paul Moller in California [and other such cars] ever be used on a widespread basis? It has been used for years. It will become more and more popular each year. Cars in the future will be more flying and be used as a boat.

Within the next two or three generations will the majority of cars continue to use solely gasoline as power? Indeed not, sir. They will use little fragments of oil, something that does not exist now.

Within the next century will there be a proliferation of robots that are practically indistinguishable from humans created by our technology? Indeed, sir. Some of those robots will be virtually indistinguishable from humans and will be designed to serve as sexual partners for humans. They will look just like humans but will not be biological. They will be very popular.

Will technology ever reach the point where nearly all of the internal organs of humans could be replaced by mechanical means? Are they not now? A mechanical heart could be installed inside a person. A liver and other organs, too.

Do we have the capability of transplanting the head of a person onto the body of another person as they have done with monkeys? It can be done but it may not all be successful. It is not possible to put the head of one species of animals onto the body of another species.

Will the time ever come when human-like robots will be self reproducing? (R) Robots won't be able to reproduce.

The U.S. technology now has an unmanned space shuttle that was in orbit for two years. Is that shuttle capable of disabling enemy satellites? (Q) Absolutely. What is already in space can disable satellites. Disabling satellites has already been done. Ask Israel that made the satellite. They know what to do with their satellite. This [the unmanned satellite] has to do with North Korea's satellites misfiring. You are protecting yourselves through that satellite.

We now have remotely controlled flying drones which take photographs or move small objects from one place to another. Will that technology ever develop to the point where drones will be used on a widespread scale for moving people from one place to another? Indeed, sir, as you well know. Otherwise you would not have gotten that idea. That will be in the lifetime of the people here.

5. Miscellaneous

Are there subatomic particles smaller than quarks? Indeed, yes. We would call them waves. I would call them dangerous waves.

Are some of the crystals that the Atlanteans used to transmit energy still in operation under the sea today? Is that the cause of the disappearance of so many ships and airplanes in the area known as the Bermuda Triangle? (PW) Yes. They are the cause of the disappearance of planes and ships. They are not causing disturbance. They have power. It is caused by your friends that are not visible to you. Some are not friends that are visible and some are not visible to you.

Are there many more elements on Earth (such as iron or calcium etc.) that have not yet been discovered by scientists? Indeed sir. There are many more elements on your planet Earth. And wait until you visit the other planets. In reality you will find more for your use.

Is there truth to the theory that, because of modern technology, humans are being excessively bombarded with positive ions and this is having a negative effect on our health? Are devices that are imbued with negative ions of benefit to our health? (S) No, this is not true. Such devices are not of importance.

Did Helena Blavatsky's writings have a significant influence on Einstein's thinking? Indeed, sir, indeed. He thought of her constantly. He did indeed.

Do the thoughts and feelings of humans have an effect on the properties of water? Water is very important, sir. If there is a glass of water in front of you, your thoughts and feelings have an effect on the properties of the water. Mostly positive thoughts.

Are what we consider the laws of science, such as the Law of Gravity, implemented automatically or are there conscious forces overseeing the implementation of those laws? (D) At times there are conscious entities overseeing that that occurs. With all of what you call the laws of science you can say that conscious entities, whether they be angels or some other kind of entities see that those laws occur [are implemented].

Did the German stealth aircraft exist during World War II? Indeed sir. It did actually exist and it was not successful.

Is gold an element that is treasured throughout the physical universe? (M) Gold, silver and platinum are treasured in other star systems.

Is instant teleportation of a person from one place to another possible both through the use of technology and also through the use of the human mind? (K) Indeed, sir. Some humans can instantly appear in a different place from where they were before. and you can do the same. The answer is yes.

Can major weather events, greater than just rain or snow, be manipulated by the use of technology? Indeed, sir.

Throughout history has the majority of great scientists been influenced by extraterrestrials? (D) Indeed, sir. Their creations are not necessarily emanating from their own minds but their minds are being influenced by the external. And being controlled. Thomas Edison, for example, received a lot of his information from other sources. He had information on what we call electricity. He channeled the information from extra terrestrials.

We have always been taught that there are three states of matter: solids, liquids and gasses. Now scientists say that there is a fourth state called plasma. Theosophists believe that there are three more subtle states of matter. Is that correct? Is has always been such. It has only been newly discovered. There are seven states of matter.

W. THE EARTH: THE PLANET, MYSTERIOUS PLACES, ANCIENT STRUCTURES AND ARTIFACTS

1. The planet in ages past

All questions in this section, except the last 2, have appeared in previous chapters.

Some scientists believe that the earth's crust has moved and that Atlantis was an island in the middle of the Atlantic Ocean that went south. Is that true? (P) Indeed, but we have no trace of it. You have no trace of it but it did exist. It is the origin of the Great Flood.

Was Antarctica once an inhabited continent? Did a shift of the crust of the earth cause it to be at its current location at the South Pole? Did it have anything to do with the Atlanteans? (P) Indeed it was once. The earth has shifted, rotated. Regarding the Atlanteans, I will simply say "yes".

Was the cause of the destruction of Atlantis created by man or was it a natural disaster? (P) It was a natural disaster. It was nature's harm or nature's good.

Was the Gulf Stream engineered by the Atlanteans or other intelligent entities? (MP) Not manmade. I would like to say other intelligent entities. Not a natural phenomenon. Not the Atlanteans. By many people, extraterrestrials. The purpose was to keep the lands to the north warmer.

Did the Nile river flow into the Atlantic Ocean at the time of Atlantis? (P) Yes.

Were the land masses of this world before the Great Flood considerably different from the way they now are? (Q) Indeed, sir. Considerably different.

Was the Libyan Desert Glass created by a nuclear explosion thousands of years ago? (P) Indeed sir, indeed. It was not caused by people. It was caused by gasses. It was natural.

Was there a time when India and the area around it were not connected to the rest of Asia? (P) Indeed.

What is the story of Lake Titicaca in Peru and its underwater city with sunken ruins? It has been in Peru many, many times [eons] ago. It was covered with earth and then with water. It was there before the Great Flood. Indeed an earthquake occurred and then water. The earth opened up here and allowed the water to overflow. I was not there. That is what I have been told. There are many cities that existed before the Great Flood. There are still remnants now.

Since it is reputed to having once been a land with lush vegetation, what was the cause of the creation of the Sahara Desert? The storm. The wind. The breeze. It was not an earthquake or a meteorite. It was the wind and the breeze and the shifting, a natural phenomenon.

2. Mysterious places

What is the cause for the disappearance of so many ships in the Sargasso Sea? Is the same true of the Lake Michigan triangle? Sir, I do not want to open up a door again but there is a black hole on Earth. The same is true of the Michigan triangle, why so many ships disappear there.

What is the cause of the events that have occurred in the Bermuda Triangle? The Bermuda Triangle is a mystery. It is a vacuum on Earth. There are other vacuums on Earth as well. People disappear never to be seen again. They are joining us.

Are some of the crystals that the Atlanteans used to transmit energy still in operation under the sea today? Is that the cause of the disappearance of so many ships and airplanes in the area known as the Bermuda Triangle? (PV) Yes. They are the cause of the disappearance of planes and ships. They are not causing disturbance. They have power. It is caused by your friends that are not visible to you. Some are not friends that are visible and some are not visible to you.

People say that is ghostly spirits that are the cause of so many people committing suicide at Aokigahara at the base of Mount Fuji in Japan. Is that correct? (C) Japan, sir, has its own influence and has been inundated by much water. The concern there in Japan is the water, the overflow. There is very little truth in ghostly influence. They are committing suicide because they are mentally disturbed and they are in fear.

Is there a connection between the Grand Canyon and star beings as thought by native American Indians in that area? (M) Indeed sir. Star beings are from the Grand Canyon. They are imbedded in the Grand Canyon and remain so for protection.

Is there a human or humanlike civilization beneath the surface of the earth? Indeed, sir There are entrances at both the North Pole and the South Pole. The bodies of those entities need air. They do not need water. The world beneath the surface of the earth resembles yours in many ways: such as having sky, rivers, mountains etc. The Nazis entered this world. They are also part of the ISIS. The same group of reincarnated Nazis are now ISIS members. What you have to fear from the civilization beneath the surface of the earth are the animals.

Are there currently people living beneath the surface of Antarctica? There is life, yes, my dear sir. They are not like you or me.

Were the prehistoric paintings in caves throughout the world drawn by those we traditionally think of as nearly savage cavemen or were they drawn by people from a more advanced Earth civilization that preceded ours? Preceded, sir. The cavemen were not savage either but they were addressed as savage because they were learning. They were not coded messages left for you. They were writing their own history before they left. You may have to study the messages in order to understand what they mean. They are more than what meets the eye. It was not meant for code, sir. It was their way of expressing themselves. They had no other way to speak English.

Do such places exist in the physical world where you can go through some kind of portal and emerge in faraway places in the universe? (LM) Indeed. Not only through one's mind but in the future. You can go into the future and into the past. They are what you may call black spaces. It is available to you. There is a network of underwater portals used by extraterrestrials. We look above but we do not look below. We must look below. Some are in our lakes and oceans and they are near here.

Are there many stargates within the borders of our country? Indeed, sir. They are mostly in the water. Earth is made of water. Those that are on land are not mostly on mountain tops as some people believe.

When something goes through a specific stargate, does that something always arrive at the same place somewhere else in the universe? No. I have said that the Michigan Triangle is a place where there is a stargate. So if a ship goes through that stargate it can arrive at different places in the universe but it is all the same anyway because there is no such thing as time or space.

What was the purpose of the serpent mounds in Ohio? Who made them? The earth. It was a naturally occurring blister. It was not some conscious entity that created them.

Could you tell me if the area of St. Augustine is a power place? Indeed, my dear lady, 'tis safe and it is covered with many human abilities protecting it. In other words, there are ghosts waiting.

What caused the creation of the Valley of Death in Siberia? What causes the people to become ill? People. The vibration in the Valley of Death, just a coincidence, sir. People become ill there. First of all it starts off to be mental stimulation and when people are fearful, that will contribute to their fear.

Why are there no animals or insects in what is called the Dead Zone in the Algerian desert? Something happened in the past that no animal life can be there. An atomic explosion. It is a certain kind of radiation.

Are there what could be called evil places on Earth; that is, places with negative energies? Indeed, sir. There are also negative people. Negative places and negative people. Positive places and positive people.

3. Mysterious structures and artifacts

All questions in this section, except the last four, have appeared in previous chapters.

Can you tell us something about the construction of the Coral Castle in Homestead, Florida? (MV) Aliens were involved to help him [Edward Leedskalnin] to do so. He was too little to do this himself. His ability to communicate was remarkable.

Do the Dogu (Dogoo) statues found in Japan represent aliens in space suits? (M) Indeed, sir.

Can you tell us about the origin and original usage of the huge statues on Easter Island? (M) Manmade, sir. They were products of people they worshipped. They were worshipped. Extraterrestrials had an improvement in them. They improved it. They had more strength. The Lemurians played a role in the creation of the many large statues on Easter Island. The statues represented extraterrestrials and people that are [of] stature.

Were some of the ancient structures on Earth built by melting rock and then reformed by putting it into molds? (V) Absolutely, sir.

How can we explain the existence of the same type of hieroglyphs and cuneiform writings that are found in both ancient Sumer and near Lake Titicaca in Peru? (P) The same way as in some caves or such other areas that were left. They were writings and messages left for the future. Some were left by extraterrestrials.

Regarding the Nazca Plateau in Peru, what was the purpose of the numerous very long lines, drawings of animals, geometrical shapes and mathematical diagrams that can only be seen from the air? (M) For those that are up high in the sky they can read it easier when above the land it is written on. I am talking about extraterrestrial UFO's. They were constructed by extraterrestrials for the purpose of providing instructions or information to the people of Earth. The same could be said about the various crop circles that have been appearing throughout the world. They are messages or instructions to Earth people from extraterrestrials. They are in your face. They are right there. They are trying to assist you and aid you. They are trying to be heard.

Have extraterrestrials imbued certain objects with special powers, perhaps such as the crystal sculls or other physical objects? (M) Yes, they have been cleansed and have special powers. Again I think about that. They have been cleansed. They are very clever. They are very intelligent. If they gather together that will be a tremendous powerful force, a controlling force. When those glass skulls are brought together power will occur. Power to the extraterrestrial groups that made them. Extremely powerful. There are other objects located on Earth that are endowed with powers, such as you humans have power that was endowed by extraterrestrials. Humans will be using the crystal skulls relatively soon to communicate with extraterrestrials.

Does the St. Louis Arch have any effect on the weather in that region? (M) Indeed. Extraterrestrials were instrumental in providing information for its design. They want to know if they were good designers. Part of the purpose was to affect the weather.

What caused the formation of the Devil's Tower in Wyoming? (M) Extraterrestrials were involved. We have been there and we created it. Extraterrestrials are still involved in the Devil's tower. We are everywhere, sir. We have been here for centuries.

Can the prehistoric cave paintings throughout the world be considered something like a key to our understanding of the history and future of mankind? (P) There is hidden meaning in those drawings. The interpretation of those drawings tells of your history and your future.

Are there ancient stone monuments on Earth today that predated the Great Flood? Indeed, sir, there are monuments that predated the Great Flood. There were many, many floods before the Great Flood. There wasn't only one Great Flood. There were many floods over and over and over. They are correcting me to tell you "and over and over". There will be more Great Floods. The Sphinx was created before the Great Flood.

There are stone wheels carved into the earth in Syria, Jordan and Saudi Arabia. Did they precede the Great Flood? What was their purpose? They are older than the Flood, sir. They were again leaving their announcements that they were here. It was a way of sending a message telling you about them. You have yet to learn the secret of how to read them. You are trying to interpret them now. They are trying very diligently to inform you about the past.

There is a deep mysterious pit in the ground on Oak Island in Nova Scotia in which it is believed there is treasure buried in that pit. Is that true? Yes. The Ark of the Covenant is buried in that pit. It was hidden so many years ago, before the Europeans settled America. A lot of your answers will come out. Some of you will be alive when they get to that, not just the younger ones. It doesn't matter how old because there are people who will be alive who were not aware that they would live so long. Life will be much longer for them as you well know. Life will be much more. There are many more people above a hundred, many more who are existing. I see the average lifetime of humans being 120 years. And with new medications coming out, many diseases will be conquered and people will live to be over 150.

Is there knowledge left by the Atlanteans under a paw of the sphinx inscribed on tablets of gold? (Laughing) Indeed. Gold is used because it is virtually indestructible and desirable. That knowledge will become available to you in the future, not that near but it will be exposed within a hundred years.

4. Pyramids, obelisks and Stonehenge

Who were the architects and builders of the pyramids in the Yucatan and Guatemala? (MP) People that are striving from your past are reaching out and wish to serve in your future. They were actually built by those of another star system, the Pleiades. They also built the pyramids in Egypt and that is how they got to the top. The Pleiades are one of the most advanced groups. Our secret people were building your pyramids that they could reach from the top down. Humans provided a lot of the labor but extraterrestrials provided the technology.

What was the purpose of the construction of the great pyramid at Giza? (P) The great pyramid was built for electricity. It was a power plant to provide energy. Many Egyptians built it. The labor was made by humans and extraterrestrials too, as they are now with you. The extraterrestrials designed the pyramid and the humans built it using extraterrestrial technology. Slaves were forced to. It was not fun, sir. It was very difficult with slavery. Most of us have been slaves. The pyramid of Giza was built before the Great Flood.

What was the purpose for various ancient pyramids being strategically placed throughout the world? There was no danger, sir. It was just exploring, learning and growing. They were created by extraterrestrials for radiation, lightening and experimenting. They created them to produce energy. Your energy was given throughout the universe. That is why they are placed all over the place. That means of producing energy is already no longer a secret.

Are there pyramids beneath the ice in Antarctica? Indeed, sir. Absolutely, sir. They had to do with the continent of Atlantis. It will come out to be. Antarctica once was Atlantis and the earth shifted and pyramids were on Atlantis.

Is there any esoteric significance to the fact that the Washington monument is in the form of an obelisk? Yes. It is not for me to express more about that. There is a reason based on ancient wisdom why the monument is shaped such. It is correct because it was interpreted in that form. The interpretation was given to mankind.

What was the purpose of some of the many ancient obelisks found throughout the world? The purpose is the same as we are told all over the world where everyone is being shared. Some share to have the obelisk existing. That is to produce both communications and energy.

When you said that the purpose of Stonehenge was to provide shade, can we infer that you were referring to the shadows caused by the stones as the sun moved through the sky, perhaps to be used as some sort of clock or calendar? If you wish to refer that way, indeed. It was used as a clock. That was the way of telling time. I was involved with the building of Stonehenge. Stonehenge was basically not for healing people. It was basically for telling time.

Was at least part of the purpose of Stonehenge to be an extraterrestrial spaceport? Indeed, sir. Stonehenge and some of these other recently discovered structures predated the Great Flood. He's telling me that it was a clock. It was like telling time. The shadows cast by the columns were like a clock and a calendar.

Did humans of long ago use the power of sound, taught to them by extraterrestrials, to accomplish such feats as moving extremely heavy objects? (PV) Indeed. You don't need an education to find that interesting. Sound was used in the construction of some of the unusual ancient monuments we find throughout the world. Sound was used in the construction of the great pyramids. Sound was also used when the Israelites went around the walls of Jericho and made the walls crumble. The frequency of the sound. And do you not have a place of interest [i.e. the Coral Castle in Homestead, Florida] in the area where you live? He used sound to raise those heavy stones. That is the same way you have seen opera singers break [drinking] glasses. Sound was used to move stones at Stonehenge.

5. The effects of humans on the planet

Is global warming caused by man or is it a natural phenomenon? Global warming is a natural phenomenon. It has happened many times before and will happen time and again.

What can human beings do to stop or slow down the acceleration of the inundation of many coastal areas, and the extinction of some animal life forms? (Q) It is the rotation of the earth. Nothing can be done. This is going to happen in many years to come. You won't be here. There's nothing we can do about global warming. That is the existence of your past and your future.

Is the earth hurting because of the greenhouses gasses created by man? The substance created by man is not hurting. 'Tis not hurting.

Would it be advisable for mankind to take better care of the planet Earth than we are now doing? Planet Earth is well taken care of as you may well know. It has many successions and will have again many successions. Planet Earth will continue to multiply. We will continue to eat and defecate on our planet Earth. Other planets are seeking to be involved as you well know.

Are the actions of humans harming the earth in ways that will result in bringing harm to physical humanity? They are harming themselves, sir. We [spirits] do not kill each other. We are already dead. The earth itself is not being harmed by mankind, not at all. This whole concern about global warming is ridiculous.

Is the health of our planet affected by the way people treat one another? Yes. If we treated each other better, our planet would be better.

Are there more people now on the planet Earth than can be successfully sustained; too many people to feed and shelter? Are there programs underway right now to thin out the population of the earth? Indeed, sir.

Is there a most efficient way to dispose of bodies that will help the soul and the earth at the same time? Cremation is probably the simplest form unless you are hungry.

6. Earth changes

Do you foresee a major Earth shift in the next thousand years, such as when Atlantis virtually disappeared? (R) Indeed yes. Not in your lifetime.

Edgar Cayce predicted that the earth would shift on its axis in 1998 but this did not occur. Did conditions change to avert this or are events predictable but not the timing of the events? He was wrong. Timing, sir. It will occur but at another time. The gentleman that made the prediction was a gentleman. It was not in order for it to occur. Time cannot be predicted, sir. Those changes may occur but at a different date. Do not feel that they will have to occur.

Will the planet Earth be struck by a comet, asteroid or something else from outer space within the next few centuries? I do not see a few centuries ahead as the planet Earth being struck but it will be divided and it will go on and on. It will be politically divided.

How many more years do you think we have in south Florida before the rise of the ocean makes it not a good idea to buy land here? (R) Well, it's a good idea to buy land because you will be here. It is true about the water rising. I do not have dates about the water rising. It will not be in your lifetime but it looks like the rising of the water is eminent in Florida. Water from the rising seas will intrude into your community in the next century.

Is the earth on a 25,580 year cycle and at the end of each cycle are there great changes regarding the earth and humanity? That is correct, sir. It has to do with the planet Niburu approaching the earth.

With the earth changes and the vibration and quickening, will the people who live beneath the surface at Mount Shasta be able to live on the surface? No, they will not.

Is the Gulf Stream gradually losing its ability to bring warm air currents to the British Isles? Yes, sir. The reason for that is because of the fresh water polar glaciers melting into the salt water oceans. The salt water helps to bring movement.

7. Miscellaneous

In our study of the earth, various dimensions, spheres etc., the expression "Fluid Earth" is used and it is not water. Can you tell us about it? It is a more hydrogen earth, in your language.

When there is a major disaster such as an earthquake or a tsunami in our world in which many people are killed, does that cause repercussions in your world? (B) We are aware of what is to be and we are always there to welcome those who are coming into our world.

Is the planet Earth a conscious entity? Indeed, sir.

Can earthquakes be caused by intelligent entities or are they always what we might call natural phenomena? Was the 2014 strong earthquake in Haiti caused by intelligent entities? Both, sir. The earthquake in Haiti was natural, not orchestrated.

ABOUT THE AUTHORS

Sondra Perlin-Zecher has been active in the metaphysical field for more than forty years. She is a clairvoyant, clairaudient medium whose life's work has been devoted to helping others through psychic readings and counseling. She is probably best known as the psychic who solved the Son of Sam mass murder case. She works with law enforcement in solving crimes. As a medical intuitive, she often works with medical doctors in diagnosing problems. Her educational background includes graduate degrees in art, social work and psychology. Her formal training, combined with her psychic sensitivity, has enabled her to provide help to numbers of individuals, medical doctors, and law enforcement officials including the FBI.

Charles E. Zecher has been a student of metaphysics and the paranormal for more than fifty years. His professional career spanned nearly forty years as an educator and school administrator at the secondary school level and universities in New Jersey and Pennsylvania. He is certified as an advanced clinical hypnotherapist. For nearly thirty years, he has worked with his wife in offering programs of interest in their homes in Bridgewater, New Jersey and in Coral Springs, Florida.

Charles and Sondra are former directors of the Central Jersey area Mutual Interest Group of the Association for Research and Enlightenment. They currently sponsor the Coral Springs Metaphysical Group. They have two adult sons and reside in Coral Springs, Florida. They can be contacted at zecher@myacc.net.

Printed in the United States
By Bookmasters